TEACHING AND LEARNING IN HIGHER EDUCATION
Fourth edition

RUTH M. BEARD and JAMES HARTLEY

P·C·P
Paul Chapman
Publishing Ltd

First published 1984
Harper & Row Ltd

Reprinted by
Paul Chapman Publishing Ltd
144 Liverpool Road
London N1 1LA

British Library Cataloguing in Publication Data

Beard, Ruth M.
    Teaching and learning in higher education.—
    4th ed.
    1. College teaching—Great Britain
    I. Title   II. Hartley, James
    378′.125′0941   LB2331

    ISBN 1 85396 093 4

Typeset by Inforum Ltd, Portsmouth
Printed and bound by Butler & Tanner Ltd, Frome and London

A B C D E F G   5 4 3 2 1 0 9

TEACHING AND LEARNING IN HIGHER EDUCATION
Fourth edition

**Centre for
Medical Education**

Professor R.M. Harden

The University
Dundee

Ninewells Hospital
and Medical School
Dundee, DD1 9SY
Scotland
Telephone: 0382   60111
Ext. 2286/7

With Compliments of

THE AUTHORS

Emeritus Professor Ruth Beard is the holder of two degrees in mathematics and two in education, from the University of London. She has taught in secondary schools, a college of education and three universities. Between 1965 and 1973 she was senior lecturer in charge of the University Teaching Methods Unit at the University of London Institute of Education. She was Professor of Educational Studies at the University of Bradford between 1973 and 1982. Her other books include *An Outline of Piaget's Developmental Psychology* (1969), *Objectives in Higher Education* (with F.G. Healey and P.J. Holloway) 2nd edition (1974), *Research into Teaching Methods in Higher Education* (with D.A. Bligh) 4th edition (1978) and *Motivating Students* (with I. Senior) (1980).

James Hartley is Reader and Head of the Department of Psychology at the University of Keele, Staffordshire. His other books include *Designing Instructional Text* (1978) and *The Psychology of Written Communication* (1980).

CONTENTS

Preface

The first edition of *Teaching and Learning in Higher Education* was published in 1970. The second edition appeared in 1972 and the third in 1976. In
essence each edition contained modifications and additions to the first
edition. In the Preface to the third edition, however, it was noted that
because of rapid change, 'it seems probable that within a few years' time a
new book rather than a fourth edition will be required'. This fourth edition
is in fact this new book. The earlier text has been reshaped and the content
revised and expanded in many ways.

Unlike the previous editions we have subdivided this edition of *Teaching
and Learning in Higher Education* into five sections. In Part One we discuss
changes in the educational scene since 1975, and problems concerning aims
and objectives. Here we were surprised to note that the CNAA (Council for
National Academic Awards), which validates degree courses in the public
sector, is now the largest degree-awarding body in the UK. It is perhaps less
of a surprise, but no less remarkable, also to note that the Open University is
now the largest university in the UK. Institutions such as the CNAA and
the Open University have laid great store by the 'objectives method' of
teaching and learning. Teachers presenting courses for validation by the
CNAA, for example, are required to prepare proposals beginning with a
specification of the aims and objectives of the course, and moving on to
outline the contents of the course and the chosen methods of teaching and
assessment. Such proposals are fully discussed internally before they are
argued before a body of external assessors representing the Council. In

other areas of higher education, new courses are introduced without such scrutiny or such attention to detail. But, even here, consideration must be given to the aims and objectives of teaching.

Teachers do not teach in a vacuum. Their aims, beliefs and values affect all that they do. Students' learning is similarly affected. Hence, in Part Two we spend some time discussing the psychology of learning and differences between individuals. Our aim here is not to provide a set of tips or guidelines, nor to present information which can be taken 'off the shelf' and immediately used. Psychology is not like that. The psychology of learning provides information about the difficulties involved – general information which might be more or less relevant. When planning a course, or an individual lecture, tutorial or class meeting, teachers need to be aware of the problems that students face in learning and to try and take these into account in their own specific contexts. Teachers need to examine both the problems they have in teaching and those that their students have in learning.

It is for reasons such as these that we wrote Part Three. Here, although our text is addressed primarily to teachers, we focus particularly on the concerns of students. We discuss the problems of coping with new situations and recent work on study skills – work that has increased rapidly since 1975. It is important for teachers to know about this research, largely because they can contribute to it by observing and helping their own students. Teachers, in effect, can become experimenters – trying out new approaches and assessing for themselves the relative merits of different ways of doing things.

In Part Four we describe different ways of teaching, that is, we discuss some of the more standard issues and problems that face new teachers in particular. Each chapter presents an up-to-date account of research in particular areas (lecturing, small-group methods, laboratory work, etc.). Not all teachers need to read all of these chapters, but each one is important for those who wish to be updated. Certainly the chapter on new methods should be relevant to those teachers who are planning new courses and who wish to be aware of modern developments.

We also include in this part of the book some new material – discussions of issues that have become important in recent years. Thus we consider the counselling of students who find themselves in difficulty. In addition, we consider the problems of promoting and reporting research, whether it be with postgraduate students or through academic writing, or both of these.

Part Five of the book is concerned with evaluation and assessment.

Assessment is a vital issue in educational practice – and regrettably it seems to be the tail that wags the dog rather than the reverse. Assessment is important because different assessment systems implicitly convey different assumptions about the nature of teaching and learning, and indeed the nature of knowledge itself. In Part Five we present a discussion of three issues: the assessment of learning, the assessment of teaching and the assessment of new courses. In each case we illustrate current developments by reference to an assortment of new studies.

Despite the fact that most of the time we discuss fundamental and complex problems, we hope that this book will also provide some suggestions about how teaching can be improved immediately – by eradicating errors, by using new methods or by modifying existing courses – but, of course, it would be sanguine to assume that all the answers to the problems of teaching could be provided in a textbook. A text can provide a coherent background of concepts and principles where these exist (and, so far they do not for teaching and learning), and it can supply knowledge about techniques. But to teach successfully individuals must practise the skills of teaching, and receive feedback on their performance in order to discover their own particular abilities and failings.

This book, therefore, is concerned with much more than teaching techniques or 'teaching tips'. We hope that the readers will become more sensitive to factors in their teaching which might give rise to discontent, and that by becoming more aware of modern developments in our understanding of how students learn they will be able to adapt their curricula and methods of teaching and assessment accordingly.

Acknowledgements

We are grateful to many people for their assistance in the preparation of this text, not least those who so willingly gave us permission to reproduce their materials. Marianne Lagrange at Harper & Row deserves our special thanks and so too do John Coleman for assistance with the figures, and Doreen Waters, Alice Slaney, Dorothy Masters, Margaret Woodward, Eleanor Gordon and colleagues for labouring with our typescript.

PART ONE

THE BACKGROUND TO TEACHING AND LEARNING

CHAPTER 1

TEACHING AND LEARNING: THE CHANGING SITUATION

In this chapter we outline current worldwide influences which have led both to greater concern with students' learning and to growing provision for staff development. The views of students and teachers are quoted and commented on. Finally, we discuss provision for staff development and the growth of research into higher education.

During the past 30 years or so there has been a worldwide growth of interest in teaching and learning in higher education. This growth has been most marked in industrially advanced countries but it is evident, too, in countries that are rapidly developing. There are three main causes: (1) a growth in subject matter and numbers of specialities which places new demands on students and teachers; (2) social changes which have led to increases in numbers of students, to the inclusion of different kinds of students in higher education and to changing demands for higher education; and (3) advances in theories of learning and technology which combine to offer new methods of learning and greater independence to students.

1.1   The growth of knowledge and higher education

The rapid growth of knowledge during the past 30 years has introduced into higher education new specialities and new emphases in older subjects, such as macromolecular science, atomic physics, social aspects of medicine, and computer science with its numerous applications in other subjects.

The developments in some areas have been extraordinary. Some subjects now develop so rapidly that knowledge is out of date in as little as two years, making the preparation of textbooks impossible. The National Register of

Scientific and Technical Personnel in the United States lists about 1000 distinct specializations in the natural sciences alone, whereas 30 years ago there were about 50. The vast increase in available information and the rapidity with which it becomes out of date have necessitated changes in students' learning. Students need to know how to obtain information and how to apply it in new situations. They need to be flexible. New changes in techniques and developments in knowledge result in a demand for students with a broad background and the capacity to respond adaptively to new materials and methods.

The need to prepare students to cooperate with specialists in other disciplines has also grown considerably during the past 30 years. In planning a new town or even a single school or hospital, for instance, architects must cooperate not only with colleagues but also with officials of local authorities, engineers and borough surveyors, builders and their clients. Industrial designers and commercial artists have similar problems, and doctors in large town practices need to cooperate with personnel in a number of ancillary services. In space programmes thousands of scientists and technical experts have had to work together. Indeed, in almost all professions, individuals are being called on to cooperate to an increasing extent, perhaps by working in teams or by communicating information to committees consisting of specialists in other fields who make different assumptions, employ different vocabularies and concepts, and have somewhat different modes of thinking.

The belief that applied science subjects should be studied in relation to their social consequences has led to an increasing number of interdisciplinary courses. For example, Jevons (1970) described an undergraduate course at Manchester which was designed to give an insight into the role of science in relation to politics, economics, industry and philosophy while offering a broad coverage of physics with some engineering and computer programming. A newer MSc course in the same department requires a more extended study of social issues relating to the sciences. Courses such as these force one to consider how the course content can be integrated into coherent and meaningful curricula.

Cooperation implies skill in communication. Consequently there is an increasing need to promote skill in spoken and written language, together with the capacity to understand other people's point of view. In countries such as Britain, where communication skills are not sufficiently encouraged in secondary schools, it is important that they should be developed in courses in higher education. In addition, if students are to learn how to work in groups, it would be beneficial for students and their teachers to have some knowledge of group dynamics. Both teachers and students must therefore know how to lead discussion and how to contribute effectively to it.

In times of rapid change it is also essential to think productively. Productive thinkers are resourceful people, capable of working in different conditions from those in which they were trained. They are able to learn rapidly from their own experience or that of others, to take responsibility when they have the greatest skill, and to accept other people's leadership if a different expertise is needed. To learn to do this requires that students should be skilful in communication and have insight into personal relationships. The value of individual resourcefulness is not only greater than it formerly was, but also additional skills and qualities are needed.

These more demanding requirements for students point to a reorientation in higher education. Whereas formerly the progress of many students was deemed satisfactory if they could reproduce a body of knowledge or acquire skills with minimal understanding, increasingly more is expected of them today. Such a reorientation requires changes in the traditional methods of teaching and assessment.

1.2   Social change, developments in technology and higher education

The increasing numbers of students in higher education, mainly in the 1960s and 1970s, led to new demands on teachers. Developments included the creation of new universities and colleges, the upgrading of tertiary colleges to the status of polytechnic or university, and the introduction of 'universities of the air' or other kinds of 'distance education'. In Britain two developments in particular stand out: the creation of the Council for National Academic Awards (the CNAA) and the Open University. The CNAA is an autonomous institution which was established by Royal Charter in 1964. Its main function has been to 'validate' degrees (and other academic awards) given by various (non-university) institutions. The CNAA (1979) reported that by that date more than 120 institutions were offering more than 1500 separate courses which had been validated by the Council. The actual procedures used for validation are outlined in Chapter 14. Here we may note that the CNAA is now the largest degree-awarding body in the UK; about one-third of all the students who are studying for a degree (over 120,000) attend CNAA-validated courses.

The Open University was established in 1971. It now enrols over 75,000 students per year, and they study for degrees on a modular or credit system. The Open University is characterized by the fact that it was established to provide a route to higher education for those people who had not managed by traditional methods, and is 'open' in the sense that anyone (over 21) can apply and admissions are allocated on a first-come, first-served basis. Students study by means of correspondence texts, assignments and (a small proportion) television and radio broadcasts. An interesting account of the development of the Open University is provided by Walter Perry, the first Vice-Chancellor (Perry, 1976).

These developments had two main effects: the number of students entering higher education from school greatly increased and growing numbers of mature students studied for degrees amd other qualifications. Until the mid-1970s, the continued growth of higher education was taken for granted. It was assumed that, in time, its growth in Europe would approach that of the United States of America, Canada and Japan. In the 1980s this seems improbable. Partly due to the recession colleges have closed or merged, and reductions have been made in the number of places available in many areas of higher education. In addition, the wisdom of so great an expansion has been questioned.

The economic recession, however, may not be the sole cause of decline in most Western higher education systems since the 1970s. The strategies used to deal with the recession may differ. Geiger (1980), in studying three national systems, noted that (1) the Belgian system maintained rigorous standards and that this led to stagnation in enrolments; (2) in the USA – where the numbers of black and women students are increasing – there was a decline in enrolment of male whites due to both worsening labour markets and the falling academic achievement of high-school students; and (3) in France, the devaluation of university degrees led to decreasing study time and effort.

One prediction – that home-based and distance education may increasingly take the place of that provided in schools, colleges and universities – deserves serious consideration. It follows from the rapid development in use of video-tape, videotex and microcomputers. Increasing numbers of students take part-time courses such as those provided by the Open University.

There is no doubt that self-instruction from computer-based courses can lead to good understanding in some subjects, including those which now frequently present difficulty, such as mathematics. Yet, however effectively a programme meets a student's intellectual needs, it cannot always supply the stimulus of working with other students or the opportunity to raise questions directly with experts in the field; nor can it teach the abilities required for effective cooperation or oral communication.

It seems likely, therefore, that the new technology, like the individualized methods of learning introduced in the 1950s and 1960s, will not replace teachers. Those who are skilled in clear exposition and in promoting in their students understanding, the will to learn, flexibility, and depth in thinking will be equally in demand, or more so than at present. Nonetheless, teachers must be prepared to meet the challenge of the new technology if they are not to be partly superseded by it, and since many teachers in higher education do not attain perfect standards, our students will still have much to say about teaching.

1.3 Students' comments on teaching and courses

In the past, there were few records of students' views of teachers and teaching. Most of those that we have are spontaneous comments about distinguished, eccentric or poor teachers. Thus, a professor of psychology in Norway who entered university as a mature student after the last major war recalls that, in contrast with trained army instructors: 'Some university teachers failed to catch attention, let alone to hold it, partly obscured illustrative material and failed to make clear what were the main points of their lectures' (Raaheim and Wankowski, 1981).

By the time that extensive inquiries into students' views were made in the 1960s, anecdotal reports such as this were becoming rare. The students' main complaints were about overloaded syllabuses which left them little time to think, about narrow specialization or about courses which were 'irrelevant'. In lectures they objected mainly to the dictation of notes, to the too rapid delivery of subject matter, to the writing of notes so rapidly on the board that they could be neither copied nor understood, to the failure to give illustrative examples and, generally, to the insensitivity to students' need to ask questions with a view to comprehending what was presented.

These complaints, of course, were justified. In dealing piecemeal with problems arising from rapidly developing subject matter, many teachers had allowed courses to become overcrowded, or too specialized, or they had presented students with a number of apparently unrelated courses failing to stress common principles. Many, again, had not developed new teaching methods to deal adequately with the larger numbers of students, and the new audiovisual techniques tended to remain the province of relatively few enthusiasts despite their great potential for class and individual teaching. This was hardly surprising, for until the late 1960s, the majority of teachers in higher education had not been offered courses on teaching methods and the few courses available were usually far too brief to be effective.

Comments by students from four universities or colleges, recorded by Marris (1964), indicate some causes of their frustration:

> . . . you want to do so much, and you're only given the chance to do so little – for instance attending lectures in the evenings by other societies, reading more widely. I can remember when I first came up, the Vice Chancellor said that the essence of university was that you should be intellectually excited. But if you are, there is very little chance of fulfilling or satisfying that excitement.
> (Southampton law student)

The complaints about those who covered too wide a field in the time available showed that some students had little time to think or to grasp essentials:

> The trouble is, there are so many branches of civil engineering and you do need an understanding of the whole field: it would be difficult to specialize any more. But you need a bit more time to think about the basic principles. There's a fantastic amount of course work – lab reports, writing up experiments, questions, drawing work you have to do – and it takes up two-thirds of your time, and leaves you very little time for revision or trying to understand the lecture . . . It doesn't train you to think, it's just mechanical, it's trotted out to you all the time, as though you were machines.   (Northampton)

To these criticisms by students must be added the very general one that contact with members of staff in large departments can be insufficient. In some departments increasing numbers have led teaching staff to feel this themselves and to institute group discussion to supplement lectures, and to provide students with the opportunity to discuss problems. The advantages of group discussions that almost all teaching staff mention are that they get to know the students and they obtain feedback on their teaching. One may question, however, whether it is desirable to double the work of staff and students in this way, especially if during the lecture students spend the time writing down subject matter which they have no time to take in. It would be better to devise methods where both objectives are achieved simultaneously wherever this is possible. For example, a shortened lecture followed by questions to which students write answers, discuss them briefly with their neighbours, and then put any outstanding questions to the lecturer, gives the student an opportunity to use, and so better understand, the subject matter. It also allows lecturers to circulate round their classes (if they do not exceed about 50 members) listening to discussion and thereby discovering difficulties and points which they may have failed to make clear.

The complaints in the early 1970s about teaching in higher education and, more especially, about teaching methods in universities and technical colleges, subsided as a measure of reorientation began. This reorientation consisted mainly of greater student participation in decision-making and of greater provision for the improvement of teaching. Reports from the Nuffield foundation (1974–76) showed that many innovations (albeit often on a small scale and unrelated to each other) were completed or in progress and there was a growing number of courses offering 'training' in teaching skills in the universities.

Despite these changes, many of the comments on teaching made in recent studies are similar to those made 10 years earlier – although comments on unsatisfactory, overcrowded courses seem to be rather less common.

Fairly extensive studies in the late 1970s showed that university teachers were often found to be ineffectual, but were unaware of their shortcomings. In one study by Brennan and Percy (1976) for example, teachers and students agreed that the main aim of teaching should be to stimulate students' independence, flexibility and critical thinking, and both described 'poor' teachers as those who lacked interest in students and failed to communicate with them. Although the teachers believed that such persons were rare exceptions, the students thought that the latter description applied to a majority of their teachers. For them, the 'good' teacher who combined enthusiasm for the subject with concern for the students was rare.

Further student comments

In 1974 Sheffield asked 7000 Canadian graduates to give the names of excellent teachers that they had experienced while at university and to indicate what it was about these teachers that had made them so effective. Approximately 1000 students replied and 23 'star' names emerged. These 'stars' were then each asked to write an essay about how they went about teaching, and in Sheffield's text these essays are juxtaposed with the students' comments. It is clear from the results that no one way of teaching is seen as best, nor will any one way suit everyone. Nonetheless the students thought highly of teachers who were masters of their subject matter, teachers who prepared their lectures well and could relate their material to practical issues, and teachers who encouraged questions and were enthusiastic about their subject matter.

In 1977, Bliss and Ogborn reported students' reactions to undergraduate science studies. In this well-planned investigation, students were invited to tell 'good' and 'bad' stories as well as an additional story about their experiences in reply to questions such as 'Tell me about a time when you found yourself working really hard'. In this way the researchers hoped to get at the general through the particular, and at abstractions through concrete examples.

Since it is impossible to give in brief the full flavour of a book, it must suffice to say that 'good' stories all mention interest, success, enthusiasm and similar feelings on the part of students, for example increased interest in the subject, feelings of pleasure and satisfaction or, more low key, feeling stimulated to read. The stories also mention increased self-confidence or security, usually in association with appreciative comments about teachers; or they may record a sense of achievement, for which the students themselves take the credit. About one-third explicitly mention a desire to learn more about a topic. Good and bad stories both stress understanding – or not understanding – as the single most frequent reason for feeling 'good' or 'bad'.

In the 'bad' stories, the students may feel bad in themselves or about themselves, feeling either a real sense of failure, personally inadequate or insecure; they feel puzzled, depressed or confused. Others react against their teachers, directly blaming them, or withdrawing by expressing their lack of interest, not caring or commenting that lectures are time wasting. Although the views of students in the three years differ very little, feelings of confusion and bewilderment are more common in the first year and blaming teachers is more frequent in the later years.

The effect of teachers and teaching on learning was also considered in a major study in 1981 by Ramsden and Entwistle. In this study 2208 students from 66 academic departments in 6 contrasting disciplines from British universities and polytechnics completed an 'approaches to studying' inventory and a 'course perceptions' questionnaire. The authors note that some departments and some lecturers seem to facilitate a deep, or meaningful approach to study, encouraging learning for pleasure, while others use methods of teaching or make coursework demands which force students into surface approaches, emphasizing learning by rote and interest in the courses solely for the qualifications they offer. Departments that excelled in 'meaning orientation' were perceived as having good teaching and allowing freedom in learning. Departments gaining high scores on 'reproducing orientation' were seen to have a heavy workload and a lack of freedom in learning.

The authors quote two students of English, the first one explaining how enthusiastic teaching could develop a positive attitude to studying a subject, while the second one, following an independent studies course, describes the effect on his attitudes of being able to choose method and content.

> If they have enthusiasm, then they really fire their own students with the subject, and the students really pick it up . . . I'm really good at and enjoy (one course) but that's only because a particular tutor I've had has been so enthusiastic that he's given me enthusiasm for it and now I really love the subject.

> If you're doing independent studies you're obviously interested in what you're doing. Therefore you're in a much more relaxed mental state for approaching work.

In their concluding remarks concerning what might be done to help students, Ramsden and Entwistle stress the need for good teaching, freedom in learning and an appropriate workload. As instances of what students mean by the first two of these, they cite:

Good teaching:
Staff here make a real effort to understand difficulties students may be having in their work.

> The lecturers in this department always seem ready to give help and advice on approaches to studying.

> Lecturers in this department seem to be good at pitching their teaching at the right level for us.

Freedom in learning:
We seem to be given a lot of choice here in the work that we do.

> Students have a great deal of choice over how they are going to learn in this department.

1.4 Teachers' attitudes and opinions

In Britain there have been few inquiries into teachers' views and attitudes; teachers have rarely been asked what they consider most important in teaching, what their opinions are concerning the characteristics of good teachers or what characteristics they look for in students.

Teachers' expectations of students and views on what teaching should accomplish may be little changed where teachers have not had occasion to reconsider the aims of education or the variety of students' needs. Thus, some university teachers still expect to be offered as students only potential scholars, who will devote themselves exclusively to the acquisition of knowledge and the development of prowess in research. They tend to neglect students who seek a higher education with other kinds of advancement in mind, or who take their subject as a subsidiary study. Although Hunter (1971) calls this the 'scientific view', it is commonly seen in arts departments also. Even where attitudes are less extreme there is often a tendency for such teachers to use uncritically those teaching methods which they themselves experienced as students. Little thought is given to the purpose of higher education in its social context, nor is an analysis made in any detail of the requirements of the professions in which the students will serve.

Other teachers still subscribe to the view, more commonly held in the previous century by those who catered for the leisured classes, that a university education should not be concerned in any sense with vocational training; to these teachers education consists in 'enlargement of the mind' which comes about through contact with scholarly and cultured companions. This has been termed the 'philosophical view' by Hunter (1971), discussing the teaching of law, and it features as the 'country-house-party model' in Becher's (1971) discussion of the effectiveness of higher education.

There is, of course, some merit in this approach for very able students, who can direct their own studies independently and who have acquired standards of criticism to apply to their work. But as a method it is inefficient in transmitting these skills to less able, or less well-prepared students even if a high staff–student ratio and concern for students' welfare result in ample tutorial supervision. Moreover, it seems reasonable to question the value of enlarging the mind when it leads to uncongenial and limited prospects for the rest of life, as it so often does for many young students who face unemployment after their degree course unless they have resources to undertake further extensive training.

A different kind of attitude – more common among teachers in vocational schools and teachers of the applied sciences – leads them to concentrate on drilling students in information and in practical skills. They see no need to provoke students into thinking about the subject but tend to maintain, on the contrary, that acquisition of 'a body of knowledge' is essential before any genuine thinking is possible. This, too, is an attitude which students accept with resignation at best, for increasingly they are coming to believe that higher studies should not be narrowly useful but should also be educational in a wide sense.

These three kinds of teachers' expectations described above might be classified respectively as academic, liberal and vocational. There is some correspondence between these sets of teachers' expectations and 'orientations' studied in students. Investigations among students, by interview and questionnaire, show that they view their university experiences in different ways and that this affects their priorities in working and choice of activities. Henman (1981), for example, attempted to see whether teachers' and students' orientations in a pharmacology department might differ significantly, and so perhaps influence their interactions adversely. In fact, Henman found that there was a similar spectrum of orientations and aims in both staff and students. Thus every student could expect to find a congenial orientation on the part of some members of staff.

Nonetheless there were some discordances. The staff, for example, were unanimous in their aim to improve the students' understanding of the basic principles of pharmacology, whereas the students were more interested in increasing their awareness of the clinical implications of pharmacology. Another, unexpected result was that a greater proportion of the students than the staff were concerned to improve their manipulative skills in the laboratory. Henman notes that students' common dislike of practical work might, therefore, be due to a feeling that they do not have the skills to complete their assignments. He suggests that a laboratory orientation course at the beginning of the year might help them to overcome their lack of confidence.

In the light of these findings and the students' comments in the previous section, it may be interesting to consider a not uncommon belief on the part of university teachers that students are often not 'motivated'. Teachers add, in explanation, that their students show no enthusiasm for studying over and above what is essential to obtain a qualification. Walkden and Scott (1980), for example, discuss the difficulties students encounter in learning mathematics. The authors proceed, seemingly without inquiry among teachers in other universities or colleges, to explain these difficulties on the basis of the attitudes of present-day undergraduates. According to Walkden and Scott, mathematics students: (1) expect to assimilate new ideas without mental effort; (2) are reluctant to devote time to study and to practice; (3) lack the necessary persistence to tackle exercises of a non-trivial nature.

We suspect that these are the views of mathematicians with an academic orientation who fail to appreciate the needs of their more vocationally oriented science students. Certainly it is difficult for specialists in one field to work with students in another, unless they have knowledge of that field also. At another university, Bradford, some students of life sciences take a very different view of mathematics. As one student said: 'Maths is interesting. You get more involved in lectures and can sit and talk after. We're given points of the lectures so we don't have to take notes and can work through examples with her which I think is much more interesting. She took degrees in both maths and biology so she can relate things' (Beard and Senior, 1980).

Whereas the students of Walkden and Scott seem to have lost confidence in their ability to understand mathematics, those taught at Bradford have been met with carefully prepared papers and a teacher who sees their point of view. The result in the former case is 'withdrawal' by the students; in the latter, understanding and a sense of achievement, with appreciation of the teacher, as described by Bliss and Ogborn (1977) in the previous section. So long as teachers are 'untrained' such disappointments and failures on the part of both teachers and students are inevitable.

Needless to say, some students really do lack motivation. They are usually those who have been persuaded to enter university by parents or teachers (Beard and Senior, 1980), who have personal problems which consume their energies (Pentony, 1968), or who are so extroverted in personality that they find solitary study uncongenial (Wankowski, 1973; Entwistle and Wilson, 1977). But when a whole class seems unmotivated then the fault must lie with the teaching.

1.5   Provision for staff development

An interesting, informative book by Matheson (1981), called *Staff Development Matters*, reviews the growth of academic training and development in the universities of the United Kingdom during the years 1961–1981. Prior to that time, because of the traditional belief that academic staff did not require any formal training in teaching, there were few books about teaching methods and no courses for teachers.

Initiatives on a national scale resulted partly from the well-known reports of the Robbins Committee on Higher Education (1963), the Committee on University Teaching Methods (UGC, 1964) and the Brynmor Jones Committee on Audio Visual Aids (UGC, 1965). In view of the complaints about teaching which they received from both teachers and students all three committees recommended that newly appointed lecturers should receive some training in lecturing and tutorial teaching, and that each institution should establish a central service unit in order to improve teaching and communication in higher education. In addition, the Brynmor Jones Committee recommended the establishment of a national centre to exploit new aids, to train staff for central service units, to provide a coordinated cataloguing and library service and a comprehensive information and advisory service, and the National Council for Educational Technology was established by the government in 1967. Within the next two years recommendations for action were made in reports of the Association of University Teachers Working Party on the Training of University Teachers (1969) and the Commission on Teaching in Higher Education of the National Union of Students (1969a). All recommended that university lecturers should be trained.

In their first report on university pay in December 1968, the National Board for Prices and Incomes recommended a probationary period of four or five years for all academic staff entering university at assistant lecturer or lecturer level. A letter to the universities from the University Grants Committee in May 1969 indicated the method of implementing this recommendation, and in February 1972 these conditions were further spelled out. With regard to selection, training and development, they stated that it was incumbent on universities to provide training for the probationer of a helpful and comprehensive nature: 'Advice and guidance by a senior colleague nominated for this task, and encouragement to attend formal courses of instruction should be included'.

When, in May 1971, the Society for Research in Higher Education published the results of a survey of provision in universities for training university teachers, 39 of the 45 universities and 9 constituent colleges of the Universities of London and Wales had some kind of training provision for their staff (Greenaway, 1971).

In 1972, the Committee of Vice-Chancellors and Principals (CVCP) agreed to establish a Coordinating Committee for the Training of University Teachers (CCTUT), in January 1973. The main work of this committee involved the promotion of training in individual universities; encouragement of inter-institutional training activity; the provision of national training conferences and workshops; cooperation in training at international level; relations with other organizations; and the production of publications.

In December 1978 the CVCP decided on a full review of the work of the CCTUT. The Review Group felt that the major concern of training should be the teaching function and that opportunities for in-service training should be offered to staff at all levels of seniority. The Group stated its belief that the termination or diminution of the work of CCTUT at that juncture would put all its past achievement at risk. It therefore established guidelines relating to a new national body which, at 1980 prices, would cost about £40,000 p.a.

Despite these recommendations, the CVCP felt unable to support the proposed large increase in budget at a time of financial stringencies. And, as each of the universities faced financial cuts, they were unwilling even to contribute to the continuance of the coordinating officer's post on a full-time basis.

This does not imply, of course, that staff development activities have now ceased. Most universities still make provision for it. In addition, specialist teachers can attend courses organized by their professional bodies and read the educational journals that they publish. Nevertheless there is a real danger as universities are forced into more stringent economies that, without external impetus, this activity will be increasingly starved of funds.

Williams and Blackstone (1983) argue that there should be three or four prestigious staff development units strategically placed throughout the country, rather than the present inadequate facilities in many institutions. While sympathetic to this proposal, we may note that significant accomplishments have been achieved by small teams in various institutions both in the UK and abroad. The key to the success of these units seems to be a willingness to assist the staff with problems that they bring, rather than attempts to impose solutions on them, and to have a successful in-house newsletter which tells people what is going on. Three such newsletters which we can recommend are Birmingham University's *Teaching News*, Loughborough University's Academic Staff Training and Development Committee's *Newsletter*, and the University of Waterloo's *Instructional Development at Waterloo*. Furthermore, if small financial resources are made available for the unit to allocate to individuals in departments in order to assist developments in teaching practice, this seems helpful (see Lacey, 1983; Rutherford and Mathias, 1983).

1.6   The growth of research in higher education

Parallel with the growth of staff development came a growth in funding for research. Predictably this was greatest and came earliest in the USA. When the *Handbook of Research on Teaching* first appeared (Gage, 1963) it contained a chapter by McKeachie, 'Research on teaching at the college and university level', in which he discussed learning principles relevant to the study of teaching methods. He drew attention to difficulties in comparing teaching methods, prior to summarizing investigations into lecturing, comparisons of lectures with other methods of teaching, studies of various group discussion methods, laboratory teaching, project methods, individual study and automated techniques. In addition McKeachie also commented on studies of students' characteristics, notably the effects of independence, anxiety, authoritarianism and sex differences on learning. His chapter concluded with a survey of studies of the role of faculty attitudes in teaching and learning.

Ten years later, when the second handbook appeared (Travers, 1973), emphases in research had changed substantially. Trent and Cohen (1973), authors of the chapter 'Research on teaching in higher education', grouped their survey of investigations under five main headings: research on the effects of teaching environments; student characteristics and the learning process; teaching technology and methods; teaching recruitment, training and resources; and the evaluation of teaching. In their concluding remarks the authors noted evidence of resistance to change in colleges and universities and the generally disappointing quality of the research, despite a few excellent studies. They commented that the need was 'for more comprehensive and sophisticated research, for more evaluation based on the research, for better dissemination of its results, and for the institutions to make use of these results'.

It is to be expected, therefore, that in the *Third Handbook of Research on Teaching* (due to appear in 1984), there will be greater emphasis on the evaluation of courses and teaching. Other topics which seem likely to receive more attention include students' study methods and strategies, relationships between personality traits or cognitive styles and academic success, and effects of teaching styles and of interactions between teachers and students on learning. In addition we may expect to see changes not only in topics but also in the approach to research itself. There is increasing concern with students' and teachers' views of the educational process and correspondingly less interest in testing performance.

In Britain, since the 1960s, the Department of Education and Science has funded an increasing number of research projects. The Social Science Research Council was set up in 1966 to administer funds for selected research projects in social sciences, including education, and a number of bodies such as the Leverhulme Trust and the Nuffield Foundation gave substantial sums to support a diversity of projects.

From the United States, a flow of new ideas prompted further experimentation. And, at about the same time, complaints from students about the quality of teaching and methods in assessment, together with a changing climate of opinion, led to the introduction of courses and conferences for university teachers. These in their turn, through the sharing of ideas, led to growth in research by the teachers themselves. Professional bodies also became active in promoting investigations into the content of examinations, the effects of new teaching methods, and so on.

The Society for Research into Higher Education (SRHE) introduced a series of publications on teaching, of which *Research into Teaching Methods in Higher Education* (Beard, 1968) was the first volume. This brief survey was designed to be read by new lecturers prior to the annual course for new lecturers organized by the University Teaching Methods Unit of the University of London. Further volumes of the series dealt with audiovisual aids (Flood-Page, 1971), objectives in higher education (Beard et al., 1974) and group discussion methods (Abercrombie, 1979). Although some useful conclusions could be drawn from the research reported in these volumes, the small scale of many investigations, the lack of adequate control groups and the absence, on the whole, of a series of related researches, made generalization from the results difficult or impossible. However, by the time the fourth edition of *Research into Teaching Methods* was published (Beard et al., 1978) there was a number of surveys of related researches to draw on.

In 1971, in order to boost efforts in the area of staff training, the UGC decided to earmark a substantial sum of money and to invite proposals for 'experimental projects in the training and development of university teachers and administrators'. In the end £130,000 was assigned to 19 projects, selected from among 35 proposals. Matheson (1981) lists the 19 successful ones. A particularly relevant cooperative project was undertaken by the London University Teaching Methods Unit and the Department of Educational Administration. This provided organizational models for different approaches to staff development. A collection of resource material produced for some of the training sessions is now available for use elsewhere (Piper and Glatter, 1977).

The growth of research in higher education is in part symptomatic of changes within the educational system. A development of considerable interest has been the growth in contributions by teachers in universities, polytechnics and colleges to educational research, and to systematic design of new curricula both in their own subjects and in interdisciplinary studies. In the view of one sociologist (Gorbutt, 1974), the transition of a rapidly changing society forces teachers to play a more dynamic and self-conscious role, re-examining the content and underlying assumptions of the curriculum at all levels. He suggests that we need to generate a new model of teacher education and educational practice, the basic aim being to produce the self-critical researching teacher who will constantly monitor the effects of his own and colleagues' activities and modify his behaviour accordingly. Teaching itself should become a self-critical research act, and educational research, far from being the remote preserve of a few, should be part of the normal activity in schools and colleges.

1.7   Reorientating staff development

Since the development of skills in teaching and learning has been taken up enthusiastically by some teachers, it may seem puzzling at first sight that teaching in higher education has not been more generally improved.

In discussing a project in the USA in which he studied professors as teachers, Eble (1972) commented: 'If college teaching is to be improved, diverse forces must change both attitudes and practices. The project has emphasized affecting faculty members, administration, and institutional structures in ways favourable to teaching.' He added that there was independent support for the belief that values dominant in higher education failed to give adequate support to teaching; but that few concrete suggestions had been made about how to change these values. In Eble's view the graduate school was the place where the college professor's values were most firmly established. He therefore thought that help should be given with teaching around the time of obtaining a doctorate.

Eble further commented that 'within the College or University, the reward system can be affected by defining in ways favourable to teaching the policies and practices which determine appointments, promotions, and salaries. But equally important, it seems to me, is substantial financial support for teaching from the top of the university budget. Faculty development has been shamefully neglected.' Other suggestions included the appointment of university professors who would exemplify teaching of extraordinary excellence and the provision of a central source for gathering, selecting and digesting information about teaching and getting the information into the hands of those students, faculty and administrators who could use it.

In Britain, except for brief courses for new teachers, programmes vary in success and tend to be ignored on the whole. In 1978 Greenaway and Harding observed that it was rare to find coherent policies, institutionally approved, and that it was key persons rather than committees who were catalysts for policy initiative for staff development. It is of interest, therefore, to read a paper by Mack (1978) concerning staff development courses at the University of Loughborough; courses which, although similar in content to those elsewhere, are always filled to capacity. He attributes this (1) to the university's supportive attitude to staff development as shown by provision of funds, and by promotion and salary increments for those who take advantage of the training offered; (2) to the use of genuine expertise in organizing training programmes and in using an organizer who is an ordinary member of staff; and (3) to the fact that information about the courses is distinctively produced and leaflets sent in good time to every member of staff.

There may be little that staff developers can do to influence the reward system. They can, however, devise courses which appeal to their colleagues and advertise them in a way that attracts favourable attention. Investigators and inquiries suggest that courses are more likely to attract staff if they are seen as relevant to their needs. For example, Moss (1977) circulated a checklist to his colleagues on which they could indicate areas of special and subject interest, with a covering letter promising to supply relevant information in these areas. A much larger number replied than would have attended staff seminars.

Bruhns and Thomsen (1979) found that the major concerns of new staff in Copenhagen related to personal knowledge of subject matter and to the adequacy with which they could organize and verbally present subject matter and arouse students' interest. In comparing these concerns with the major components of introductory courses for university teachers, they noted that some had little relevance for beginner teachers. In Britain, Taylor (1980) writes critically of courses that separate curriculum and pedagogy, offer indirect instruction and fail to address the (often) poorly articulated anxieties of university staff with respect to their teaching.

Fox (1981), however, notes that staff do not always perceive their need for training as teachers and he recommends taking steps to increase their instructional awareness. That this can be done is evident from the success of workshops at the Centre for Medical Education, Research and Development at the University of New South Wales. Associates of the Centre – Blizard et al. (1979), for instance – report on the favourable responses of nearly 600 Indonesian medical academics, from 10 different medical schools, to a series of two-week workshops in educational science. These workshops had the limited purpose of helping participants (1) to acquire skills in constructing educational objectives, at all levels, from those to do with the running of the institution to those connected with a particular course, and (2) to develop positive attitudes towards the use of these skills in curriculum design and planning. The method of planning the workshops is outlined by Cox (1982) in the Centre's *Newsletter*, and the book *The Workshop Way* (Mack, 1978) shows that this method has also been used with some success in Britain. Workshops can lead to a change of attitude towards curriculum design and teaching, and this leads participants to encourage their colleagues to attend.

Another related method specifically designed to assist teachers in verbally presenting material is micro-teaching. Here teachers have a limited number of objectives in teaching a small group of students, and the process is video-taped. New teachers, in particular, find it very helpful to see themselves lecturing on video-tape; they are more likely to appreciate some of the errors that they are making, finding it easier to accept their own criticisms and those of peers rather than comments by staff developers. Brown (1976) outlines the objectives of the method, together with the pros and cons of the technique.

For some teachers reading about teaching and learning may be sufficient for them to decide what is understood by 'good teaching' and whether their own needs to be improved. Two widely differing books might be of assistance. Meyer and Veenstra (1980) at Cape Town have prepared a 'practical guide to effective teaching and learning', principally for teachers in higher education. The contents are arranged alphabetically beginning at 'Aids' and ending at 'Visualisation'. The shortest entry is 'Chalkboards' and the longest is 'Course evaluation'.

In the USA Gilbert Highet has published *The Immortal Profession* (1976). This book is unusual in that it is not a set of chapters on lectures, tutorials, practical work and so on, but discusses topics such as 'the scholarly life' and 'the need for renewal'. A chapter entitled 'Teaching college teachers how to teach' does not contain research findings but simply opens the discussion on what new teachers should be taught, and how, when and from whom they should gain this information. New teachers, Highet argues, need to be taught how to communicate clearly, how to prepare for class, how to set examinations, how to be sympathetic to students and so forth. But more than this they need to recognize that active energetic teaching is good for self-esteem. These things, he argues, cannot be learned in short courses on teaching methods: one learns best by watching other (master) teachers, and by the constant monitoring of one's own progress.

So far, on the whole, we have limited 'staff development' to mean the development of teaching skills, while recognizing that its meaning can be wider. Centra (1978) conducted an inquiry in 756 colleges and universities in the USA in an attempt to find out what staff development was in progress. As a result he distinguished four types of faculty development practices: traditional practices (sabbaticals, temporary teaching-load reductions); instructional assistant practices (senior teachers with expertise to help); those that emphasize the assessment of faculty (ratings by college administrators, students); and those that involve faculty in improvement activities. Over 300 of the institutions had established Staff Development Units, but most of these were very small.

As staff development has come to be interpreted more widely, the need for clearer definition has been felt increasingly. Rose (1978) comments: 'Anything a faculty member does outside the classroom is now called "staff development" '. He adds: 'In this mélange most development programmes have little potential for contributing significantly to instructional improvement'.

In Britain, as a result of his work with CCTUT, Matheson (1981) feels the need to define staff development more clearly. He wishes also to redirect it, in its sense of instructional improvement. In his view it is essential that it should become a normative mode of activity involving 'the monitoring and maintenance of values' and the endorsement of 'canons of scholarship and codes of good professional practice'. In addition, Matheson notes that many staff development activities are intellectually below par in comparison with other professional academic pursuits: as Matheson puts it, 'pedagogy in higher education is in a pre-professional state'. He comments, too, on the deficiency of discipline-based training, advanced courses, training of tutors and inter-institutional cooperation. While there are undoubtedly some promising beginnings in each of these areas, there is still far to go and, regrettably, the resources required to expedite progress are diminishing.

1.8   Summary

- Social and technological changes affect the pattern of university provision and ways of teaching and learning.
- Students need to know how to obtain new information and how to share

it with colleagues from other disciplines.

● Teachers – via staff development – are becoming more aware of changes in methods of teaching and learning.

● Teaching is undervalued in university reward systems compared with research, but some teachers are now combining the two activities by carrying out research into their own teaching.

CHAPTER 2

AIMS, GOALS AND OBJECTIVES

In this chapter we distinguish between aims, goals and objectives in higher education, and discuss the importance of these with respect to course planning. We also consider how the aims, goals and objectives of students may differ from those of teachers and what might be done to reconcile these differing viewpoints – or at least to clarify the issues.

When students first enter higher education many of them have little idea what to expect. Their knowledge about what their new teachers do (when they are not teaching) is sparse, as is the teachers' knowledge about what their students are doing when they are not in class. One way for the staff to help students to recognize what the new situation is about is for the staff to make clearer their aims, goals and objectives. This is one of the reasons, for example, that Open University course units almost invariably start with a list of objectives, and the CNAA also lays great store by them.

2.1 Aims

What are aims? Aims are broad general statements of intent. If, for example, you ask a member of staff what a particular course is for, you are apt to get answers like 'to help students learn to think', 'to enlarge the mind', 'to provide a body of knowledge from which students can go further', 'to fill lacunae in knowledge', and so on. Aims are broad general statements which attempt to set the scene for later, more detailed statments which will specify how these aims are to be achieved. Because of their breadth and encompassing nature it will sometimes be difficult to evaluate whether or not one's aims have been achieved.

2.2   Goals

Goals are more specific statements. Goals explain how aims are to be achieved. If aims are general, and are perhaps rather grandiose or vague, then goals are specifically directed to the more immediate ways in which one might start to try to achieve the aims. If aims answer the question 'What is the course for?', goals answer the question 'How shall we achieve all this?'

An example of this difference is shown indirectly in *Table* 2.1, which lists the aims and goals of a subsidiary course in psychology. It can be seen that the third aim is the most general (i.e. to consider the advantages and limitations of psychology as a discipline and as an approach to knowledge), and that the goals are concerned with methods of achieving it – by using three specific textbooks, and related lectures, tutorials, essays and examinations.

Although goals are more specific than aims, goals are still general statements. Indeed, in *Table* 2.1, they are largely statements about methods. These goals still have to be refined in terms of content: What are the three areas that are to be taught? Which one should be taught first? What about

Table 2.1   An example of aims and goals taken from a course handout for subsidiary psychology at the University of Keele. The goals explain how the aims will be achieved

---

Aims
This course offers students the opportunity
- to find out something about three main areas of psychological enquiry;
- to assess for themselves the competence and usefulness of research work done, evidence obtained, and the conclusions drawn in these areas of psychology;
- to consider the advantages and limitations of psychology as a discipline and as an approach to knowledge.

Goals
Students will learn about psychology in three ways during the subsidiary course:
- from the three course textbooks;
- from lectures which discuss and expand aspects of each course text;
- from tutorials where students can discuss work and raise questions with a tutor.

Students will be required to write three essays (one each term) setting out their ideas and conclusions based on evidence from each of these three areas of psychology.
Students will be assessed by the marks obtained on these three essays (33 percent) and on an end-of-year essay-type examination (67 percent).

---

major and minor topics within each area? and so on. Thinking about goals leads one to consider the various teaching methods that can be used, and the sequences in which the instruction will be given.

For many teachers this seems sufficient. Specifying the topics and methods seems to be all that is required in course planning. For some, however, there is a need to go beyond this – beyond the choice of content and methods to further considerations of what the students will actually do in the course and what they will achieve.

2.3   Objectives

Objectives provide specific statements of what students *will be able to do* at the end of instruction. They attempt to do this in the clearest terms possible. So, if aims are general statements of interest, and goals state how that intent may be realized, then objectives provide statements which enable one to assess whether or not that intent has been realized. Objectives describe what the students will be able to do to demonstrate mastery of their topic. Aims, goals, objectives and assessment are thus inexorably inter-linked.

Most objectives contain three elements. These are:
1. A description of what the student should be able to do or to produce after the instruction.
2. A statement of the conditions under which the student should be able to do this.
3. A statement of the criteria, or standards of performance that will be used to judge what has been done.

In describing the first element of an objective it is important to specify clearly and exactly what it is that the learner is expected to do when demonstrating competence. To do this one uses verbs which express actions which can be measured. For example, instead of saying that students should understand X, one has to say that students will be able to explain, or to define, or to distinguish between X and non-X, etc. All of these verbs imply understanding, but we have now stated what we mean by under-standing in this context, and thus the achievement of this understanding can be assessed.

Once one has determined what the student should be able to do, then statements of conditions and criteria follow fairly automatically. These statements supply further information to make the objective as complete as possible. Will the student have to get his or her answer completely right, or are small mathematical errors irrelevant, provided the procedure is correct? Will the student be able to use reference books or calculators in the exam or not? Are there time standards to be met? and so on.

Figure 2.1   The three parts of an objective (adapted with permission from Figure 7.2. of Davies, 1976)

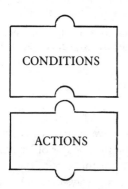

	Example 1	*Example 2*
CONDITIONS	From a legal contract and a list of contract laws,	Given a reproduction of David's *The Oath of the Horatii*,

ACTIONS	the student will be able to show which of the laws are violated by the wording of the contract	the students will be able to outline in writing six reasons that may be used to substantiate the argument that this painting represented a new type of revolutionary classicism in art
STANDARDS	the student is expected to be right at least eight out of ten times	reference should be made to composition, action, expression and accessories in the reasons

Davies (1976) suggests that these three components (conditions, actions and standards) are like three pieces of a jigsaw (*Figure* 2.1). However, as he points out, it is limiting to think of single pieces: objectives have to be fitted together to form a set, and sets of objectives have to be fitted together to make a course or programme. One problem with using objectives is determining just how much detail is necessary. There seems to be an assumption by some people that one should specify almost every task that a student should be able to perform. Such an approach, carried to extremes, can only be time consuming and wasteful. The notion, however, of considering more generally just what students should be able to do at the end of instruction, is an extremely valuable one. Thus one needs to distinguish between general and detailed objectives, and to write objectives at appropriate levels (*Figure* 2.2).

Figure 2.2   The same objective expressed in three levels of detail (reproduced with permission of the publishers from Dick and Carey, 1978)

Level 1:   The student will be able to write a paper which illustrates the application of scientific investigation techniques to the identification, investigation and discussion of a problem.

Level 2:   The student will be able to formulate and write a statement of null hypotheses and logical alternative hypotheses for given problem situations.

Level 3:   Given several hypotheses, the student will be able to rewrite the hypotheses using the following notation system: Ho $G_1 = G_2$, Ha: G_1, G_2; Ho: $G_1 = G_2$, Ha; $G_1 > G_2$; Ho: $G_1 = G_2$, Ha: $G_1 < G_2$.

2.4   Different kinds of objectives

Although stating and using objectives in education have a lengthy history, perhaps the best-known attempt to describe different kinds of objectives was made by Benjamin Bloom and his colleagues in the 1950s (Bloom, 1956). What Bloom and his colleagues did was to classify ways in which one could describe the intended behaviour of students after instruction. To do this they devised three sets of descriptions. It was claimed that objectives could be classified as 'cognitive' (i.e. to do with comprehending knowledge and information), 'affective' (i.e. to do with attitudes, values and emotions) and 'psychomotor' (i.e to do with physical skills). The plan was to arrange objectives within each of these three areas from the simplest to the most complex. This was achieved for the first two areas (cognitive and affective) but the task was not completed for the third (skills). However, other investigators have attempted to complete Bloom's work. *Table* 2.2 illustrates the hierarchical nature of the framework that Bloom and his colleagues envisaged for each major category of objectives.

Cognitive objectives

At the lower levels of cognitive learning one is concerned with knowledge – knowledge of facts and the correct use of terminology. As the objectives become more complex one wants learners to be able to demonstrate their comprehension and to be able to apply what they know to new situations. Finally, one wants them to be able to analyse and synthesize disparate information into new wholes and to make judgements about the value of materials and methods for given purposes – in a word to evaluate.

Cognitive objectives		Affective objectives		Psychomotor objectives	
Major categories	*Associated action verbs*	*Major categories*	*Associated action verbs*	*Major categories*	*Associated action verbs*
1.0 Knowledge	to describe, recall, state, identify, recognize, name, list, etc.	1.0 Receiving (attending)	to listen, attend, to be aware, favour, accept	1.0 Reflex movements	to flex, stretch, straighten, extend, inhibit, tense, relax
2.0 Comprehension	to comprehend, understand, predict, interpolate, extrapolate, interpret	2.0 Responding	to state, answer, comply, acclaim, applaud	2.0 Basic movements	to crawl, creep, glide, walk, run, jump
3.0 Application	to apply, show, use, demonstrate, perform, relate, construct, explain	3.0 Valuing	to accept, recognize, participate, support, debate, appreciate, prefer	3.0 Perceptual abilities	to catch, bounce, write, draw from memory, distinguish by touching, balance
4.0 Analysis	to analyse, separate, breakdown, discriminate, distinguish, detect, categorize	4.0 Organization	to discuss, organize, judge, relate, correlate, formulate, weigh	4.0 Physical ability	to stop and start, move precisely, improve, endure strenuous activity
5.0 Synthesis	to synthesize, combine, restate, summarize, generalize, conclude, derive, deduce	5.0 Characterization	to revise, change, face, accept, judge, resolve, resist, reject, identify with, believe	5.0 Skilled movements	to type, saw, play the piano, file, skate, juggle, dance
6.0 Evaluation	to evaluate, judge, decide, choose, assess, contrast, criticize, defend, support			6.0 Non-discursive movements	to gesture, carry oneself, perform skilfully, to smile knowingly

Source: Adapted with permission from Davies (1976).

Affective objectives

A similar notion held by Bloom concerned how one might categorize and classify affective objectives – those to do with attitudes, values and emotions. At the lower end of the hierarchy are objectives like willingness to receive and to respond to instruction. After this one moves up to the development of internally consistent and coherent qualities of character and conscience (see *Table* 2.2).

Psychomotor objectives

A similar classification of psychomotor objectives was provided by Harrow (1972), but this classification was concerned more with primary than tertiary education. However, as shown in *Table* 2.2, at the lower end one is concerned with reflexes and basic fundamental movements. After this one moves up to perceptual and physical abilities and finally to skilled movements and what Harrow terms 'non-discursive communication'. This is defined as comprising those behaviours which involve expressive communication in certain gestures and postures.

There are four things to note in particular about the classification scheme described above:

1. It was more complex than is apparent from this brief description. Each numbered level in the hierarchies shown in *Table* 2.2 were in fact further subdivided.

2. Its purpose was to help teachers to evaluate instructional outcomes. For each level in the hierarchy Bloom and his colleagues provided samples of the kinds of questions that one might ask to determine if that level of objective had been reached.

3. Bloom did not intend, by separating his objectives into the three main kinds, to argue that they were separate entities. Learning anything involves to some degree the achievement of all three kinds of objectives. What the classification schemes did indirectly was to point out that many methods of assessment concentrate on one kind of objective at the expense of others.

4. The scheme proposed was not intended to be the final word. It was a guide to ways of thinking about aims and assessment. Other taxonomies have been proposed (see Davies, 1976).

What in fact happened, as we shall see below, is that Bloom's approach turned out to be a major guide for curriculum development. Many teachers developed it for their own disciplines, and some specific references are as follows: Bishop (1971), art education; Ross (1972–1977), law; Naaera

(1972), physiology; Stones and Anderson (1972), educational psychology; and Short and Tomlinson (1979), medical sciences. Other examples may be found in virtually all of the Open University course units and five specific examples are given in an appendix to this chapter (see pp. 38–43).

2.4 Planning with objectives

The use of objectives is associated in many people's minds with the notion of rational or systematic planning. The basic idea here is that a set of goals and related objectives can be stated, a set of methods to achieve these aims can be devised, and techniques of assessment can be developed to assess whether or not the course has been successful. If, as expected, one is not as successful as one would wish at the first attempt, then the course can be revised, improved and retested until it is performing satisfactorily. This approach (although it has its critics) has been used quite successfully in many areas of higher education: some approaches to computer-assisted and programmed instruction provide specific examples. Rational or systematic planning may be diagrammed as shown in *Figure 2.3*.

It is relatively rare, however, for teachers to plan an entirely new course from scratch. Most new courses have to fit in with the ones that already exist and thus they are bound by the constraints of the organization of which they are a part. In fact we suspect that the most common sorts of planning that teachers do are (1) 'expedient' and (2) 'piecemeal' planning.

Expedient planning involves first considering the methods available, and then determining those objectives that will best fit in with the limitations or the constraints imposed by this approach. For example, new lecturers planning new courses are typically told, 'Well it's a 10-week course, with two lectures and one tutorial a week'. The limitations of this approach are that teachers focus on the methods rather than on the objectives and that the methods are not seen to arise out of course aims but appear to have an independence of their own.

Piecemeal planning is possibly the most common form of planning in higher education. This, putting it crudely, involves making alterations to what was done this year in order to make it work better next year. Alterations may arise because of suspected weaknesses in a course (perhaps there was a dramatic drop in attendance) or because of changes in personnel (a colleague has left, or a new colleague with different expertise will be taking part) or because of alterations in conditions (a different lecture theatre, a new time slot). Piecemeal planning, unfortunately, is often neither rigorous

Figure 2.3   A systematic approach to planning instruction

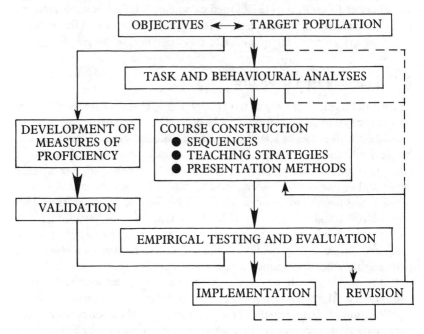

nor systematic. How often do we decide to make changes next year, and then when the time comes do not do so, either because we have forgotten what was planned, or because it now seems to take up too much effort!

Piecemeal planning without objectives seems a little aimless. Consider this example. In one university department it was considered that the final-year students had gaps in their basic theoretical knowledge. To remedy this, a once-weekly lecture course was mounted by the staff for two terms. The lectures were given by different members of staff, each talking about his or her own speciality. Together with the lecture course an optional tutorial system was set up. Students could sign up in each lecture whether or not they wanted to attend a tutorial on that topic later in the week. Tutors were then provided to match the number of students who signed up. The course appeared to work well (although as far as one could tell there was no attempt to see if the gaps in theoretical knowledge had been closed), but it was felt that the course was 'bitty': the lectures lacked cohesion. So, the next year the process was repeated, but the lectures were grouped into topics and the groups of lectures were given all-embracing titles. This seemed reasonable (except that the lectures, despite the titles, were much the same as in the previous year). However, this year it was felt that the students did not take part sufficiently in the tutorials: attendance dropped markedly. To remedy this in the following year regular weekly tutorials for all students were introduced. This solution was thought to work well but this was then abandoned the following year because four of the staff concerned were on leave of absence and student numbers had increased dramatically. In this year of the course the lecturers were asked to devise new sets of related lectures, to give tutorials if they wished, or to use the tutorial time for other things (more lectures, films, etc.).

This example illustrates, as noted earlier, that piecemeal planning can come adrift. Changes were brought about on the basis of intuition and their effects were not properly assessed. For example, it was never really clear whether tutorial attendance did decline markedly from one year to the next, and certainly no attempt was ever made to assess whether or not the theoretical 'lacunae' were ever filled (or, indeed, were even there in the first place!). To solve all these problems more attention should have been paid to what were the course aims – was it in fact necessary and, if it was, how could these aims be best achieved? If the aims and objectives had been specified more precisely then the underlying assumptions of the different teachers involved would have been made more explicit. Indeed one might have expected greater clarity of thinking about all of the elements involved (aims, methods, topics and assessment). At the same time, piecemeal planning can be useful if it is taken seriously. One can build from what is already known; one can consider afresh course objectives each time a change is made; and one can assess the effects of modest changes.

Outlining specific objectives has a vital role in systematic rational planning – when one is creating a new course, whether this be for internal consumption or for approval by an outside body such as the CNAA. Objectives play a modest role in expedient planning but they can make a useful contribution in the area of piecemeal planning – perhaps the most frequent type of planning.

2.6   Objectives in practice

It is probably already clear that thinking about and producing objectives produce proponents for and against the kinds of ideas expressed by Bloom and others. The main limitations appear to be the difficulty of doing the task and the relevance of this approach for certain subject matters and skills. The main advantages appear to lie in the usefulness of specifying objectives as far as teachers and students are concerned.

Objections to objectives have been raised on practical, theoretical and philosophical grounds. Detailed discussions are presented by Popham (1968), Macdonald-Ross (1973) and Davies (1976), to name but three contributors to the debate.

Some of the *practical* objections that have been raised are that:
- it is difficult to specify measurable activities in certain subjects (e.g. the arts);
- there are no well-defined prescriptions for writing objectives;
- the problems of how many, and how detailed the objectives need be, have not been solved;
- it is very time consuming and very difficult to produce lists of detailed objectives for complete courses;
- the easiest objectives to specify are the trivial (lower order) ones, but these are the least useful;
- specifying objectives in advance does not allow for dealing with unpredicted events or 'voyages of exploration' – either by students or staff – and it is these that are really important.

Some of the *theoretical* objections to objectives are:
- there is an extremely large number of paths through any body of knowledge. Lists of actions do not, therefore, adequately represent the structure of knowledge;
- there are no consistent views as to the origin of objectives (thus there is no 'one way' to instruct);
- the presence of objectives, therefore, does not make the related test items used for assessment automatically valid.

Some of the *philosophical* objections to objectives are:
- objectives smack of behaviourism, and suffer from many of the weaknesses of any operationalist dogma;
- the suitability of goal-referenced models of education can be questioned;
- the use of objectives implies a poverty-stricken model of student– teacher interaction.

All of these objections are important, and it would be difficult to deny them out of hand, but there are counter-arguments too. Our view is that although the case against objectives must be taken seriously, this is not an argument for not using them in appropriate circumstances.

First of all, it would seem reasonable to suggest that one has to consider the appropriateness of objectives. Agreed, it will be more difficult to state objectives in some subject areas than in others. The problem lies therefore in recognizing where objectives are appropriate, not in their blanket acceptance or dismissal. As it happens, a number of people have attempted to specify objectives in arts curricula. In the appendix to this chapter (p. 38) we include as examples schemes from courses in history, French, design and art education.

People using objectives have testified to their value as:
● a guide to planning new curricula;
● a means of exposing underlying assumptions;
● a stimulus to clearer thinking;
● an aid to precise rather than vague communication;
● a guide to actual teaching and choice of teaching method;
● a guide for learners – both in dependent and independent study situations;
● a guide to developing comprehensive modes of assessment.

2.7 Sharing objectives: staff and students

One of the claims of those who advocate specifying course objectives is that providing such objectives for students clarifies for them (and for the teachers) what it is that is being attempted. The research suggests, however (Davies, 1976; Melton, 1978), that objectives help in some situations but not in others.

Melton (1978) suggests that objectives are ineffective when students fail to pay attention to them, when they are too general, too trivial or too difficult, and when they are of little interest to most students. He also points out that if students are conscientious or well motivated they are likely to achieve objectives whether or not they have been specified.

Davies (1976) summarizes the results of over 40 studies directed at testing the effectiveness of objectives. He concludes that the results (mostly from studies with children) are somewhat conflicting, that providing objectives helps learning in some situations and not in others, and that it helps some kinds of learners more than others. In particular, Davies suggests that objectives are more helpful with more traditional methods of teaching and with middle-ability learners, rather than the less able or the very able. Dependent rather than independent learners also do better with objectives.

Various ways of providing students with an outline, or even detailed statements of objectives, have been developed during the past few years. In

Table 2.3   Objectives in university education (for consideration and comment)

Objectives	Teaching method or student activity	Evaluation or feedback
Knowledge At the end of a university career, a student should:		
know the basic terminology of his subject	lectures; assigned reading; practicals; demonstrations, etc.	multiple-choice question examinations; correct use of forms in essays, discussion, etc.
know the principles (basic laws and concepts) of his subject; understand some of the uses to which his subject is put	lectures; assigned reading; practicals; demonstrations, etc. contact with research, industry, professionals in own field; experiments, projects, where appropriate	correct reference to laws, etc. arguments; essay writing, etc. informative assessment of project essays, etc.
be acquainted with principles and application of related subjects	general studies; background reading	synthesis of data from various sources
Skills University teaching in general should enable the student:		
to write coherently	essays; laboratory reports; dissertations; papers to be given in tutorials	informative assessment of those
to be verbally articulate	giving papers; effective argument in discussion groups; tutorials	criticism by other students and tutors
to make his own independent judgements	etc. meets contradictions; contrasting points of view; use of discussion to expose student's assumptions, etc.	e.g. 'compare and contrast' questions in examinations; evaluation of arguments, etc.
to obtain information efficiently	use of library, abstracts, etc.; preparation for essays, projects; open-ended experiments	informative comment on performance; open-book examinations
to think creatively, imaginatively and in abstract terms	research projects; tackling unsolved problems; use of concepts in arguments, discussion	quality of writing (publications?); assessment of method in tackling problems; credit for originality
to cooperate with colleagues and other professionals in future career	joint projects; role-playing; group discussion to give insight into group interactions	evaluation of student's behaviour in a group by tutors and other students
to develop adaptability, i.e. to cope with changing patterns of knowledge (both general technological advance and new ideas in own subject)	exposure to new ideas (not accepting everything given as 'facts')	follow-up after graduation
Attitudes An aim in university teaching is to foster in the student:		
enthusiasm for learning	non-assigned reading; extra-curricular meetings (e.g. science clubs)	extent of extracurricular activity; posing new problems for own investigation

Table 2.3 *Continued*

Objectives	Teaching method or student activity	Evaluation or feedback
scholarly concern for accuracy	contact with teachers and researchers displaying such accuracy; continuous checking of own results	assign marks for accuracy in examinations
awareness of moral, social, economic, political and scientific problems of society	general studies; some projects; modern history, literature, sociology	impressionistically, from student's writing and discussion

one engineering department, for example, students have a list of objectives showing what formulae and principles they are expected to learn during the course (Hill, 1969). In one department of architecture, decisions relating to the making of designs have been outlined in sequences of network analyses (Darke, 1968). A basic network shows the major decisions and their inter-relationships against a time-scale, and each step is analysed further in additional networks. This is to ensure that no essential steps are omitted and that preparations are made in good time for subsequent steps.

Thus, in various ways, students can be spurred on by knowing what is expected of them and by being able to assess the extent to which their tasks have been completed. The traditional kind of syllabus, which consists of a list of topics or books to be read, does not suffice for this purpose. It fails to specify just what it is that students should learn to do. No doubt teachers have this at the back of their minds, but there is some evidence that unless objectives are both stated and deliberately catered for they tend to be neglected. For example, in the medical field, where many of the experimental inquiries into teaching have been made, Miller (1962) found that an aim high in the prospectus at the Medical School at the University of Illinois was 'critical thinking', yet in observing teaching in the school he found that students had little opportunity to ask questions or to take part in discussion. When the students' grades were compared with scores on a standardized test of critical thinking, it appeared that the 25 least critical students obtained high grades whereas the 25 most critical had low ones.

In Britain, critical inquiries into examinations and courses show similar discrepancies with stated aims. Although teachers of sciences commonly say that studying their subjects should teach pupils to think as scientists, an investigation into A-level papers by the Institute of Physics in 1966 (see

Spurgin, 1967) showed that 85 percent of questions could be answered by recalling information alone. Thus these examinations were encouraging memorization rather than thinking.

This final observation brings us back to the statement we made earlier – that aims, goals, objectives and assessment are inexorably interlinked. In Table 2.3 we have attempted to show this in general terms. In the appendix (see below) we have provided more specific examples of how different people, working in different disciplines, have tried to specify more clearly than usual just what it is that they and their students are attempting to achieve.

2.7   Summary

- Aims are general statements of intent, goals explain how aims are to be achieved and objectives state what learners will be able to do upon completing a course.
- The three kinds of objectives – cognitive, affective, psychomotor – are not independent: all play a part in learning any subject matter.
- Objectives play an important role in rational planning, and a lesser (but still important) role in expedient and piecemeal planning.
- The practical, theoretical and philosophical objections to objectives can be met in part by considering how appropriate it is to use objectives in certain situations.
- Sharing objectives between staff and students can clarify what courses are all about: students know what is expected and are able to assess the extent to which they have achieved their goals. Aims, goals and assessment are thus inextricably interlinked.

Appendix

1   Excerpts from aims and objectives from an OU history course (Marwick, 1970)

Part I   What History is and why it is important
1. Definitions
You should understand that the word 'history' is used in various different ways: the 'history' we are mainly concerned with is 'the historian's attempt to reconstruct and interpret the past', not 'the past' itself. You should be able to distinguish between the different uses of the word 'history'.
2. Justifications for the study of history
You should be able to list the various justifications which can be given for studying history. Beyond that you should familiarize yourself with the idea that history is a

social necessity – the idea that history is as necessary to man and society as memory is to the individual, that without history man and society would be totally disorientated, would have no real sense of identity. You do not have to agree with this justification, but you should be able to argue about it.

3. The basic concerns of the historian

You should be aware of the three basic concerns of the historian, which are:

(i) Man in society.

(ii) Change through time (a vital ingredient in history, and one which distinguishes it from the more static studies of the social scientist).

(iii) Particular unique events (as opposed, again, to the abstract conceptualizations of the social scientist).

You should also understand that history involves *explanation* and the study of the *interconnection* between events: *history* should be distinguished from *chronicle* – mere narration of events without explanation or interpretation. You should therefore be able to distinguish history from other types of writing which occasionally bring in the past, such as sociology, political science, biology, astronomy, etc.

4. The subjective element in history

You should understand why it is that although the historian should try to be as objective as he can, it is never completely possible to suppress the personal and subjective element in history. You should understand why it is that history must always in some sense be, as E.H. Carr has said, 'a dialogue between the present and the past': that is, in reconstructing and interpreting the past the historian is always influenced by the attitudes and prejudices of the age and society in which he lives.

5. The development of the modern discipline of history

It is not necessary for you to have a complete knowledge of the history of history, but you should know the names of, and the main achievements associated with, some of the really outstanding historians in the last two hundred years. You should understand how in the twentieth century there has emerged the concept of 'total history' – that is, history which looks at man's past in all its aspects, cultural and social, as well as economic and political.

6. History as science, history as art, history as art and science

You should understand the various basic arguments which are put forward on the different sides of this quite difficult problem. You should be able to reach some conclusions of your own about how far history is scientific, how far it is an art.

2   *Aims, objectives and methods of teaching and evaluation in a medical sciences course (from Short and Tomlinson, 1979)*

Aims	Objectives	Means
The student should:	The student will:	We arrange that:
(1) Appreciate problems of the design of significant experiments	Select objectives Write protocol Include controls Keep to protocol	Laboratory manuals and briefing describe the scope but often require student group to lay down its own plan of action

Aims	Objectives	Means
	Change protocol in the light of experience Finish protocol	and later defend it
(2) Develop precision and appropriate confidence in observation and measurement	Calibrate apparatus Exclude artefacts from measurements Instruct the subject Repeat the readings	Students are required to make and record observations and perform or confirm calibrations of instruments
(3) Competently collate, assess and interpret results	Keep to the protocol Make contemporary records Present tabulated and graphed results Draw suitable conclusions	Students are required to preserve an intelligible record of their findings and use the data to prepare a seminar
(4) Develop appropriate attitudes to people under his care	Instruct subject Take safety precautions	Classes using human subjects may be the students' first experience of formal responsibility for the safety and comfort of another person
(5) Acquire some basic clinical skills	Use and explain the steps on checklists of nine published procedures	Checklists for procedures are published. Students rehearse procedures in labs and arrange critical 'clerking' contacts
(6) Practise clear, concise communication	Deliver audibly a seminar presentation in an orderly manner Show diagrams Discuss results Present succinct written report	Students meet in rooms equipped with seating for 12, and an over-head projector. Seminar preparations assessed, report assessed
(7) Reinforce his or her learning by other modes in the medical course	Relate results to other information where appropriate	Classes are timetabled to relate to rest of the integrated course

3 Excerpts from objectives for a French language course

Objectives: theoretical grasp	Related activity	Evaluation
1. Reorientation: the student will come to understand what is meant by (i) active command of language, (ii) independent reformulation of a given content, (iii) learning from first-hand observation instead of from second-hand instruction.	1. The paraphrase exercise.	

Objectives: theoretical grasp	Related activity	Evaluation
2. Remedial tasks: he or she will begin to eliminate commonest first-year errors (identified over past five years). He or she will observe the structural analysis *implied* in the remedial tapes, in their organization. This structural analysis not presented until year 2.	2. Fortnightly laboratory taped exercises on selected grammatical structures (pronouns, infinitives, articles).	2. Undergoes multiple-item test related exactly to content of tape, before and after performance. Statistical analysis of results shows overall measure of improvement, individual variation, weak areas of the tape.
3. Constructive tasks: he will acquire elementary vocabulary for presentation of ideas, processes of thought, argument (abstract vocabulary).	3. Attends expository lecture, with examples and discussion. Observes the corrections made in this field to his own writing.	

Objectives: aesthetic perception	Related activity	Evaluation
1. Reorientation: he will begin to distinguish: (i) spoken and written registers, (ii) concrete, abstract and figurative language, (iii) archaic and modern usage.	1. The commentary accompanying the paraphrase exercise	No method of evaluating student's performance yet devised. Evaluation mostly directed towards the *materials* being used: how good are they?
2. Constructive tasks: developing speed and suppleness of the ear, so as to catch all kinds of non-academic language (song, cabaret, parody, theatre, interview, formal discourse not previously written).	2. Attends language laboratory, weekly one hour, listening, trans-cribing, responding to short questions, under guidance of monitor.	

4   Excerpts from objectives in design education

The fundamental aims of the course and their related performance requirements (charts 1 and 2) were derived from the initial statement concerning the nature of the course. Aims 1 and 2 (chart 1) embody the context in which the design takes place. Aims 3–7 (chart 2) cover the cycle of operations which is the *design process*. The *design cycle* is then further developed on the next page (chart 3) (not given here).

The context   Chart 1

1. To enable the student to have a defensible concept of the designer's responsibilities.	The student will be systematic in his professional decisions (systematically evaluating his decisions against general social criteria).

2. That the student will be successful in establishing a relationship between the designer and managers, acceptable to both.

The student will be able to:
(a) recognize and fit in with those managers' norms which are not critical to the solution of design problems.
(b) be successful in changing those managers' norms which are critical to the solution of design problems.

The design cycle   Chart 2

3. That the student will state design problems in manageable terms.

The student will ensure that a comprehensive brief is produced. (This means a systematical appraisal of the problem area.)

4. That the student will solve design problems well and economically.

The student will be able to:
(a) discover and evaluate existing solutions,
(b) reach the best solution via the best method (both sets of values measured against explicit criteria).

5. That the student will communicate the solution of a design problem in a way most likely to ensure its acceptance.

The students will be able to:
(a) effectively present the solution of a design problem,
(b) overcome irrational resistance to its acceptance.

6. That the student will implement the solution of a design problem successfully.

The student will be able to ensure that the process of good decision-making is continued through the development of the production process.

7. That the student will secure maximum improvement in the quality of his or her future performance.

The student will be able to validate the accepted solution of a design problem.

---

5   *Objectives in art education* (adapted from Bishop, 1971, pp. 153–154, by permission of Harper & Row, Publishers Inc.)

Listed below are some general objectives in art education published by the National Art Education Association in the USA in 1968. These are numbered 1–8. Beneath each of these general objectives are some more specific objectives labelled a, b, c, etc., designed to show how these general objectives – involving information, attitudes and skills – might be specified more precisely for a course in pottery.

At the end of the art programme, each student should demonstrate his or her capacity to:
1. *Have intense involvement in and response to personal visual experiences:*

a. by voluntarily *attending* ceramics classes and labs an average of three hours a week for at least one term;

b. by voluntarily *attending* an exhibit, display or studio of ceramic work and *discussing* it with others.

2. *Perceive and understand visual relationships in the environment*:

a. by being able to *describe* the relationship between foot, belly, neck and rim in any given ceramic pot;

b. by being able to *identify* and *discuss* examples of good form/function relationships in objects of everyday use.

3. *Think, feel and act creatively with visual art materials*:

a. by voluntarily *making* ceramic objects of his or her own design.

4. *Increase manipulative and organizational skills in art performance appropriate to his abilities*:

a. by being able to *prepare* and *care* for clay and objects of clay from construction through the final firing;

b. by being able to *construct* properly unique objects of clay.

5. *Acquire a knowledge of the world's visual art heritage*:

a. by being able to *describe* generally the differences in the construction of pottery from basket-maker to the wheel, and the general relationship of these methods to the culture of the times;

b. by being able to *distinguish* and *discuss* the differences between the pottery of the American Indian, the Hellenic Greek, the medieval Japanese and the contemporary American.

6. *Use art knowledge and skills in his or her personal and community life*:

a. by voluntarily *purchasing* or *trading* his or her own work for a piece of pottery for himself or herself or for someone else;

b. by voluntarily *sharing* his or her points of view about the existing examples of ceramics in the student's community with others.

7. *Make intelligent visual judgements suited to the student's own experience and maturity*:

a. by being able to *discuss*, on the basis of judgements formed while taking this class, what are examples of good pottery from a group of given examples;

b. by *making* objective *critiques* of the relationship between form and material in his own and the pottery of others.

c. by *keeping* that work of his own which is good and by voluntarily *destroying* that which fails to meet the criteria which he has set for good pottery.

8. *Understand the nature of art and the creative process*:

a. by voluntarily *attempting* projects that are unique to him.

b. by voluntarily *discussing* with others events or objects which seem both unique and important to him.

PART TWO

THE PSYCHOLOGY OF LEARNING

CHAPTER 3

THE PSYCHOLOGY OF LEARNING

In this chapter we first consider main historical trends in the psychology of learning, we then look at today's teaching methods which reflect these earlier views, and finally we consider some new directions suggested by more modern approaches. Our aim here is to make teachers more aware of the implications of the psychology of learning for their own instructional situations.

3.1 Theoretical approaches to learning

In the first half of this century there were two major groups of learning theories – behaviouristic and cognitive – and a third group of less pre-eminence.

The behaviouristic theories, dominated by writers such as Pavlov, Watson, Thorndike, Hull and Skinner, were often termed 'stimulus-response' or S-R theories, and this name reflects their mechanistic view-point. Behaviouristic theories were concerned with what organisms actually did – how they responded to stimuli – and not with what they thought. Thorndike, for example, thought that animals learned by trial and error: habits were automatically 'stamped in' if the consequences were favourable or 'stamped out' if they were not.

Perhaps the best-known and most influential behaviourist is B.F. Skinner (b.1904). Skinner is most closely associated with what is termed 'operant conditioning'. Here, in its basic form, a hungry animal (say a rat) is placed in a box that contains nothing except a lever and a food dispenser. After casting around a while the animal will accidentally press the lever. When it does so a food pellet is released. The animal learns fairly quickly that pressing the lever leads to food. Once this is learned many other variations can take place. Animals can be rewarded by food – or more technically their movements 'reinforced' – for responding to one stimulus and not to another, thus making discriminations. Animals can be rewarded for carrying out certain actions, and not others. If actions are complex they can be taught in simple sequential stages.

The key concept of operant conditioning is that behaviour is affected by its consequences. Blackman (1980) calls this the A:B:C of conditioning, where A = the antecedent conditions, B = the behaviour and C = the consequences. All three elements are closely inter-related.

These simple notions have been elaborated at great length elsewhere (see, for example, Skinner, 1974, 1978). We simply wish to note here three concepts that are important for teaching and learning.

1. There are general reinforcers that will reinforce a variety of different responses (for example, money, the esteem of colleagues, or words and phrases such as 'good', 'well done', etc.).

2. There is no need for reinforcement to be regular and consistent: in fact once a link is established, irregular reinforcement is more powerful in maintaining behaviour than regular reinforcement.

3. In order to change behaviour one has to seek out how the present behaviour is being reinforced, to remove the existing reinforcers and to substitute different reinforcers for more desirable behaviour. If, for example, lecture attendance is falling rapidly then something needs to be done (i) to reduce (if possible) what is reinforcing non-attendance, and (ii) to make the lectures themselves more reinforcing to the students and thus increase attendance.

The early cognitive theorists (for example Wertheimer, Koffka, Kohler, Tolman and Katona) rejected the mechanistic viewpoint of the behaviourists. For them learners were not perceived as passive organisms that mechanically responded to stimuli: the meaning of the stimuli themselves was important. The cognitive theorists argued that organisms select out specific information, process it and act upon it, perhaps in different ways in different circumstances.

Cognitive theorists were important for stressing the effects of prior knowledge and assumptions on new learning, and for indicating how teachers might help learners to perceive and select information. Indeed, many of the theorists in this tradition illustrated their thinking with examples drawn from visual perception. *Figure* 3.1, for instance, can be used to show the interaction between prior assumptions and a search for meaning. It represents a section of a ship's boiler riveted in the usual way

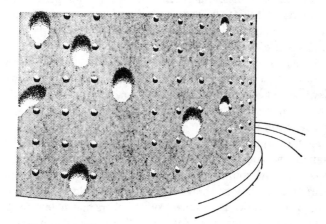

Figure 3.1

but also having indentations due to gun-fire. If readers turn it upside down they will find that the rivets have now become indentations while the gun-fire indentations now stick out. The reason for this is because readers are accustomed to a world in which light comes from above. If you had been handed the picture upside down it would probably not have occurred to you to reverse it; you would simply have accepted a natural, but erroneous, interpretation of it. Doctors, whose interpretation of X-rays would be seriously affected by error, or astronauts, whose multi-directional movements extend their experience so that light may reach them from any direction, would probably display more caution in interpreting the picture.

This tendency to interpret events in accordance with past experience is termed 'set'. In normal circumstances 'sets' of all kinds facilitate effective action since individuals need not waste time considering what a perceived image implies or pause to decide what action they will take. In other situations, 'sets' can hinder objective reaction because they are inappropriate or misleading.

Cognitive theorists introduced two other important notions. These were (1) that animals (and humans) could reorganize or be shown how to reorganize their existing knowledge in order to solve problems, and (2) that there was a phenomenon called 'latent learning'. The idea here was that learning could take place incidentally and not show itself in performance until some future date. If this is true, then it follows that teachers can profit from this by introducing at an early stage those ideas which will facilitate the later acquisition of more difficult concepts.

As stated earlier, in contrast to the rival behaviouristic and cognitive theories of learning there existed other, less influential viewpoints. Many views were held, for example, about the issue of motivation. We are well aware that students need to be motivated to learn, but what is motivation, and how can it be encouraged?

At the simplest level motivation is to want something. Suppose, for example, we consider a need for esteem as being of prime importance, then, to take a behavioural view, factors which lead to esteem are reinforcers. These factors may be things such as good marks for contributions in oral and written work, and praise from teachers and fellow students.

The work of Frederick Herzberg (1966) suggests, in fact, that there are two quite different groups of factors which might affect a feeling of esteem. Herzberg argues that high esteem is associated with factors in the learning task itself: learners feel good if the learning task is organized so that they obtain a sense of achievement by completing it, a sense of recognition when they have accomplished their objectives, and a sense of responsibility towards their own learning. Low esteem, however, is associated with extraneous environmental factors, such as poor teaching methods, dreary working conditions and feelings of low status. Here students feel the situation is unfair, unpleasant and unsatisfactory. Herzberg suggests that environmental factors are not the same in their effects. When environmental factors are changed or improved, students feel less dissatisfied, but this does not necessarily mean that they feel completely satisfied. It is making the task more worthwhile that leads to improved motivation.

The views that teachers hold about how students are motivated affect their methods of instruction and, indeed, how teachers are themselves judged as persons by their students. McGregor (1960) has described two broad sets of assumptions about the nature of humans – assumptions labelled theory X and theory Y (*Table* 3.1). Clearly X and Y are extremes drawn to point out differences, but note how a theory X teacher would be traditional and autocratic while a theory Y teacher could be democratic and participative. One might also expect that students might behave in ways that match the theoretical stances held by their teachers. If teachers treat students as irresponsible, they will probably behave irresponsibly; if students are treated as mature and responsible, then (hopefully) they will behave that way.

Obviously there are many different views about motivation. Other approaches are discussed in more detail elsewhere (for example, Beard and Senior, 1980). The point we wish to make is that theories in this area (and

Table 3.1 An outline of the underlying assumptions behind theory X and theory Y teaching strategies

A theory X teaching strategy	A theory Y teaching strategy
The average student has an inherent dislike of work, and will avoid it if he can.	The expenditure of physical and mental effort is as natural as play or rest.
Because students characteristically dislike work: EITHER They must be *coerced* by controls, directions and threats of punishment to get them to put forward an adequate effort towards the achievement of the desired learning objectives. (Hard line) OR They must be *coaxed* with rewards, praises, permissiveness and blandishments. (Soft line)	*Since learning is natural* external control and threat of punishment are not the *only* means of bring about effort towards learning objectives. Students will also exercise self-direction and self-control in the service of objectives to which they are personally committed.
Commitment to learning objectives is a function of the controls that are exercised.	Commitment to learning objectives is a function of the rewards associated with their achievement.
The average student prefers to be directed, wishes to avoid responsibility, has relatively little ambition, and wants security above all.	The average student learns under proper conditions, not only to accept but to seek responsibility for his or her own learning.
The capacity to exercise a relatively high degree of imagination, ingenuity and creativity in the solution of learning problems is narrowly distributed in the population.	The capacity to exercise a relatively high degree of imagination, ingenuity and creativity in the solution of learning problems is widely, not narrowly, distributed in the population.
Under the conditions of modern life, the intellectual potentialities of the average student are, as far as possible, completely realized.	Under the conditions of modern life, the intellectual potentialities of the average student are being only partially utilized.

Source: Adapted by I.K. Davies, with permission, from McGregor (1960).

indeed in the previous two areas that we have discussed) have clear implications for teaching methods, and how students learn.

3.2 Learning theory in practice

In their authoritative text *Theories of Learning*, Hilgard and Bower (1975) present a list of principles drawn from learning theory that they consider to be potentially useful in practice. They divide the principles into three categories which match the three kinds of learning we have discussed so far in this text. These principles are (1) principles emphasized within stimulus-response (S-R) or behaviourist theory; (2) principles emphasized within cognitive theory; and (3) principles which stem from theories of motivation, personality and social psychology. The following account is somewhat shorter than the one presented by Hilgard and Bower, and we have, on occasions, suggested rather different principles.

Principles emphasized in stimulus-response theory

Activity Learning is better when the learner is active rather than passive. As Hilgard and Bower put it, ' "Learning by doing" is still an acceptable slogan'. This does not imply that people do not learn anything if they are passive but rather that they are likely to learn more if they are actively involved in their learning.

Repetition, generalization, discrimination If learning is to become appropriate to a wide (or narrow) range of stimuli, then this implies that frequent practice, and practice in varied contexts, is necessary for effective learning to take place. Skills, for example, of any kind, are not acquired without considerable practice.

Reinforcement Reinforcement is the cardinal motivator – the effects of the consequences on subsequent behaviour are important, whether they be extrinsic (reward from a teacher) or intrinsic (self-reward). As Hilgard and Bower put it, 'While there are some lingering questions over details, it is generally found that positive controls (rewards, successes) are to be preferred to negative controls (punishments, failures)'.

Principles emphasized in cognitive theory

Learning with understanding This is better than learning by rote, or without understanding. For people to acquire something new it must be meaningful, for example it must fit in with what they already know. The job of the teacher is to show how new material fits in with what has gone before, and to indicate in what ways it is new or different.

Organization and structure   The hallmark of efficient instruction is that it is well organized by the instructor (although one person's type of organization may be different from another's). Organized material is easier to learn and to remember than unorganized material. In the same way, subject matters are said to have inherent structures – logical relationships between key ideas and concepts – which link the parts together. Well-structured materials are more easily understood and better remembered than are poorly structured ones. Organization – how the teacher sequences the material – and structure – the inherent logic of the material – are thus closely related issues.

Perceptual features   Human beings are bombarded with stimuli from all directions – internal and external. The way we cope is to attend selectively to different features of the environment. The way in which a problem is displayed to learners is therefore important in helping them to understand it. (Lecture handouts which convey the structure of a lecture to the listener in advance provide an appropriate illustration.)

Cognitive feedback   This is the provision of information to learners about their success or failure concerning the task in hand. This feedback may be intrinsic or extrinsic. In S-R theory the term 'reinforcement' is often used in the sense of 'providing information' rather than just 'reward'. Information is only of use, of course, if learners understand it, for example if it is appropriate to the tasks which they have set themselves. Another term commonly used here is 'knowledge of results'. One can have learning without such knowledge, but learning is more likely to be effective and efficient if the learners are informed as to how well they are doing.

Differences between individuals   These differences can also affect learning. As well as differences in intellectual ability there are differences in personality (such as extroversion and need for achievement). Individual differences are relevant, of course, to both cognitive and personality theories.

Principles emphasized in theories of motivation, personality and social psychology

Learning is a natural process   Human beings have a natural propensity for learning – indeed one cannot stop people from learning. By nature we are curious beings who constantly absorb information: we are natural decision-makers and problem-solvers. Learning is not something that is 'done' at school and university, and nowhere else.

Purposes and goals   Learning is not conducted in a vacuum. Learners have needs, goals and purposes which provide important motivators for learning and for the setting of future goals. Many decisions about what to learn result from long-term goals which may have been established much earlier. (The importance of goals is, of course, also relevant to cognitive theories.)

The social situation   Learning is rarely an isolated event. We are almost always learning from or with other people. The group atmosphere of learning (competitive vs cooperative, and the value systems held by teachers and learners) affect both success and satisfaction in learning.

Choice, relevance and responsibility   Learning is better when the material to be learned is personally relevant, and when learners are responsible for their own learning. Significant learning, it is argued, only takes place when learners choose what they want to learn, how they want to learn it and when they want to learn it.

Anxiety and emotion   According to Carl Rogers (1983) learning which involves the emotions and feelings as well as the intellect is the most lasting and most pervasive kind. Significant learning only takes place in non-threatening environments.

Comments

These three groups of principles are, of course, not mutually exclusive; in fact, it is difficult to envisage a learning situation where they do not all apply in varying degrees. What has happened, in practice, as we shall see below, is that the influence of these three major kinds of theory is still strong in new teaching methods, but that many of the principles are now being used in combination. It is now no longer fashionable to believe that any one psychologist or group of psychologists has the monopoly of truth. Theories that actually attempt to combine learning theory, subject matter and individual differences are rare, although some (ambitious) attempts have been made in this direction (for example Pask, 1975; Gagné, 1977; Scandura, 1977).

3.3 Applications: some examples

Applications in the stimulus-response tradition

There are today several examples of teaching methods which demonstrate an application of the traditional S-R approach. In school learning, operant conditioning has been clearly influential in behaviour modification schemes and the use of 'token economies' (see Thoresen, 1973). In schools and higher education, programmed instruction has played a dominant role. However, in the area of higher education perhaps the best example is that of the so-called 'Keller plan' or the 'personalized system of instruction' or just simply 'behavioural instruction', which has become so popular in introductory courses. The main feature of this kind of teaching is that students work on their own at their own pace with units (or chapters) of text. Each student has to demonstrate mastery of the unit (by taking a test) before he or she is allowed to proceed to the next unit, and most of the organization and testing are carried out by fellow students or 'proctors'. Lectures are occasionally given as a source of motivation rather than instruction. Many different procedures are possible within this general framework (e.g. the mastery of the units may be paced, contracts may be established or grades given for various amounts of work done, and so on) but, in general terms, behavioural instruction combines the ideas of the students doing the work when they want to do it, learning with peers, self-paced instruction, immediate knowledge of results and mastery performance. Assessments of behavioural instruction by Kulik et al. (1976) and of variants on it by Robin (1976) have shown it to be remarkably effective. Kulik et al. found in 39 studies comparing behavioural with conventional instruction that 34 were significantly in favour of the behavioural method, and that the remaining five were not significantly different from each other, thus none favoured the conventional approach.

Modern applications of cognitive theory

It is not so easy to point to a particular method of instruction and label it 'cognitive' as it is to point to examples in the S-R field. The principles drawn from cognitive psychology are not so clearcut, and to some extent they are already absorbed into common practice. So in this section we report influences rather than direct applications.

To get the feel of an experiment in modern cognitive psychology we invite you to read the following passage:

> Rocky slowly got up from the mat, planning his escape. He hesitated a moment and thought. Things were not going well. What bothered him most was being held, especially since the charge against him had been weak. He considered his present situation. The lock that held him was strong but he thought he could break it. He knew, however, that his timing would have to be perfect. Rocky was aware that it was because of his early roughness that he had been penalized so severely – much too severely from his point of view. The situation was becoming frustrating; the pressure had been grinding on him for too long. He was being ridden unmercifully. Rocky was getting angry now. He felt he was ready to make his move. He knew that his success or failure would depend on what he did in the next few seconds. (Anderson et al., 1977)

Now, did you interpret this passage as being about a convict planning his escape? Or about a wrestler trying to break the hold of an opponent? Or perhaps both?

Ambiguous passages of this kind indicate that readers interpret their meaning by making them fit in with what they already know. Information is selected to fit an appropriate frame of reference. Actual convicts and wrestlers, one would assume, would readily interpret the above passage quite differently.

Thus cognitive psychology emphasizes that learners approach tasks with different backgrounds, select different pieces of information and recall different things. In terms of instruction the implications are that learners can be helped (if it is appropriate) to make the interpretation that the teacher or writer wishes. There are many devices (such as titles, subheadings, question in text, and so on) which can be used to remove the inherent ambiguity which is present in text per se, and which allow readers to construct an appropriate frame of reference.

To take a second and different example, let us consider the notion of sequencing in instruction. We noted earlier that cognitive psychology emphasizes organization and structure. Here we may illustrate how two cognitive psychologists have tackled this problem rather differently.

Robert Gagné (1977) claims that much subject matter is organized *hierarchically*. *Figure* 3.2 shows some schematic diagrams of topics with different structures. All that one has to do to discover this structure is to ask, 'What skills does a learner have to have in order to perform a particular task when given only the instructions to do it?' Answers to this question provide material to which one can apply the same question, and so on, producing a subset of skills, or more technically a cumulative hierarchy of subtasks. *Figure* 3.2 shows different examples, but basically the argument is the same: success at the task on one level requires the ability to perform successfully at the task on the level below, and so on, reading down the figures. The phrase 'cumulative hierarchy' simply implies that in order to learn successfully the learner must be able to succeed at one level before he can continue to the next.

In his earlier work Gagné stressed that in order to achieve full mastery of a skill a pupil should master each subskill in order up the hierarchy, and he applied the hierarchical notion to all kinds of subject matter. Today these views are not so strictly held. Some people have argued that if situation D requires knowledge of A, B and C then it is preferable to present D as a problem-solving situation involving A, B and C, rather than start straight away with A.

Gordon Pask (1975) talks more about a *network* of connections forming an 'entailment structure' to describe the structure of a topic. *Figure* 3.3 provides examples to show that in some respects the end result is very similar, but Pask draws more attention than Gagné to the logical inter-relatedness of all the elements in the structure and to how these inter-relations can match the cognitive structures of the learners involved. *Figure* 3.3 in fact grossly oversimplifies Pask's examples: the more detailed networks provided by Pask (1975) are extremely complex.

The aim of both of these workers, however, is to try and determine the nature of subject matter in order to derive teaching sequences from it. Again, Gagné and Pask differ between them concerning how the sequences are to be derived from the structure. Oversimplifying once more, we might say that Gagné would be more prescriptive than Pask – deciding the sequence for learners in general on the basis of the hierarchy, whereas Pask would be more likely to show the structure (in a simplified way) to particular learners and let them, by means of computer-assisted instruction, determine their own way through it. Gagné is thus more concerned with probable sequences for groups of learners, Pask with individuals.

Modern applications of principles derived from theories of motivation, personality and social psychology

Modern applications of the principles derived from these areas of

Figure 3.2   Simplified examples of the hierarchical nature of topics (after Resnick, 1973)

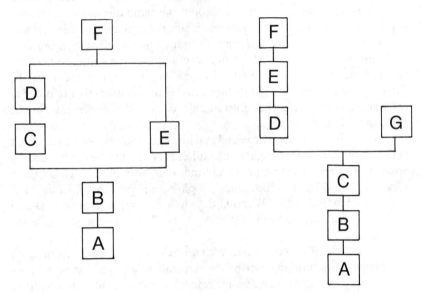

psychology are perhaps best illustrated in an extreme form in the debate about 'traditional versus progressive' teaching, particularly in our primary schools.

How these principles tie in with attitudes and value systems in education is summarised in *Table* 3.2, which presents a more sophisticated version of McGregor's theory X and theory Y shown earlier in *Table* 3.1.

In higher education there have been a number of attempts to be more 'progressive' and to offer more freedom to the student than that which is normally available. DeCecco (1971), for instance, offered his students the choice of a formal course of lectures around a set text or the opportunity to work independently, on their own projects. They all chose the latter. Faw (cited by Rogers, 1969) compared a traditionally taught introductory course in psychology with a system in which the students were free to choose the method and the content of their study. Faw found in terms of written work (1) that no students wrote about the same thing in the optional course and (2) that the amount of reading was far wider in the optional course. Faw's experiment, and several others, are cited in greater detail in Roger's *Freedom to Learn*, in itself a testament to student-centred learning. Hartley

Figure 3.3   Simplified examples of the relationships between topics (after Pask, 1975)

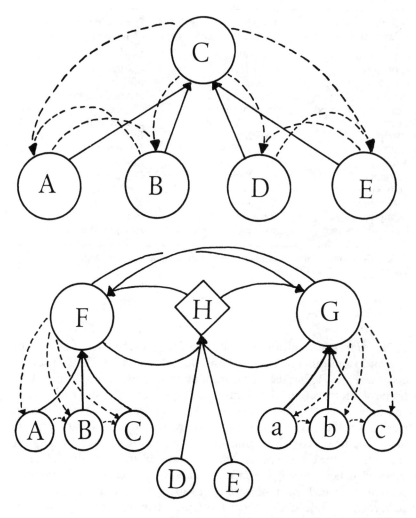

(1972a) describes 12 other studies that vary the amount of choice that they offer to students – choice of topics, teaching methods and techniques of assessment.

To cite another example in this area, let us consider the medical school programme of McMaster University in Canada (Neufeld and Barrows,

Table 3.2 Some contrasting value systems behind different perspectives towards the curriculum

S–R theories (Classical perspective)	Cognitive theories (Modern perspective)	Personality theories (Romantic perspective)
Class teaching	Flexible grouping	Individualized learning
Autocratic	Participative	*Laissez-faire*
Conservative	Liberal	Abdication
Subject emphasis	Process emphasis	Method emphasis
Teacher dominated	Inquiry centred	Child centred
Teaching aids	Learning resources	Audiovisual
Discipline	Experience	Freedom
Skills	Creativity	Discovery
Active	Transactive	Reactive
Certainty	Probability	Confusion
Competitive	Growth	Cooperative
Other directed	Self-fulfilling	Inner directed
Discipline	Responsibility	Freedom
Doing things to	Doing things with	Doing things for

Note: It is recognized that most teachers subscribe to some values in all three categories.
Source: After Davies (1976).

1974). Here, in contrast to many medical programmes, students are assumed from the start to be responsible and motivated adults. They are encouraged to define their own learning goals (within a tutor-presented frame of reference), to select appropriate experiences to achieve these goals and to be responsible for assessing their own learning progress. Students work in small groups together with a tutor, and goals are worked out with his or her help. The achievement of these goals is assessed by both the students and the tutor. The tutor too is assessed by the students, and can be replaced if not deemed satisfactory. The instruction is largely problem centred, and a wide range of learning resources is available to help students achieve their objectives – actual patients, live simulations, computer simulations, 'problem boxes' – containing programmed texts, tape/slide instructions, study outlines and notes – and a reference library. One key idea is for students to learn that few problems are ever actually solved and that trying to solve one problem opens up many more: thus the notion of sequential learning is abandoned.

3.4 Future trends

The discussion so far has shown that there are distinctly different viewpoints about the psychology of learning, and that these differences of emphasis can be detected in many of the teaching methods used today. Although many psychologists are eclectic – and indeed there is now an area of research called 'cognitive behaviourism' – the old controversies still exist and surface from time to time. At present cognitive psychology seems to be enjoying a renaissance. Glaser (1979) puts it thus: 'In psychological research, at the present time, modern cognitive psychology is the dominant force'.

According to Gagné (1980) modern cognitive psychology forces us to pay attention to four integrated factors in learning: (1) selective perception, and factors which influence this; (2) encoding – the processes by which material is stored in memory; (3) prior learning, and its effects; (4) metacognition – the knowledge that learners have or may acquire about their own learning processes and how to improve them.

Each of these four factors is being subjected to considerable research at the time of writing, and quite what the outcome will be is difficult to tell. We describe work on metacognition and self-controlled learning in more detail in Chapter 12. Here we note that the research that has been done so far would suggest that teachers might do well to pay attention to:

1. What features of a display (for example a text or lecture) are likely to stand out, and how learners can be trained to pay attention to significant features if they cannot readily discriminate them.

2. How material can be presented in such a way that it can be easily encoded by the learner (for example making it fit in with what has gone before).

3. How prior knowledge can be activated to aid learning (for example techniques can vary from simple reminders to the use of pretests).

4. How they can help students become more aware of the differences between them, and the variety of learning strategies that are available to them.

Clearly development along these lines could have a profound effect on teaching methods. The lecture method, for example, can hardly be described as a method of learning which emphasizes active responding with immediate feedback or which stresses individual difference in perception, encoding and prior knowledge. Thus the principles of learning we have described above actually contradict many traditional teaching methods.

We suspect that other factors will also lead to changes in traditional teaching methods and more individualization in teaching and learning in higher education. One such factor is the change in objectives of students entering higher education (see Chapter 5). Another is the development of educational technology (see Chapter 11).

3.5   Summary

● The key issues raised by the older theories of learning are:
   1. the effects of consequences on subsequent performance;
   2. the effects of prior knowledge on initial learning; and
   3. the effects of motivation and personality on learning.
● A number of principles derived from theories of learning are still reflected in modern-day practice – with different degrees of emphasis in different situations.
● Current developments suggest that there might now be more success in putting learning theory into practice than there has been so far. If this is the case it will markedly affect current methods of teaching and learning.

CHAPTER 4

PERSONALITY AND LEARNING

Learning varies between individuals. In this chapter we first examine some of the more stable differences between people – teachers and learners – and then we consider some which are more adaptable. Finally we comment on the implications of these differences for teaching and learning.

People come in many shapes and sizes, so do their ways of learning. In this chapter we shall first examine some of the differences between personalities that seem relatively stable, such as ability, and certain personality characteristics like extroversion. We shall then consider what are often called elsewhere 'cognitive styles' – more flexible predispositions to respond to certain kinds of stimuli in certain ways. We shall then show how, by using certain statistical techniques, we can examine the different paths taken by different groups of students to achieve common aims and finally we shall report on different ways of tailoring teaching to meet individual needs.

4.1 Stable characteristics of people

Ability

Entwhistle and Wilson (1977) reviewed many of the studies which examined the relationship between ability, as measured by intelligence test measures and university degree performance in the United Kingdom (and elsewhere). They report that Eysenck (1947), following a review of 34 (mainly American) studies, suggested that the highest correlation likely to be found between intelligence test scores and degree performance was 0.58, and that Himmelweit (1950) obtained a multiple correlation between various measures of 0.55.* These early results seem rather higher than the

---

* A correlation coefficient expresses the degree of relationship between two variables. The relationship may be perfect and positive (+1.00) or perfect and negative (−1.00). As we shall see from the correlations we shall be reporting, however, most relationships are somewhere in between. A low correlation (say up to 0.40) means that the relationship is negligible in actual practice.

ones more recently obtained, but different measures and samples have been used. Most investigators seem to find correlations of between 0.20 and 0.30 between intelligence test scores and degree results. Choppin et al. (1973), for example, validated a British test of academic aptitude, which was especially developed for use with sixth-form pupils. They found correlations of the order of only 0.30 between test scores and degree performance. Adding in A-level results increased this correlation to 0.42 but this value still did not represent any great improvement on prediction which was made from A levels alone.

Indeed many studies have found that, after first-year university results, secondary school examination results are the best predictors of university performance (hence the use of A-level results as a major tool in the selection process). However, the degree of relationship is still very low. The Universities Central Council of Admissions (1969) reported from a sample of 11,000 students correlations between A levels and degree success of 0.33 in technology and 0.17 in the social sciences. Entwistle (1974) also found higher correlations between A levels and degree success for science and mathematics (0.33 to 0.50) than for languages, arts and the social sciences (0.12 to 0.27). *Figure* 4.1 shows these relationships, together with how they related to the quality of the three A levels obtained.

Possibly the most useful information provided by A-level grades is to indicate where to put the 'cut-off' point when selecting students – and this is of course what happens in practice. However, it is disturbing to note that different cut-off points are used for different disciplines (largely because there are more applicants for arts than science courses), and that there are variations between universities in this respect.

Sex differences in ability   It has long been acknowledged as far as education is concerned that after the primary school girls face an ever-decreasing set of possibilities. In this chapter it is not our purpose to explore the reasons for this, but simply to comment on certain differences between men and women in higher education.

The proportion of men to women students in higher education differs dramatically. Nearly twice as many men go to university, and three times as many do postgraduate work. In addition, although the numbers of university teachers increased sharply between 1965 and 1975, the actual proportion of women teachers did not. In 1961 only 2 percent of professors and 9 percent of readers and senior lecturers were women; in 1971 the figures were 1.6 and 6.6 percent respectively (Rendel, 1975). Szrefter (1983) docu-

Figure 4.1 The average degree results of approximately 1200 students who entered seven universities in 1968 with different A-level requirements and who studied different subjects. (Reproduced with permission from Entwistle, 1974)

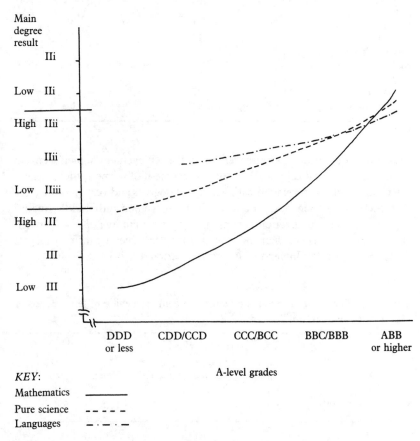

KEY:

Mathematics	————
Pure science	– – – –
Languages	– · – · –

ments further the inequality of women as university teachers.

Not only is the proportion of men to women in higher education very different, but there are also big differences in the subjects studied. This in part reflects earlier differentiations made at school. The numbers of boys and girls obtaining A-level passes in England in different subject matters in 1981 are shown in *Table* 4.1.

However, once at university, do women do as well as men? And does this vary for different subject matters? There seem to be two related answers to

Table 4.1   A-level passes in 1981 (in thousands)

Subject	Boys	Girls
Art	6	11
Music	1	2
English	13	31
Modern languages	8	20
Biology	12	16
Physics	30	7
Chemistry	22	11
Mathematics	46	16

these questions. First, speaking generally, the achievement of men seems to be slightly more widespread than the achievement of women; that is, there are proportionally more men with very good degrees and very poor degrees than there are women, and proportionally more women with middle-quality degrees. This generalization is supported by the data in *Table* 4.2, which show the percentage of men and women students achieving different levels of degree at Keele University during the period 1954–1979.

Table 4.2   Percentage of men and women students achieving different levels of degree at Keele University, 1954–1979

		Degree class			
	First	Upper second	Lower second	Third	Pass
Men (N=3872)	4.1	33.8	45.8	13.2	3.1
Women (N=2809)	3.1	30.2	52.2	12.5	2.1

Secondly, if one compares men and women with equal A-level entry requirements, it appears that the women make better progress than the men during the first year, but the men do slightly better than the women at degree level (Miller and Dale, 1972). Of course these are broad generalizations, and there may be subject-matter differences. Studies in medical education, for instance, have suggested that women do worse than men in the initial stages (Weinberg and Rooney, 1973) but as well as, or better than men by the end of the course (Walton, 1968; Tomlinson et al., 1973).

Extrovert–introversion We all know that some students (and indeed some staff) are enthusiastic and outgoing, whereas others are shy and retiring. Most are somewhere in between: indeed, some seem to vary according to the situation in which they find themselves. This distinction between the outgoing extrovert and the inward-looking introvert reflects one of the basic 'dimensions' of personality. *Table* 4.3 describes extreme cases of extroverted and introverted people. Although we are concerned here with extroversion, we should note that *Table* 4.3 concludes by emphasizing neuroticism as a third important personality characteristic.

There are several major reviews of the effects of extroversion on the learning of both children and students in higher education (e.g. see Entwistle, 1972; Eysenck, 1972a, b). These indicate that at primary school, and during the first stages of secondary schooling, extroverted children do slightly better (in terms of academic achievement) than do introverted ones, but that during the later stages of secondary schooling, and in tertiary education, introverts do better. The size of the correlations between extroversion and academic success in institutes of higher education of course varies with different institutes and with different subject matters but they range from zero to 0.30. Similar findings have been reported from many different countries (e.g. see Orpen, 1976).

The pen portraits shown in *Table* 4.3 indicate why the findings are like this. They suggest that extroverts at university will be easily distracted from studying by social activities, and/or by an inability to concentrate for long periods of time, whereas introverts would seem to be predisposed to engage in good study habits. Eysenck (1972b) also points out that extroverts are better than introverts at immediate recall on verbal tasks but that introverts are better after a period of delay (say 20 minutes). This might suggest that introverts are better able to encode verbal materials into long-term memory.

The generalizations made above are clearly oversimplifications. A careful reading of the research literature suggests a lot of 'ifs and buts', and caution is necessary to prevent drawing oversimple conclusions. Eysenck (1972a), for instance, comments that it is foolish to suggest that introverts *always* do better at scholastic and academic tasks than extroverts. And, he says, it is necessary to recognize the problems presented by ability differences, sex differences, differences in educational objectives and many other factors – including the nature of the theory on which the predictions are based.

Nonetheless, it is probably useful for teachers to be aware of such personality differences between their students. It is likely, for instance, that extroverts and introverts will react differently to particular styles of verbal

Table 4.3

[. . .] The typical extravert is sociable, likes parties, has many friends, needs to have people to talk to, and does not like reading or studying by himself. He craves excitement, takes chances, often sticks his neck out, acts on the spur of the moment, and is generally an impulsive individual. He is fond of practical jokes, always has a ready answer, and generally likes change; he is carefree, optimistic, and likes to 'laugh and be merry'. He prefers to keep moving and doing things, tends to be aggressive, and loses his temper quickly. Altogether, his feelings are not kept under tight control, and he is not always a reliable person.

The typical introvert, on the other hand, is a quiet, retiring sort of person, introspective, fond of books rather than people; he is reserved and distant except with intimate friends. He tends to plan ahead, 'looks before he leaps', and distrusts the impulse of the moment. He does not like excitement, takes matters of everyday life with proper seriousness, and likes a well-ordered mode of life. He keeps his feelings under close control, seldom behaves in an aggressive manner, and does not lose his temper easily. He is reliable, somewhat pessimistic, and places great value on ethical standards.

In all that I have been saying, it is not suggested, of course, that these two dimensions are the only ones in terms of which personality can be described, or into which it can be analysed. There are presumably many others, but these are the only two which have been found again and again by many different investigators, using many different methods, and it may perhaps be agreed that these two dimensions are the most important ones in describing human behaviour and conduct. If we were reduced to describing a person in just three figures, then I have no doubt that we would get the closest approximation to his real nature by using these figures for an assessment of his intelligence, his extraversion, and his neuroticism.

Source: Reproduced from Eysenck (1965) with permission of the author and Penguin Books Ltd.

criticism, and indeed, as already indicated, to different styles of instruction. It may be that in the future extroversion could be one of the measures used for individualizing instruction in computer-assisted learning courses. More immediately, however, in conventional situations there is a need to be aware of the fact that extroverted teachers might be hostile towards introverted students and vice versa.

Motivation   One of the most popular explanations of failure by students is that, despite their ability, they lack the necessary motivation. However, as we saw in Chapter 3, there are many different ways of interpreting what we mean by motivation. In this section we shall distinguish between motivation in general (or need for achievement) and motivation in an academic context (academic motivation).

The work on *need for achievement* (often abbreviated to 'N.ach') is associated with the work of McClelland (1953, 1970) and his colleagues. McClelland devised an ingenious technique for assessing this need in children and adults. Respondents are shown a series of pictures and asked to tell brief stories about them, answering four main sets of questions: (1) What is happening? Who are the persons? (2) What has led up to this situation? What has happened in the past? (3) What is being thought? What is wanted? By whom? (4) What will happen? What will be done? These stories are then assessed for signs of achievement by means of a complex set of scoring procedures. (A clear summary of this research and its overall findings can be found in Brown, 1965.)

However, despite the widespread acceptance of this approach by many psychologists, the research has not demonstrated clear relationships between need for achievement and academic success (see Lavin, 1967; Hartley and Hogarth, 1971). Two particular difficulties have been pointed out: one lies in the method used (i.e. the projective technique) and the other is that 'N.ach' is a very broad concept. It was thought that if a more precise measure was used (e.g. a questionnaire), and that if this measure focused on more specific areas (e.g. academic motivation), then this would lead to clearer results.

Academic motivation questionnaires thus ask specific questions about academic work (e.g. Is doing well at university an important aim in your life?) compared with more general questions about 'N.ach' (e.g. Would you describe yourself as an ambitious person?). Most of these questionnaires ask for a simple yes/no response although clearly a five-point scale (always, often, sometimes, rarely, never) for each term would be preferable.

The results obtained with such scales, however, have not been any more encouraging. Entwistle et al. (1971b), using approximately 900 university students and a scale that measured both study habits and academic motivation, reported correlations ranging from 0.10 to 0.41 between the scale scores and end-of-year assessments; the average correlation, however, was 0.18. Similar results were reported by Entwistle et al. (1971a) for college (0.23) and polytechnic students (0.23). Somewhat better success was achieved by Entwistle and Wilson (1977) using a retrospective technique. They asked a group of 72 graduates to fill in both scales relating them to their work during the previous year – the year leading up to 'finals'. The results obtained are shown in *Table* 4.4.

Table 4.4 The relationship between level of degree class and scores on scales of academic motivation and study habits, when the judgements were made retrospectively.

Degree result	N	High scorers on both scales	High scorers on one scale	Low scorers on both scales
Good honours	24	13	9	2
Honours ordinary	24	8	11	5
Poor ordinary	24	2	8	14

Source: Data from Entwistle and Wilson (1977) with permission.

However, in general the correlations between measures of academic motivation and academic performance are much the same as those reported for intelligence tests and A levels: that is, they are often there, but they are usually small. This may partly reflect the measures used, and the difficulties of classifying educational performance, but the results suggest that simple measures of motivation taken on their own are not good predictors of academic success.

Nonetheless, the point we wish to make here again is that it is likely that teachers will respond differently to students who differ in their motivation and achievement. Although we know of no work with students in higher education, related research with schoolchildren (e.g. Brophy and Good, 1970) suggests that teachers often:

● pay less attention to low achievers;
● ask low achievers to contribute less often;
● demand less from low achievers;
● wait less time for low achievers to respond;
● do not stay with low achievers in failure situations;
● criticize low achievers more frequently than high achievers;
● praise high achievers more frequently than low achievers.

Such findings suggest that teachers interact less with less able and less motivated students. Less able students present more difficulties and are thus treated differently. This could lead to worse performance and, as a result, poorer motivation.

4.2 Cognitive styles and learning

We now turn to another set of differences between and within teachers and students which have been characterized by the term 'cognitive styles'. By 'cognitive style' we mean a preference and ability for certain kinds of information and for certain ways of processing it. Brumby (1982) makes a useful distinction between measures which concentrate on how students perceive problems (convergers, or serialists, as discussed below) and measures which concentrate on how students integrate new material with existing knowledge (deep or surface processors as discussed below). We want to suggest at the outset, however, that people have more flexibility and control over the various styles of thinking that we shall now discuss than they do over the differences we discussed in the previous section.

Convergent and divergent thinking

In recent years there has been a growing feeling that typical intelligence tests of the kind used to measure ability do not measure all aspects of intelligence (e.g. see Butcher, 1968). It has been argued, for instance, that such tests measure only what is termed 'convergent thinking'. By this it is meant that students are required to find a single correct solution to each of the problems set: their thinking focuses down – converges – to the one right answer.

The opposite of this approach – which, it is argued, is not measured in typical intelligence tests – is called 'divergent thinking'. 'Divergent thinking' refers to the capacity to generate responses, to invent new ones, to explore and expand ideas, and, in a word, diverge. Divergent thinking demands fluency and flexibility. The implications for instruction in this matter centre on two issues: (1) it seems that students who are good at one style of thinking may not be necessarily good at the other; and (2) conventional tests may only measure one of these aspects and thus neglect whether a student is good or bad at the other, or indeed good or bad at both.

Divergent thinking is usually measured by 'open-ended' tests. Typical items in such tests are such things as 'How many uses can you think of for the following: a barrel, a paper clip, a tin of boot polish, a brick, a blanket?' 'Write down as many meanings as you can for the following words: bit, bolt, duck, fair, etc.' In general these tests do not require the individual to produce one right answer and in practice they take many forms. Difficulties arise in their administration and in their marking but these technical difficulties should not prevent us from acknowledging the existence, or the importance, of this mode of thinking.

It seems from using such tests that there are wide individual differences between people in this respect. *Table* 4.5 illustrates the responses of two secondary pupils, one an extreme converger and one an extreme diverger, to the question 'How many uses can you think of for a paper clip?' (Again,

Table 4.5

Question: How many uses can you think of for a paper-clip?

Extreme converger
Keeping papers together, repairing page of a book.

Extreme diverger
For holding papers together. To clean wax out of one's ears. Red hot, to bore holes in a cork. Unwound, as a pin or needle for rough work. To clean the dirt from between floorboards, and from under finger-nails. As a fuse wire. As a keeper for a magnet. As a safety-pin. As a hair clip. As a tooth pick. As a stylus for working on wax or in clay. As a fish-hook. With a thread passed through it as a sort of hook. As a charm on a necklace or bracelet. As a collar for a pet mouse, or as a ring for a bird's ankle. To tie labels on with. Unwound, to clear out a small hole, bind something together, or as solder wire. As a sort of shoe-lace. As a tie-pin. As a means of barter. As a counter in a game of cards. As a piece of a board game such as draughts. As confetti. To sabotage a clock. To match with a spring. To make into chain mail.

Source: Reproduced from Hudson (1966) with permission of the author and publishers.

remember that most of us are neither entirely convergent or divergent, but that extremes better illustrate the differences.)

In the United Kingdom there has been some attempt to relate convergent and divergent thinking to specialization in the arts and sciences. Hudson (1966), for example, has suggested that science students will show a bias towards convergent thinking. By this he means that such students will score well on conventional intelligence tests, but less well on open-ended ones. Conversely Hudson suggests that arts students will show a bias towards divergent thinking, that is, they will score well on open-ended tests but less well on conventional ones. Hudson's methodology for arriving at these conclusions is complex but there has been some support for his position. Child and Smithers (1973) found that 66 percent of convergers ($N=53$) at Bradford University were studying science subjects (and 22 percent languages), and that 74 percent of divergers ($N=51$) were reading non-science subjects and only 8 percent were physical scientists or mathematicians.

Findings such as these have caused some consternation among science teachers because of another link in the argument: the suggestion that divergent thinking is associated with creativity. Scientists naturally object to the view that they are less creative than their arts colleagues! In fact the attempts to link up responses on open-ended tests with creativity in the more normal sense of the word – a creative process, product or person –

have not proved entirely successful. It seems better to think of open-ended tests as measures of fluency and divergent thinking, than as tests of creativity per se. Furthermore, creativity demands other skills, such as evaluation and judgement.

Nonetheless, this concern, particularly among science teachers, has paid off. It has drawn attention to the fact that teachers generally react more favourably to convergent than to divergent students. Putting it plainly, teachers find divergent thinking difficult to deal with. It seems that teachers often confuse divergent thinking with frivolity: the divergent student is seen as a threat to discipline; the teacher finds it difficult in discussion to deal with divergent responses – they 'put him off his task' and they 'waste valuable time'. Many teachers do not like guessing or playfulness, they like a 'serious' approach.

However, the link in people's minds between divergence and creativity raises an apparent contradiction. Most teachers would think it important to encourage creativity and yet they have problems with divergent thinkers. New attempts are therefore being made to make teachers more aware of (and to encourage) signs of creativity, and to persuade them to be less hostile to divergent thinkers in their class.

It is interesting to note that it is not always obvious from their behaviour whether or not students are divergent thinkers. Administering open-ended tests can produce surprising results: some students (and teachers) seem to be able to produce endless supplies of answers, others only two or three. Yet is this difference fundamental? Can this behaviour change?

A number of studies have shown that to a certain extent it can. Hudson (1968) once found when he was angry with a class of schoolboys and shouted at them that their divergent thinking scores all increased. Had he, as it were, 'released the brakes'? Others have shown that if you provide examples of what is required (e.g. examples of extreme divergers' responses) then again responses are increased. Encouraging fluency and indicating where it might be useful (for example in 'brain-storming' sessions) might indicate to students and to staff that they both have more abilities than they thought.

Serialists and holists   A number of investigators have drawn distinctions between students who work step-by-step, and those who look first at the 'big picture'. Vernon (1962), for instance, distinguished between 'analytic' (step-by-step) problem-solvers, 'synthetic' (big picture) problem-solvers and 'plastic' (those who could use either approach) problem-solvers. Other investigators have used similar terms, for example 'scanners' and 'focusers', 'sharpeners' and 'levellers', and, perhaps crudest of all, 'splitters' and 'lumpers'!

Gordon Pask (1976) has followed this line of thinking by distinguishing between serialist and holist learning strategies. Both of these strategies reflect the way in which learners respond to uncertainty. The serialist will learn most efficiently by proceeding one step at a time, thus eliminating uncertainty in a steady manner. The holist learns most efficiently by establishing an overview or structural framework for the task, and then filling in the details once this framework has been established. Despite personal preferences for one strategy or the other, the choice of strategy depends upon the level of uncertainty at which the student is prepared to operate. Consequently different strategies can be adopted for different tasks.

Pask makes a further distinction between tasks which do not clearly demand a serialist or holist response: here students who are disposed to act like holists he calls 'comprehension learners', and those who act like serialists 'operational learners', whereas students who are able to act in either way, depending on the subject matter, he calls 'versatile'. Using such strategies inappropriately or unsuccessfully can lead to learning difficulties. Pask distinguishes between 'globe trotting' (holists with inappropriate links between concepts) and 'improvidence' (serialists who do not properly understand the links that have been made).

Pask's papers are difficult to understand and it may be that in this simplified account we have misrepresented him. However, the point we wish to make here is that this distinction between strategies of approach to new and difficult learning materials is an interesting one. Furthermore, it suggests implications for instruction, particularly when it is provided by computer. If, as Pask (1975) suggests, students should select their own way through material (see Chapter 3), then the material will have to be arranged in such a way that it can be learned successfully by holists or serialists. If there is a mismatch between the teaching and the learning strategies then difficulties may ensue. Pask (1976), for instance, reports the results from a study where 60 students were divided into those with a tendency towards comprehension (holist) learning and those with a tendency towards operational (serialist) learning. Subgroups of these students then worked through various programmed texts, each designed according to holist and serialist teaching strategies, and each providing approximately 24 hours of instruction per student. Half of the students worked in a 'matched' condition, and half in a 'mismatched' one. The overall results are shown in *Table* 4.6.

Table 4.6 Average percentage correct on end-of-programme tests

	Holist teaching strategy	Serialist teaching strategy
Holist learners	93	34
Serialist learners	44	91

The difficulty with a study such as this one, however, is that it seems to assume, despite Pask's earlier statements, that students can be labelled 'serialist' or 'holist'. Brumby (1982) found, with a series of biology problems, that only 8 percent of her students could be labelled 'holist', 42 percent were 'analytic' (serialist) and 50 percent 'variable'.

Deep and surface processors In a series of studies conducted in Sweden, students have been asked by Ference Marton and his colleagues about how they study written text – in both natural and experimental situations. The replies of the students have been categorized as those of deep and those of surface processors. Deep processors give replies like: 'I try to get at the principal ideas.' 'I try to find the main points of the article.' 'I think about how the author has built up his argument.' Surface processors give replies like: 'I just read straight through from start to finish.' 'I try to concentrate on remembering as much as possible.' 'I didn't remember what I read, because I was just thinking of hurrying on.' Deep processors, it appears, try to extract meaning from the text; surface processors focus on the text itself.

This research has shown that the method of processing which students use has a marked effect upon how well they learn. In one study, Marton and Saljö (1976) asked students to read a 1400-word article on the topic of curriculum reform in Swedish universities. In the article itself the author had argued that a sweeping reform, aimed at raising university pass rates uniformly, was misguided because different groups of students had different pass rates. The author suggested, therefore, that selective measures should be taken which would concentrate on those particular classes of students which had low pass rates. After reading the article the students were asked, 'Try to summarise the article in one or two sentences. What is the author trying to say, in other words?'

It was found that responses could be classified in four ways:

A. Those that reported there were differences in the pass rates between groups of students.

B. Those that reported that measures were to be taken.

C. Those that reported that different measures should be taken with different groups of students.

D. Those that reported that selective measures should be taken, i.e. only for particular categories of students with low pass rates.

When these replies were analysed with reference to whether or not the students were considered to be deep or surface processors (based on further questioning on how they had read the text), the results were as shown in *Table* 4.7. Clearly the students' approach to reading the text had had a marked effect. None of the students labelled 'surface processors' adequately summarized the main points of the article, whereas none of the students labelled 'deep processors' failed to do so.

Table 4.7

		Level of outcome			
		A	B	C	D
Level of approach	Surface	5	8	1	0
	Not clear	1	0	6	0
	Deep	0	0	4	5

Findings such as these have been demonstrated many times in the Swedish studies, and attempts are now being made to replicate them in England. In our own work at Keele we have been intrigued by how difficult it has been to classify both students and learning outcomes in the same proportions as those obtained by Marton and his colleagues. Nonetheless, we have been surprised by the difficulties many students seem to have in summarizing, or grasping the main points of instructional text.

Other British studies have indicated (as indeed has later Swedish work) that students can *vary* their reading strategies (e.g. Laurillard, 1979). The same student may be a surface processor in some conditions, and a deep processor in others, depending on the nature of the task. Laurillard suggests that if students are doing the task for their own sake – if they are intrinsically motivated – then they are likely to take a deep-level approach. If, however, students are doing the task for extrinsic rewards (e.g. to pass the exam) then they are more likely to take a surface approach, that is, to learn material parrot-fashion, and to memorize key facts, names, dates and formulae.

Speaking more generally, it seems that whether or not students are deep or surface processors depends upon their conception of what learning itself involves. Perry (1970), for instance, describes students' conceptions of what learning is about in terms of nine stages of development. His scheme can be illustrated with a brief example:

> Let us suppose that a lecturer announces that today he will consider three theories explanatory of – (whatever his topic may be). Student A has always taken it for granted that knowledge consists of correct answers, that there is one right answer per problem, and that teachers explain these answers for students to learn. He therefore listens for the lecturer to state which theory he is to learn.
>
> Student B makes the same general assumptions but with an elaboration to the effect that teachers sometimes present problems and procedures, rather than answers 'so that we can learn to find the right answer on our own'. He therefore perceives the lecture as a kind of guessing game in which he is to 'figure out' which theory is correct . . .
>
> Student C assumes that an answer can be called 'right' only in the light of its context, and that contexts or 'frames of reference' differ. He assumes that several interpretations of a poem, explanations of a historical development, or even theories of a class of events in physics, may be legitimate 'depending on how you look at it'. . . . He supposes that the lecturer may be about to present three legitimate theories which can be examined for their internal coherence, their scope, their fit with various data, their predictive power, etc.
>
> Whatever the lecturer then proceeds to do . . . these three students will make meaning of the experience in different ways . . .

Perry's nine stages describe how a student can progress from an extreme absolutist position (e.g. student A), through relativism (e.g. student B) to a flexible commitment (e.g. student C).

The ideas that students have about what learning is and what it is for, are, of course, buffeted about by what happens in practice in their different courses. The work of Perry (1970) and Saljö (1979) would suggest that such ideas are deep-rooted and only change slowly. Ramsden (1979), however, has shown that different departments differ in what they require from students and that this too affects students' learning strategies.

4.3 Combining measures

Many investigators who have failed to find significant correlations between one variable or another and academic achievement have often sought to *combine* different measures to see if this increases their predictive power. In this section of this chapter we shall look at only one way in which this has been done, although there are many more.

Cluster analysis

The statistical technique of cluster analysis is one of many techniques that can be used to combine groups of data. (Others include multiple correlation, multiple regression, factor analysis, discriminant function analysis, etc.).

There are many forms of cluster analysis, but the one used by Entwistle and Brennan (1971) provides a typical example. Basically these investigators took 23 measures from 875 students. These were as follows:

Variables

Intellectual domain
1. Academic performance
2. A-level results
3. Verbal ability
4. Numerical ability

Study habits domain
5. Motivation
6. Study methods
7. Examination technique
8. Hours studied in week
9. Hard-working (self-rating)
10. Ambitious (self-rating)
11. Father's occupation (coded so that high scores indicate low social class)

Personality domain
12. Extroversion
13. Neuroticism
14. Sociable (self-rating)
15. Likeable (self-rating)

Values domain
16. Tender-mindedness
17. Radicalism
18. Theoretical values
19. Economic values
20. Social values
21. Political values
22. Aesthetic values
23. Religious values

The cluster analysis programme started by dividing these 875 students into 15 'clusters' or groups on the basis of these 23 measures, that is, each student in one group (or cluster) was more like every other student in that group than he or she was like any other person in any of the other groups. What the programme did next was to redefine the groups by combining the two most similar ones, and regrouping the remainder (in this case into 14 groups). This process was then repeated (making 13 groups) and repeated and repeated until only two groups remained.

The problem for the investigators was to decide at what stage to stop, or, putting it another way, how many clusters it seemed most useful to have. Entwistle and Brennan chose to distinguish between 12 groups of students. Space precludes listing the characteristics of all 12 here, but *Table* 4.8

Table 4.8 The characteristics of students in groups 1 and 11 as described by Entwistle and Brennan (1971)

Cluster 1 (High attainment)
This group contains a majority of male scientists with good A-level grades and high numerical ability. Combined with these intellectual advantages are found high motivation, study methods and examination technique. This group of high scores combined with introversion and stability leaves little doubt as to why this group has the highest level of attainment of any cluster, although the members of the cluster did no more than an average number of hours' study in the week prior to the test sessions.

In values, the theoretical value or empirical rationalism is dominant with high scores also on being tough-minded, conservative and ambitious. The picture is completed by indicating that while this type sees himself as being near average on the self-ratings of 'sociable' and 'likeable', the additional traits of high economic and political values linked to being tough-minded, conservative and ambitious may suggest a certain ruthlessness and seeking after personal power.

Cluster 11 (Low attainment)
This is a low-ability group of male science students, again extroverts, but tough-minded conservatives as well. Their values are typical of scientists in general – high theoretical and economic, low aesthetic and religious. This group has near-average scores on motivation and study methods, although not working particularly long hours. It appears that poor attainment in this cluster must be explained mainly in terms of low ability and poor entry qualifications, perhaps combined with rather rigid attitudes and a tendency to be extroverted. As the self-rating on sociability is lower than the extroversion score, it is possible that the group tends to be impulsive, rather than sociable.

Source: Reproduced from Entwistle and Brennan (1971) with permission of the authors.

describes the characteristics of students in two extreme groups.

Cluster analysis has the advantage then of providing a richer picture than simple correlational techniques. It is clear (from comparing the different clusters) that there is no one way to academic success: there are different types of successful students (clusters 1, 2 and 3 in Entwistle and Brennan's analysis) and different types of unsuccessful ones (clusters 10, 11 and 12). And, of course, there are many different ways of being mediocre.

As noted above, one difficulty with cluster analysis is determining how many clusters to accept as the best solution. There are no precise mathematical ways of deciding whether a particular number of clusters is better than a solution with one fewer (or one more) cluster. This is a matter of judgement and interpretation on the part of the researchers concerning which solution makes most sense.

Other techniques tackle this problem in different ways. For example, another similar technique called 'discriminant function analysis' starts with some predefined groups determined by the investigator (such as first-year, second-year, third-year students, high achievers and low achievers) and then attempts to see whether individual students can be allocated to their correct group on the basis of combining in some way the scores they obtain on a battery of tests. With this method there is the advantage that one can see how successful the solution is in terms of the percentage of students who are correctly allocated. It is then possible to determine which of the tests are best at discriminating between students and in allocating them to their predefined groups. An example of this approach can be found in Branthwaite et al. (1980).

4.4   Tailoring teaching to individual needs

Many attempts have been made in actual teaching situations to try to take into account some of the differences that we have discussed so far. In this section of the chapter we shall look at three different kinds of approach:
1. matching teaching methods to different groups of students;
2. allowing students to choose their teaching methods;
3. independent study.
One area of research which is relevant here – computer-assisted learning – is discussed in Chapter 11.

Matching teaching methods to different groups of students

Examples of this kind of approach have been provided by Leith (1969) and Rowell and Renner (1975), who have shown that introverts do better with well-structured situations and that extroverts do better in less-structured situations. A further example is provided in a study by Domino (1971). Domino divided approximately 100 students into two main groups (conforming and independent) and each of these groups was further sub-divided and taught in two contrasting ways – by the instructor encouraging either conformity or independence. (The same instructor was used in both instances.) The results showed that independent students did better than conforming students when the instructor encouraged independence; conforming students did better than independent ones when the instructor encouraged conformity.

The technical name used to describe the kinds of study illustrated above is 'aptitude x treatment interaction' studies (ATI). Such studies aim to examine the interaction between different aptitudes (e.g. personality differences) and different treatments (e.g. teaching methods). A major literature review of such ATI studies has been provided by Cronbach and Snow (1977). Drawing from this research Snow (1977) indicates that four aptitudes (or individual differences) have been shown to consistently affect education achievement, and, he argues, these should be considered first in developing any set of instructional methods that are planned to take account of individual differences. These four are: general ability (intelligence); achievement motivation (either via independence, or via conformity); anxiety; and prior knowledge.

A study reported by Hill and Nunnery (1971) provides an example of a different approach where individual students are given different instructional treatments on the basis of their personality. At Oakland Community College in the USA, students entering the college take a battery of tests which measure various cognitive styles. Then, using computer analyses of the results, a team of teachers plans personal programmes with the students which are geared to their strengths and weaknesses. The basic procedure is Keller plan-oriented (see Chapter 3). The course material is divided into weekly units. On day 1 the students attend a lecture. On days 2, 3 and 4 students are directed to different study activities on the basis of their personal programmes. Thus a student may work with programmed texts on day 2, do library research on day 3 and attend a seminar on day 4. A variety of such study activities is available for days 2, 3 and 4 and most of these have assistance from tutors and senior students. On days 5 and 6 the students are tested on their knowledge of the material, and must achieve 90 percent or more. If they are unsuccessful a parallel form of the test may be taken after a further hour of study and four attempts at the test are permitted. The tests are computer scored and the results reported to the instructors, the programme centre and the students.

Allowing students to choose their teaching methods

Another approach to ATI studies is less rigorous than the ones we have described so far. In this situation the students may be offered sets of options concerning different teaching methods and different methods of assessment. It is then up to the students to choose which methods they think will suit them best. There is (usually) no attempt to measure students' cognitive styles or to relate personality variables to the choices made.

As we noted in Chapter 3, studies by Faw (cited by Rogers, 1969) and DeCecco (1971) provide examples of this approach. Another example is provided by White (1971). White described an introductory psychology course whose aims were expressed as (1) to introduce students to various areas of psychology, (2) to allow them to study some of these in a fair degree of depth, (3) to give a grasp of empirical methods in psychology, but (4) not to require all of the students to cover all of the areas uniformly. The assumptions underlying the course design were that students came with different backgrounds and different aims, that a uniform review might turn off most of the students most of the time, and that flexibility must be the key to teaching a multi-purpose course.

The course was conducted by using one lecture/discussion period, one period for films or outside speakers, and one in which students could choose from either meeting in discussion groups, working on projects or working on their own using the instructor as a resource person. The conventional omnibus introductory text was replaced by a variety of cheap paperbacks.

The students were offered a number of options to choose between to determine their final grade for the course. There were two examinations, each consisting of multiple-choice and essay sections worth 50 percent each; two or four project reports worth 50 or 100 percent respectively; and two or four essays worth 50 or 100 percent respectively. Thus each student was able to obtain his or her grade by combining different elements.

White concluded his paper by presenting student evaluations of the course and a discussion of the grades obtained. The results were interpreted as being generally favourable, and supportive of the rationale of the course – that a flexible approach is needed to meet the demands of different students.

Independent study

Finally in this chapter we report on another approach to instructing individuals differently: that of allowing students to free themselves from orthodox arrangements and pursue what is sometimes called 'independent study'. Independent study allows the student to use available instructional resources in a rather different way. Instead of choosing between existing courses, students construct their own courses using the resources available – the staff, the library, the laboratory, parts of existing courses and other students. One example of this approach will be given here.

Lancaster University established a School of Independent Studies in 1973. Students at Lancaster, after their first year of conventional instruction, can decide whether or not to transfer from their normal courses to the School of Independent Studies and to pursue a major or minor part of their next two years in independent study. What this means in practice is that at the end of the first year or the beginning of the second students have to submit a proposal to the School. This submission typically consists of an outline of the work proposed (e.g. indicating the questions that the student will be trying to answer), a statement of what form the work will take, how it might be assessed and the name of a staff member who has agreed to supervise the work. Such a scheme may involve courses offered by departments in the normal way, but it usually consists of activities devised by the student concerned. In drawing up their schemes students typically cross traditional subject boundaries and study topics in depth from different perspectives. The submission is discussed by a subcommittee of the School together with the student concerned and it is modified if necessary before being discussed by a full committee. There are three constraints: the goals that a student wishes to pursue must be academically respectable; the student (or the School) must be able to find someone on the staff of the university who will agree to act as a Director of Studies for the student; and the work must be capable of being assessed in some way.

Assessment at Lancaster is based on the fact that in the last two years of study a student completes nine units of work. A student majoring in one subject completes six units in that subject, and three in a minor one. Thus students majoring in independent studies are required to have six assessments to contribute to the nine that will make up their final degree. All the work presented for the final assessment is marked first by the Director of Studies and then by a second internal marker before being sent to a specialist examiner. The School then awards degrees to students majoring in the School by assessing these six marks and combining them with the three other assessments that have been obtained from the other courses taken by the students.

The results obtained from students majoring in independent studies between 1975 and 1980 are shown in *Table* 4.9. These data show that on average there are about 10 students majoring in independent studies each year with over half of them getting a 2.1 or first-class degree. A large proportion of these students are mature ones, and perhaps this approach is well suited to this group (see Chapter 5).

4.5   Concluding remarks

Few people have any doubts that individual differences affect learning. What is not clear, however, is how important these differences are. Are some students disadvantaged by their personalities, do others profit from

Table 4.9   Results of students majoring in independent studies at Lancaster University, 1975–1980

Year	Degree class				
	1	*2.1*	*2.2*	*3*	*Pass*
1975	3	2	1		
1976		7	4		
1977	1	4	4	2	1
1978	3	4	5	1	
1979		4	4	2	
1980	2	6	2		

theirs, or does everything even out in the end? Much of the research that we have summarized in this chapter would seem to suggest the latter. But is this a reflection of the quality of the research? It seems remarkable how many investigators seem to want to translate the richness of experience into scores obtained on yes/no questionnaires. It is perhaps not surprising that such scores correlate poorly with academic performance – itself often reduced to a single score on a five-point scale. The more recent research has started to escape from this earlier methodological straitjacket. Descriptions of student behaviour and experience are now more in vogue. If, in fact, different students seem to arrive at much the same destination, then we know at least that they use a variety of routes to get there.

The next question, if this is true, is how far will making changes in teaching methods and techniques of assessment enable students to perform better than they do? Any change applied to a whole group would probably help some students, but not others. So we need to consider further how far courses and assessments can be individualized, and to ponder on how useful in terms of personal growth it would be for students to experience different methods and procedures from the ones they are accustomed to.

The results of the studies reported in this chapter suggest that there are groups of students who will prefer quite different styles of teaching. But if different teachers and methods are not available, what can be done? Some suggestions that have been made are as follows:

● For students who prefer structure in a lecture situation one can provide a handout giving the 'big picture' and let them look at it before the lecture. Students who are more independent can be encouraged to look at the handout afterwards.

● Lecture styles can be more consciously varied. Some lectures can be mainly factual, some more discursive. Students might be informed in advance what the main aim of the lecture is (e.g. factual information vs problematical stimulation).

● In writing essays and doing practicals students may be given lists of suggested topics or questions but instructed to choose their own topics if they want (preferably in consultation with a member of staff).

● For assessment students could be allowed to choose between different types of assessment that reflect differences in their need for security and/ or structure (as in White's study).

There are no easy answers to questions concerning individual differences, but, as we have noted before, it would seem helpful in an age of rapid change, to focus on teaching methods that demand collaboration from staff and students, and on methods which are more varied than is the case in conventional instruction. We might all at least attempt to strive for more flexibility.

4.6 Summary

● Differences between individuals affect teaching and learning.

● Some differences between individuals are relatively stable (such as ability and extroversion). Some differences are less stable and vary according to circumstances (such as serialist/holist processing, and deep/surface processing).

● Some students have clusters of traits which lead to better performance than other clusters, but these too may vary in different circumstances.

● This would seem to suggest that it would be valuable to vary methods of teaching and assessment more than is currently fashionable.

● Three ways of doing this described in this chapter are:
   i matching teaching methods to different groups of students;
   ii allowing students to choose their own methods;
   iii independent study.
Other, less drastic solutions are also suggested.

PART THREE

ON BEING A STUDENT

CHAPTER 5

ADJUSTING TO HIGHER EDUCATION

The problems of students entering higher education from schools have been relatively neglected. In this chapter we describe introductory courses designed to assist students in their choice of subjects and in the acquisition of essential study skills. We discuss possible deficiencies in knowledge and in levels of thinking, and experiments designed to remedy them. In conclusion we consider in particular the problems presented by mature and overseas students.

5.1 Problems in transition from school to higher education

For most students entry to university, polytechnic or college of higher education involves a sudden change in their way of life. They are expected to take greater responsibility for their work than they did at school and, if they leave home, must learn to cope efficiently in lodgings or halls of residence.

Just how differently students responded to their new experiences was noted in an internal report by Isabel Senior, a research assistant at the University of Bradford, who interviewed a number of students in their first term.

One student said that he was interested in the whole experience of being a student and was aware that he was already adapting his methods of studying. He found note-taking in lectures fairly straightforward and was trying to take notes sufficiently legibly to not need rewriting. He had looked ahead through the syllabus and, recognizing which were his weaker subject areas, had decided what books it was most important to buy. He had used the library quite extensively (which he said he never did at school) and always asked for help if he had difficulty in finding what he needed.

Another student in the same department said that being a student was very different from his expectations. He didn't like lectures; he found that in some he 'couldn't get enough down – it's just no use trying to get the notes down because afterwards they don't make sense'. He could not get used to the idea of working on his own, finding himself unable to concentrate for more than half-an-hour. He said that he had not expected to have all those books recommended – 'You know, you've got a heck of a lot of work to do yourself, you're not forced to do it, you have to do it yourself, use your own initiative.' He had used the library only once and had not managed to find what he was looking for then. In contrast to the first student, he felt that he was still trying to get used to everything, to cooking meals, the longer working day, getting to know people, and that he had hardly begun work yet.

Other new students may refer to feelings of bewilderment because of the differences in size between school and a large university or polytechnic. For a student who knew everyone in a small school, just being among so many people and not knowing any of them is strange. The sheer variety of possible activities can be confusing: 'There's so much you want to do that it's difficult to find time to fit anything in and you end up doing nothing.' Some students find loss of status a problem; there is no longer a role they must fulfil as prefect, games captain or team member, nor any activity they must engage in. Some students in residence or in lodgings find themselves lonely but feel reluctant to join in activities if they have no friend to accompany them.

Students who have chosen to cater for themselves may, at first, have difficulty in finding time for shopping and housekeeping. Some find noise intolerable – two sources of music at full volume making work impossible; others feel that sharing a room leads to conversation rather than study. Some students in halls of residence report that they find themselves constantly entertaining other students, or being entertained. 'One student at Bradford even mentioned the number of keys he had as a source of anxiety: 'instead of only one he now had so many that he was worried about getting them mixed up and, consequently, kept them all separately about his person!'

To these domestic problems may be added financial difficulties when grants fail to arrive, often in the case of foreign students who have no family at hand to assist them. The unsettling effect of prolonged separation from a boy- or girlfriend, or of knowing that there are problems of health or conflict at home, may lead to thoughts of early withdrawal.

Any uncertainties or confusion in work, therefore, may make 'confusion worse confounded'. Yet students report numerous problems which might be avoided with somewhat more assistance from their teachers. A frequent cause of concern to students is taking adequate lecture notes. They are uncertain whether to write the fullest notes possible or whether to concentrate on listening and only make brief notes, whether to rewrite notes neatly after a lecture and whether, and when, to add notes from books. Students sometimes contrast the lack of guidance at university or college with the greater direction they received at school where notes were dictated or read and corrected by teachers. They dislike dictated notes since 'you just copy them without taking in what they are about'; but they would appreciate an opportunity, early in the term, to practise taking notes from a few short lectures in different subjects, to discuss the notes with the lecturer and to consider how they could be improved.

Other major causes of concern are that some teachers fail to make clear what are the aims of courses and do not explain what they look for in written work. Consequently, as a series of lectures unfolds, students may have no understanding of how each lecture contributes to the greater whole. Or, if teachers give marks for essays or reports without comment, students do not know how they could improve their work. When taxed with their deficiencies such teachers commonly reply that new students do not take in what they are told, or that they have insufficient knowledge to appreciate implications of their teachers' aims, or that they will learn from experience.

Serious problems may also arise if teachers ignore gaps, or deficiencies in knowledge at entry to higher education. These difficulties can be insurmountable in subjects where knowledge is said to be hierarchical, such as pure sciences, mathematics and to a lesser extent languages, if teachers attempt to build on foundations which do not exist.

Thus, although some students are fortunate and cope well with the transition to higher education, a substantial number experience problems which could have been avoided or ameliorated if their teachers had prepared them at school, or if all teachers in universities and colleges recognized students' initial needs at entry and catered for them.

5.2 Introductory courses

Courses for pupils still at school

The growing recognition of students' difficulties in making the transition to higher education has led to attempts by school teachers and teachers in higher education to prepare students for the greater independence which will be expected of them. Three different methods are being used to prepare students for higher education before they leave school.

Raaheim and Wankowski (1981), for example, mention a course at Solihull Sixth-Form College which effectively prepares intending students to learn independently during their last year at school. By the time they enter higher education they already have confidence in their ability to organize their time, to take notes when listening to a lecture or when reading and to play a part in discussion. Consequently they have few problems in studying on entry to university or college.

Williams (1977) outlined the results of an inquiry into organized personal contacts between higher educational institutions and schools or colleges of further education. These occur most commonly when a university representative visits schools or colleges to talk with staff and pupils likely to proceed to university. The representative may ask colleagues to talk to intending students about fields of study which are unfamiliar in schools, such as the various branches of engineering. Williams points out that the advantages of this kind of contact are that less well-known or new institutions become better known to the schools, students and institutions can be better matched and those who enter higher education do so better informed, even if they cannot realize fully what their studies will entail.

A third approach, which depends mainly on the initiative of university or college teachers, is that of providing a course, or 'workshop', for sixth-form pupils intending to proceed to higher education. At King's College, University of London, for instance, an annual workshop in engineering is held for lower sixth-formers (Jolly and Turner, 1979). A main objective is to show pupils what engineering courses require from the student regarding years of preparation, education and training and, secondly, the range of opportunities available in industry after graduation. The organizers hope in this way to encourage some of the most able school-leavers to choose engineering as a professional. During the five-day course each student undertakes a half-day practical in each of electrical engineering, mechanical engineering and computing. They also attend lectures and tutorials of the kind used in undergraduate courses. Several talks are given by young engineers from industry. At an informal party, the sixth-formers have an opportunity to meet various guests – workshop staff, managers and young engineers – with knowledge of other aspects of engineering. As a result, some pupils discover an interest of which they were not previously aware:

> I had no interest in engineering before attending the course. I now know what engineering entails . . . I am now much more interested in taking an engineering course. (Girl)

The more I learned about engineering the more convinced I became that it was something I would definitely enjoy doing as a career.   (Boy)

Since courses of this kind are too costly to offer to many students the majority require introductory courses at school or on entry to higher education, and preferably both.

Introductory courses in higher education institutions

Most teachers in higher education regard some part of their first-year course as introductory in the sense that it is designed to help students study effectively. Nevertheless, the emphasis is commonly on how to acquire knowledge rather than on the learning of study skills or of appropriate attitudes.

The view of those who have discussed students' initial experiences with them, or who have given assistance to students who had serious initial difficulties, is that a main purpose of any introductory course should be to give students sufficient confidence to take increasing responsibility for their own independent work. Wankowski (1973), a counsellor at the University of Birmingham, considers it essential to avoid an abrupt change in teaching and learning styles between school and higher education. When this occurs, he finds that it diminishes the competence of all but the most independent and may lead to disorientation in some students. He believes, therefore, that courses for new students should be more teacher dependent, and that they should include work in small groups, contact between teachers and students outside lectures, and far more feedback than is commonly given on students' submitted work. Not only should the course aims and objectives be specified, but the purposes of teaching and assessment methods should be clearly explained.

New students themselves consider that a good introductory course involves early opportunities to get to know their teachers and other students, being informed of the aims of courses, assistance in acquiring essential study methods soon after entry, and the identification of initial gaps in their knowledge followed by prompt remedial treatment. A brief initial course designed only to assist with study skills, therefore, falls far short of some students' needs.

Getting to know teachers and students   One of the reasons why students wish to get to know their teachers and other students very early in the first term is that this gives them confidence in taking problems to teachers and in discussing difficulties which arise with other students. The feeling of belonging to a group reduces anxiety. In addition, increasing interaction within the group provides opportunities for students to make friends with whom to share social activities.

In more prosperous times some departments were able to send all new students with their teachers to spend a weekend together at a conference centre. At the present time the most that teachers can do is to arrange social gatherings, but these suffice for students to find out something about each fellow student. Further activities can be provided by introducing short periods of group work, say, at the end of lectures. If two or three students work together in answering questions or solving problems based on the lecture, commenting on a brief article or simply discussing a few difficult points, shy students are involved and 'peer teaching' spontaneously takes place. Various other suitable methods are suggested in Chapters 9 and 11.

Knowledge of course aims   Unless teachers specify course aims and objectives there is a very real danger that students will interpret them in terms of their own past experience. For example, when the Foundation Science course was about to begin at the Open University and students received their first books, some intending students wrote to their teachers saying that they did not find the aims and objectives at all helpful and would be glad to know what they should *learn*. Evidently they conceived of science as knowledge learned from books, failing to realize that it was primarily a method of studying the universe by means of observation, experiments and measurements and the formulation of laws and theories based on scientists' findings. Since the aims had been spelled out, a discussion was initiated in which the students acquired expectations in line with those of the scientists who taught them.

Discussion with students in various university departments suggests that some are not so fortunate. A quite common complaint is that they do not know what their teachers expect of them, or how they are supposed to use their time. At one medical school, able graduates supposed that their teachers expected them to learn the entire content of their large medical books! In this instance the teachers were astonished that graduate students had such a misconception, but it had not occurred to them to sit down and discuss with the students what they did expect. And since students may be confused initially by a conflict of new impressions and requirements, it might be most sensible to print a school manual outlining the expectations of teachers, for discussion with the students, say, within the first half-term.

Another common misunderstanding by new students, where teachers fail to communicate their expectations, is that they should read every book from the extensive reading lists with which they are supplied. Students who were never given a choice of reading texts at school may simply assume that teachers in higher education behave in the same way, but expect far more.

Failure to specify and to communicate aims and objectives may also have long-term consequences. Some students graduate from universities with their initial modes of thinking only marginally changed. Bligh (1977) has written a case study of 'Cynthia', an exemplar of a type of university student: middle-class, conventional, quiet, conscientious and rule following, who chooses to study at 'a red-brick university with a humanities bias'. There she works assiduously, absorbing information as she did at school, disappointed and perhaps puzzled by the rather poor marks she obtains, but failing to learn skill in argument or the critical modes of thinking which are said to follow from a higher education. Eventually she obtains a lower second-class degree.

While it is certainly more difficult to induce changes in students' attitudes and modes of thinking than to encourage acquisition of knowledge, the existence of graduates like 'Cynthia' suggests that the teachers' aims were never effectively communicated to them. Development in thinking was neither adequately encouraged through discussion nor explicitly evaluated in written work.

Acquiring essential study skills   It is impossible to teach all students all of the study skills required throughout a three-year course during its first few weeks. Improvements in study skills will be required as new demands are made of students. Initially practice can be offered in reading, taking notes from lectures or books and, perhaps, in writing brief reports or paragraphs. Like all skills, these must be practised, and students need to receive feedback on their performance. This need not come from the teacher. If small groups compare their notes 'surface' learners who tend to record details, rather than main points and their relationships, may be redirected by other students to the more profitable 'deep' methods.

Skill in skimming articles to select important or relevant points, and use of the index to look up a topic in a number of books, may also need practice. Science students, in particular, tend to grow accustomed to careful, sequential reading through a text and may need reminding that there are other ways of reading and using books. Although students will find a sheet of information about the library useful and interesting, those who are set exercises in their own subject, which involves use of references from the library, normally use it more intelligently and more frequently than those who are merely taken on a tour of the library by a librarian.

Students' skills in writing often differ widely on entry. Problems most frequently arise with those who seem hardly literate initially, or with some students from overseas whose command of English is barely sufficient for the course they have entered. For these students, meetings with tutors to discuss occasional essays provide insufficient practice. Frequent short exercises designed to practise specific skills in writing are more helpful. Teachers suggest making summaries of short articles or chapters, writing reports on short experiments or demonstrations, describing technical apparatus, making diagrammatic schemes prior to writing essays, etc. For students having considerable difficulty, meetings with a tutor to discuss their current written work, perhaps in a small group, may be needed to help them organize their thoughts and to write clearly and concisely. Other ways of helping students initially are outlined in Chapters 6 and 7.

Coping with students' deficiencies at entry   Students are likely to need considerable initial assistance if they missed topics in A levels which are normally considered necessary for entry to a course. The solution of revising A-level topics with all first-year students can lead to boredom among the better qualified students, who then are apt to use their energies in some other direction. Thus, in a comparison of two courses of engineering, in the one which included a great deal of revision during the first year, abler students gave less time to their work and more to social activities – with the result that at the end of the year the less able students did best in the examinations, whereas the more able did poorly (Beard et al., 1964).

In recent years, better ways of diagnosing and remedying deficiencies have been developed which enable teachers to cater for the needs of individual students. Sutton (1977) reports using diagnostic tests to identify gaps in knowledge in physics. Once diagnosed, deficiencies are remedied with the aid of concise, inexpensive textual self-teaching units, each requiring from one to three hours of study, and containing many review questions. These are supplemented by laboratory-based demonstrations undertaken by the students without supervision. This method, which has proved interesting and effective, does not involve those already well qualified in needless repetition. Similarly, Furniss and Parsonage (1975) and Galton et al. (1976) identified deficiencies in chemistry, confusions in inorganic chemistry and weakness in mathematics by the use of such short answer tests.

In some instances deficiencies can be foreseen, rather than diagnosed. Pramanik and Dring (1977), for example, describe a laboratory course for first-year students which was introduced when it was discovered that final-year students were unable to use common laboratory equipment with any degree of confidence. Experiments were chosen to teach techniques and handling of equipment, to illustrate verification of various laws, and to emphasize practical aspects of devices and their deviation from theoretical ideal situations. Some experiments were open-ended, requiring initiative to discover a solution. In this course, unlike most individualized courses, there was considerable interaction between teachers and students. As a consequence the course had the effect of increasing interest and motivation.

Students are usually unaware of deficiencies in their thinking. It takes new experiences, time to absorb them, and often considerable discussion among themselves before students' thinking develops to higher levels. It involves change from depending on teachers telling them what to think to thinking for themselves as responsible adults.

5.3 The development of thinking in late adolescence

The initial difficulties which some students have in their studies in higher education may arise from characteristics in thinking which are common to many first-year students, if not to the majority of undergraduates, whatever their field of study. Observations by Peters (1958), Veness (1968) and Gibson (1970) in various fields of inquiry indicate four main kinds of limitation: (1) students are commonly said to have a poor understanding of important basic concepts; (2) many students seem to expect a greater degree of accuracy than is possible; (3) students may believe in the 'truth' of theories and the infallibility of authorities; (4) students have difficulty in handling evidence.

Understanding concepts

Students' failures in understanding basic concepts seem not to have been investigated until approximately 15 years ago. In an inquiry at Surrey University into students' mathematical and scientific knowledge on entry to university, O'Connell et al. (1969) found that although students had sufficient knowledge of facts and formulae to form a good basis for university work, they were weak in concepts and ideas. The majority of the students were unclear about the concepts 'vector' and 'scalar', they had hazy ideas about 'exponentials' and 'wave motion' and showed some confusion of thought about 'diffraction' and 'interference'. The authors attributed these deficiencies to failure on the part of school teachers to discuss concepts. Physicists in London, discussing their objectives in teaching, also commented on students' weaknesses in comprehending some concepts, citing 'inertia' and 'entropy' as often poorly understood, and similar gaps with biology students have been reported by Brumby (1979) and with economics students by Dahlgren and Marton (1978) and Dahlgren (1981).

Although there have been few investigations into concept formation by students of arts subjects, teachers are aware of the difficulties their students experience in understanding abstractions. For instance, a group of historians, when attempting to prepare an outline of their objectives in teaching, spoke of the need to assist students in understanding basic concepts of their subject, citing 'civilization' as an example.

Perhaps a greater problem in arts and social sciences is that many concepts are already familiar as words in common use. Beginning students are apt to suppose that they already know the meanings of terms such as 'history', 'education', 'democracy' or 'liberalism'. It may not have dawned on them that people, having different values, do not agree as to their meaning; there are numerous interpretations of 'history' or of 'democracy' and there is no universal agreement as to their attributes. Consequently students must learn that it is impossible to define briefly some concepts. Instead concepts must be discussed showing how they differ to groups of people having different perspectives or making different assumptions.

'Accuracy' and 'equivalence'

Secondly, as we have said, many students expect a greater degree of accuracy than is reasonably attainable; for instance, they believe that it is possible to make a 'correct' translation from one language to another, exactly conveying the original meaning; or, if disabused of this belief, they hope at least to attain the 'best' translation. Students of science and mathematics expect to obtain 'the right answer' and continue calculations or experiments in order to obtain an unrealistic degree of precision.

Some students may also suppose that a model is virtually identical with the system it represents, instead of understanding its role in providing a simplified version of phenomena which concentrates attention on certain features. Perhaps, in school, they have been taught models as though they were 'true'. Consequently, in the absence of discussion of the different types of models and their use in the students' field of study, they may be a source of some confusion to students, especially when they are expected to change one model for another.

Gilbert (1980) discusses the use of models in teaching sciences, distinguishing five different types: scale models (most commonly used in engineering and architecture); analogue models, designed to represent a web of relationships, such as ball-and-stick models of crystals; mathematical models which represent relationships by an equation, so that each symbol corresponds with a concept in the original phenomenon; theoretical models, which tend to be communicated in verbal or diagrammatic forms, e.g. a magnetic field acts as if it consisted of lines of force joining North and South Poles; and the archetype models, such as Lewin's 'field model' in psychology which uses the terms 'vector', 'force', 'boundary', 'fluidity', etc. in describing an individual's psychological field. This requires a list of key words and expressions with statements of their interconnections and their paradigmatic meanings in the field from which they were originally drawn.

Gilbert notes that students show a general lack of awareness of properties of models; for example, they cannot generalize properties of 'waves' from sound to water; they hesitate to use the more advanced, or abstract models (as we shall see this could be a consequence of their level of thinking); and are uncertain how to relate models of different categories within the same topic area, e.g. the Kekulé model (analogue) and Ingoldian mechanisms (theoretical) in organic reactions. Understandably Gilbert suggests that a lesson devoted to models should be of some assistance.

'Belief in theories and in authorities'

A third prevalent characteristic is seen in the belief that theories are 'true' or that authorities are above criticism. The historians we have just mentioned try to wean their students from a belief that authorities are infallible by showing that even great scholars may disagree, or by drawing attention to errors, through study, for instance, of Pirenne's thesis on the dating of the collapse of the classical world. Physicists comment on the distress caused to some students when well-established theories are questioned; like the students of sociology studied by Gibson they feel that a theory which has an exception can no longer be trusted. A desire for certainty or for something 'absolute' and definitive to hold on to may be seen even among mature students when they find their beliefs and assumptions effectively challenged. As one mature student of education said despairingly after taking part in a philosophical discussion, 'If everything is relative, nothing is true, nothing matters!' Her difficulty seemed to arise from an unquestioning dependence on authority, in this instance vested in 'absolute truths' to which everything could be conveniently referred, and her assumption that, in their absence, no meaningful judgements could be made.

The change from a childlike acceptance of authorities to realization that knowledge is relative, has been observed by Perry (1970) and Saljö (1979), as mentioned in Chapter 4. Clearly such differences influence students' learning; those who are at Perry's initial stage will seek 'right answers' to learn while those who have reached the final stage can be expected to display ability for intelligent discussion.

'Handling evidence'

Fourthly, many students have difficulties in handling evidence. Gibson's findings were mainly concerned with this. Historians, too, when discussing their objectives, speak of the students' need to learn how to consider evidence in order to arrive at a relatively unbiased opinion, how to resist the temptation to manipulate evidence to predetermined ends, and how to avoid reaching premature conclusions by failing to obtain as much evidence as possible. Abercrombie (1960) noted limitations of similar kinds in first-year students of the biological sciences. Like Elton (O'Connell et al.) she attributed this to the teaching they received in their schools or at college.

Abercrombie (1960) used discussion methods in which she withdrew from the role of authority figure to that of observer and occasional commentator, so leading the students to educate each other through argument with their peers. Her method and others designed to foster thinking, and evaluation of evidence, are described in Chapter 9.

5.4   On being a mature student

The problems of adjusting to life at university, polytechnic or college of higher education can be more acute for mature students, but it does not follow that this will necessarily be the case. Many mature students will profit from their maturity. The variety of mature students, though, can cause some difficulties for teachers. Consider the following people cited by Squires (1981):

1. A young man leaves school with three O levels and works as a clerk in an insurance company for several years. He gets bored with the job and its lack of prospects, and studies at the local FE college to get some A levels. He is subsequently admitted to study psychology at a university as a full-time student. His girlfriend, later wife, who has a job with British Gas, helps to

support him while he is working.

2. A woman leaves school with two O levels, works as a typist for several years, then marries and has two children. Both of these are at school by the time she is 29, and she decides to enrol as an Open University degree student, partly because one of her friends has, and partly to prove to herself that she can do better than she did at school.

3. A man in his late thirties is suddenly made redundant by the manufacturing company for which he has worked in a managerial capacity for 15 years. He finds great difficulty in getting a similar job anywhere else, and decides to look for an intensive full-time one-year vocational course which will re-equip him for a new career.

4. A retired teacher, mentally active, wants to deepen her late-developing interest in history. She goes to an extramural class for one year, which she finds interesting but not very demanding; on the other hand, she does not really feel like committing herself to a full degree.

Squires (1981) gives a clear account of the complexity of describing mature students as a single group, and of the problems of establishing similarities and differences between these and similarly undifferentiated groups of 18-year-olds.

Nonetheless, speaking in broad terms it is possible to discern some similarities within groups of mature students that suggest implications for teaching and learning in higher education. It appears, for example, from various studies that there are three main reasons why adults take up full-time study: (1) to make a change in their career; (2) to obtain a job qualification – for such reasons as job promotion; (3) to seek personal and intellectual development per se.

Some problems

The difficulties facing adult learners can, for convenience, be categorized into three kinds – social, psychological and physiological (Elsey, 1982). Socially (and in the classroom) adults are continually faced with a set of expectations about what they can and cannot do. Adults are expected to be more socially conservative and traditional in their approach to life, and it is often assumed that older people will be less adaptable to change, more difficult to teach and too old to learn. 'You can't teach an old dog new tricks' is a common enough refrain.

Thus, for some mature students, there are age-gap problems:

This situation (lack of sleep from worry) is even more of a problem for a mature student who lives in a hall of residence where the other occupants tend to keep later hours. . . . Often students are not satisfied with four hours of punk noise at the Union disco, but decide at midnight to play their stereo or to improvise by kicking a litter bin up the stairs and along the corridor.

Frequently mature students have problems they will not admit to. They don't want to appear 'thick' in front of their younger counterparts. Instead they plod on trying to find ways round their problems, often succeeding at the expense of time, effort and worry.

But for others such problems do not seem to arise:

I had thought that one would find the age-gap between oneself and the bulk of the students a problem, but this was a non-event. Not only did I make close friends among the other mature students, but I seemed to get on well with everyone and was not consciously constantly aware of being older.

Nonetheless, the problems connected with inter-relating home, work and student life can cause great difficulty.

The mature married student faces the greatest difficulties. She has to organize herself in order to share her time between her husband, children, housework and to set aside some of the time she used to spend at leisure with her family.

The problems may be more acute, or certainly different, for students at the Open University compared with those at more traditional ones.

The psychological difficulties that accompany ageing are typically problems of remembering, less flexibility in one's thinking and an increased difficulty in dealing with more complex issues:

What I find most difficult is to switch from one subject, or one language, or even one idea to another. This makes me waste considerable time during exams.

Also, it appears, there is often a problem with discarding earlier ideas and beliefs, and with preventing errors from reoccurring:

From my observations it would seem that progress is dependent on breaking old habits and trying to work out strategies which will reduce stress and anxiety whilst allowing efficient learning to take place.

Anxiety, of course, arises from various sources:

The fear of failure is greatest among mature students at all levels.

A particular problem that faces male mature students is that this is probably their 'last chance'. Younger students have time to make up for mistakes if they fail their exams. Mature students tend to feel that they have used up all their time and are at a disadvantage in the job-market because of their age. Failing exams would seal their fate.

Finally, if we consider physiological problems, we might note that various functions start to decline in efficiency from the late teens and early twenties, and continue to decline thereafter (Bromley, 1974). This decline is hardly noticeable at first, and indeed in the middle years people can adopt various ways of dealing with things that make it hard for anyone to discern any decline in their efficiency. Nonetheless, these problems may affect teaching and learning:

> Although domestic problems are the most difficult to solve, some other difficulties must not be overlooked. These are failing eyesight, hearing loss and generally all the minor ailments associated with middle-age.

> I have great difficulty in reading the reduced-size printing of your handouts. As a psychologist you should know better.

Problems with hearing and eyesight continue to grow more acute the older one gets, but the main effect of general physiological decline can be characterized by a gradual reduction in the speed at which most activities can be completed:

> Slowing with age can result in the individual feeling harassed in a situation where younger people can do the job quicker. This could have a disastrous effect upon a mature student in, say, a practical class, if he feels that he cannot do a proper analysis of the task. If others are waiting to use the equipment he may abandon his experiment uncompleted for fear of being considered incompetent.

However, not all is gloom and doom. Maturity brings advantages too:

> I found that most mature students had a wider general knowledge on which to build, and that their greater experience of life was an asset, particularly with the social sciences.

> Generally you can handle situations in a much more confident way than you could at, say, nineteen. You are less likely to be over-awed by the tutor/lecturer and much more likely to ask if you don't understand something.

> The advantages of being a mature student far outweighed the disadvantages. I had a ball!

Mature students have a clearer view of what they want from university, and a strong motivation to succeed. The results of a questionnaire (Elsey, 1982) indicated that these factors lead to wider reading, a questioning and critical approach to lectures and an appreciation of the applications of theory to practice.

Implications for teaching

A number of investigators have considered in detail the implications for teaching that accompany the problems facing mature students, and how these might change over time (e.g. see Nicholson, 1977; Rogers, 1977; Lovell, 1980).

Knights and McDonald (1977) suggest that:

> Staff should be explicit about the requirements of the course: what is required of the students, and the amount and level of reading necessary. (For example, the Open University makes it clear to students that it is not expected that they will read every word or completely understand everything they read.)

> Staff should not make assumptions about students' basic knowledge of a subject or their approach to it without checking these with the students.

But at the same time, allowance needs to be made for the fact that mature students are able, and more than ready, to take a greater responsibility for their own learning.

> Staff should be able to acquaint themselves with the background of mature students, to enable them to use this to best advantage.

> More attention could be paid to inculcating skills of tutorial leadership in tutors. Although tutorials containing a mixture of mature students and school leavers can be rewarding, some skill is required to enable their potential to be realised.

Davies (1981) describes four main areas that require special attention when teaching older learners. These are summarized in *Table* 5.1. We need to note that the recommendations given in *Table* 5.1 are based on research that has typically looked at the performance of people whom we might regard as older than the typical mature student, and, in addition, that it has examined this performance in areas very different from that of higher education (e.g. industrial training). Because of these factors there is some debate as to how far these recommendations actually apply to mature students in higher education (especially those still in their twenties).

Furthermore, there is also some debate as to how far the difficulties that mature students report concerning learning – of the sort that we have already quoted – really exist, are shared equally with 18-year-olds, or are simply expressions of expectations that these are the issues that mature students should be worrying about. As it happens we believe that our quotations reflect genuine problems, and we note that Nicholson (1977) considers that the problems of mature students are the same as those of

Table 5.1   Adapting instruction to suit 'older' learners

Organizational factors
- Make instruction purposeful and relevant.
- Arrange for longer periods of instruction (say 60–90 minutes).
- Include breaks (say 5 minutes after every 30).
- Mix young and old in the same instructional groups.
- Respect adult status and experience.
- Give strong emotional support and encouragement.

Instructional factors
- Use discovery methods of learning.
- Restrict the range and content of lectures to essentials.
- Use written instructions as well as verbal ones for projects and assignments.
- If using demonstrations, demonstrate the whole, then the parts, and then the whole again.
- Avoid the use of audiovisual aids that have a different organizing structure or sequence from your presentation.
- Employ a great deal of practice, review and consolidation, so that overlearning takes place.
- Vary instructional methods and work assignments. Provide variety.
- Avoid formal tests and examinations. Use continuous assessment.

Personal factors
- Allow learners to participate in the planning process.
- Allow learners to proceed at their own pace.
- Avoid any sense of competition.
- Encourage learners to set their own goals, and to beat their own targets.
- Make sure that learners feel a sense of achievement and recognition.
- See that learners learn correctly from the start.
- Promote group feelings and identity.

Source: Based on Davies (1981). Reprinted with permission of the author and the publishers.

younger students, 'only more so'. Certainly one finds an increasing concern with increasing age among the first-year Open University students about the problems of coping with new methods, new subject matter, memory and the ability to concentrate (MacIntosh, 1976).

Meeting the requirements of mature students

Despite all the difficulties, both real and imagined, a number of studies show that most mature students do cope successfully with higher education (see Roderick et al., 1982). It is likely then that the potential demand for further education by adults can be exploited. Institutions can increase their enrolment and provide a greater variety of courses with more varied teaching methods and methods of assessment.

Clearly, if one is to consider greatly increasing the number of mature students, then many courses will have to be rescheduled. The rather simple but effective idea of the evening class will have to be expanded to incorporate a vast array of scheduling possibilities such as daytime courses, evening sessions, blocks (ranging from weekends to residential summer schools) and self-paced schedules (such as those provided by correspondence courses or the Open University).

Some universities and colleges are already making changes along these lines. There have been changes in lecture timetables (with lectures being given later in the day, and/or repeated in the evening), crèches have been provided, and study guides and induction courses have been prepared for mature students. However, there has been little fundamental restructuring. The Open University alone provides an exemplar of a new and positive approach to adult learning.

5.5   Overseas students

Students may be more than just mature: they may come from overseas as well. Recent changes in the economic situation have led to an increase in the number of overseas students at both undergraduate and postgraduate level. Indeed, in some institutions the recruitment of overseas students today ensures the viability of courses which might otherwise be too small.

Woodhall (1981) reported that the number of students taking part in higher education in a foreign country throughout the world had quadrupled from about 240,000 in 1960 to approximately one million. At present foreign students are heavily concentrated in five countries – the USA, Canada, France, Germany and the UK. In Britain the number of overseas students in higher education trebled from 42,000 in 1950 to 120,000 in 1978, but by 1983 this had declined to 87,000.

While most reports concentrate on the economic implications of governmental decisions with respect to overseas students (e.g. Williams, 1981; Woodhall, 1981) some authors have written about the effects of overseas students on teaching and learning in higher education.

Reed et al. (1978) interviewed groups of overseas students and asked the following general questions:

Why did you come to the UK to study?

What has your experience been here?
How has your experience lined up with your expectations?
What do you think people here assume about you?
How do you regard yourself in relation to the UK?

The responses led the authors to conclude that it was necessary to consider a wide context when considering overseas students. The students were participating in a process which had begun in their own country, which had brought them to the UK, which had led them to a place of study, and from which they would depart to their home, country or elsewhere. It became clear that the students were primarily concerned about three issues: (1) being a *student* – studying for and gaining academic qualifications; (2) being a *client* – making sure they were getting value for money; and (3) being a *visitor* to the UK – subject to government regulations concerning what they can or cannot do during their stay.

Reed et al. explored all of these three concerns in depth. We shall consider here only the first issue: that of being a student. Reed et al. were impressed with the firmness with which overseas students expressed their wish to achieve something through studying in the UK. Some saw studying in terms of a qualification:

I want a bit of paper with my qualification on it at the end of my time here.

Others wanted more than that:

You come here not only to get the academic qualifications but to meet people here . . . our assumption is to come to Britain to meet the British.

The incentive for study also varied:

I have spent so much money coming here, I cannot afford to fail.

We want to develop our character and it is important to us who we meet and what kind of values we accept.

I see myself as a mirror between the UK and Nigeria . . . to take back things important for my country.

Reed et al. suggest that everything else is judged by overseas students on the basis of how it helps them as students. This applies, for example, to accommodation, facilities, equipment and staff–student relationships.

The teaching staff in a number of colleges and universities were also asked various questions about overseas students, such as:

How do you view overseas students in your department/college/hall, etc.?

What differences, if any, do you perceive between home students and overseas students?
What do you feel overseas students are looking for?
What contributions do overseas students make?

Reed et al. reported that the starting point for many staff was to put on one side any differences which were more than individual:

> To be honest, there is not much difference between overseas students and home students . . . we treat each student as an individual, it doesn't matter where he comes from.   (Poly Course Director)

> I don't appreciate who is an overseas student and who is not. The differentiation is faced at enrolment, which is not the concern of lecturers, and once that decision is taken they don't feel any different.
> (FE College Departmental Head)

> Unless some issue crops up, I don't think of them as overseas students.
> (University Senior Tutor)

Clearly, in the light of the information given by Reed et al., these responses seem naive. The attitudes of teaching staff to overseas students can be a major problem. Reed et al. report that some academic staff treat overseas students as though they are of a lower intellectual calibre, and that some do not acknowledge that the students' preparation and techniques of learning will have been different from those of UK students. Unfortunately, too, some forget that most overseas students face difficulties with the English language.

For those staff who are aware of these concerns it is clear that overseas students present problems. To help overcome these difficulties institutions usually provide various agencies such as counselling services, courses on English for overseas students, lodgings officers, personal and academic tutors. Reed et. al. discuss in detail the value and role of an academic tutor who is solely responsible for overseas students. Sometimes these solutions work well, sometimes not. It is important, therefore, for teaching staff to ascertain what the situation is in their own institutions.

5.6 Summary

● Moving from school to higher education can cause considerable anxiety for many students.
● This anxiety can be alleviated to some extent by courses for pupils still at school, by increasing contacts between schools and institutions of higher education, and by induction courses for first-year students.

● One difficulty often overlooked is that levels of thinking used by first-year students are often inappropriate for higher education. Students have difficulties in handling concepts, theories, accuracy and evidence.

● While mature students present a particular range of difficulties that carry their own implications for teaching, most mature students adjust successfully to higher education.

● Overseas students present particular difficulties, and these are probably best solved by appointing an academic tutor responsible for overseas students.

CHAPTER 6

DEVELOPING STUDY SKILLS: ACQUIRING INFORMATION

Chapters 6 and 7 provide two chapters on study skills. In this chapter we focus on reading and memorizing, using the library, purchasing textbooks and note-taking.

6.1 Introduction

The essential aims of teachers in higher education are (1) that students should learn to think and work independently, and (2) that students' study methods should be made more effective. While these have always been avowed aims in universities, evidence from critics of teaching in higher education and from students themselves would suggest that they have never been fully realized. In fact it would seem that such aims are by no means central for all teachers for, if they were, courses and methods of assessment would give additional credit to the capacity for independent study and thinking.

The tutorial system in the older universities, if it works well, encourages the development of independent thinking and autonomous study, since a student must present an essay or a problem and be prepared to discuss his or her views or arguments with a more experienced tutor. On the other hand, those teaching methods which are derived primarily from an apprenticeship system – as in some schools of engineering, dentistry and, perhaps to some extent, education – tend to suffer from a legacy of didactic teaching which is aimed at inculcating essential knowledge and skills. Between these two approaches lie many colleges and departments which exhibit an astonishing diversity of practice but which, if examination papers are a fair indication, still tend to teach students basic information and accepted interpretations and applications. So, even here, independence of thought does not appear to be as highly valued as it should be.

Whatever the attitudes of the teaching staff, the study skills of students – reading, writing and organizing material – tend to be taken for granted and to receive little or no attention. Yet, if the ultimate aim is that students should continue their education without guidance, then the methods by which this can be achieved need to be developed until they are fully effective.

It is evident from the sales of available study guides that students themselves feel the need for guidance in these matters. Study skills have been a topic of research since the 1920s, and indeed in the 1950s it was commonly thought that one of the main causes of student failure was that the students were using inefficient study methods. Two kinds of study manual developed: the general study manual, which took different topics in turn and offered specific advice on each one (e.g. Cassie and Constantine, 1977), and the particular study manual, which described one particular over-riding approach (e.g. Robinson, 1961). Unfortunately these manuals also encourage what might be called the myth of the 'perfect student'. Such a person is one who assimilates and puts into practice all the known advice about study habits. Critics of these manuals point out that such perfection is physically impossible (e.g. see Gibbs, 1981).

Reading a manual does not, of course, guarantee effective performance. What is essential, as in learning all skills, is practice and feedback. For this reason guides such as Rowntree's *Learn How to Study* (1976) and the Open University's *Plain English* (1980) are preferable to many in that they include exercises which enable students to practise activities for themselves. Even so, it is still questionable whether or not any book or course about study methods can allow for the diversity of students' needs if only one approach is presented for each topic. A single approach may be too advanced for some students and too contrary to the cognitive styles of others. Consequently, teaching methods which provide students with opportunities to discuss their own and other students' approaches to study tasks may be more helpful. In this way students are likely to develop the self-analytic attitude to learning advocated, as we shall see below, by Gibbs (1981) and Harri-Augstein et al. (1982).

6.2 Reading and memorizing

Once children have acquired the ability to read fairly fluently it is commonly assumed that they do not need any further help. However, there is now evidence to show that even university students may need to increase their speed of reading and to improve their skills of selecting essentials and recognizing relationships. Assistance to students mainly consisted, until fairly recently, of providing instruction in how to increase reading speeds. However, there are now methods which teach specific reading skills or which increase the students' awareness of reading habits which need to be reconsidered.

There is still some doubt about the desirability of using exercises to promote faster reading. Students and lecturers who have attended 'faster reading' courses normally state that they are well worthwhile and cite considerable increases in reading speeds and greater skills in 'skimming'. Experimental tests have shown considerable increases in reading speed immediately upon completion of a course (Poulton, 1961) but, when further tests have been made, it seems that only some students retain their improvements, and there are wide individual differences here.

The fact is that people read at many different speeds depending on (1) the purpose for which they are reading and (2) the difficulty of the subject matter. One does not usually understand mathematics or appreciate literature best by rapid reading, but there are occasions, in seeking a quotation, for example, or in getting the gist of a passage, where skimming is advantageous. Fry (1963a) considers three main reading speeds: a slow speed or 'study speed' for high understanding or good retention; an average speed for easier textbooks, novels, newspapers, etc.; and a fast speed for skimming, when high comprehension is not required or time is at a premium. No doubt, most of us use all three speeds at different times without conscious thought and probably acquire preferred techniques. Some readers, for example, have the habit of skimming all the difficult material before studying it. This, they feel, helps them to put topics into context, calls to mind related subject matter and indicates which sections of the text need most attention.

Surveys of students' and adults' reading, however, suggest that poor readers are unable to skim satisfactorily. If they want to obtain a level of 70 percent comprehension poor readers have to read at about 150–180 words per minute with fairly easy material or to go more slowly with difficult material for greater comprehension. Good readers, on the other hand, achieve a level of 50 percent comprehension while skimming at more than 800 words per minute, read at 250–500 words per minute for 70 percent comprehension and reduce to about 200–300 words per minute to achieve

80–90 percent comprehension. It is clear, therefore, that poor readers will benefit from being taught to skim and that some good readers may benefit from speed reading courses – at least in terms of the time spent in study. Two methods of instruction have been used to promote faster reading. One involves the use of specially prepared passages which are read and timed, followed by perhaps a set of questions to test comprehension (Fry, 1963b). The other is to show material on film at increasing speeds so that the reader must keep pace with it; again, comprehension is tested by questions (James, R.L., 1967). Either method is initially effective but, as already noted, it is doubtful whether there is evidence that increased speeds are always maintained.

For skimming, however, some quite specific advice can be given which may lead to permanent gains. Fry advocates that students do the whole of a skimming exercise 'against the clock'. He suggests that (1) students should perhaps read opening paragraphs in full at an average speed since these may supply an outline; (2) they should then pick up main ideas from later paragraphs, probably using their first sentences; and (3) they should skip the rest of the material except for figures and key words. If the students meet a paragraph which needs to be read in full to obtain the meaning they can make up for lost time subsequently by skimming faster until they reach the last paragraph, which may be read in full. Since all this requires practice it is best done in a class or by pairs of students checking each other.

Jahoda and Thomas (1966) provided early evidence that students looked for different things when reading, and more recently Harri-Augstein et al. (1982) have discussed these considerations in a useful booklet on reading that incorporates self- and small-group exercises. Harri-Augstein et al. describe how a reading recorder can be used to throw light on readers' strategies and tactics when they are reading a particular piece of text. *Figure* 6.1 shows a simplified version of a record obtained from such a recorder. As Harri-Augstein et al. say:

A reading record like this makes one wonder:
1. What was in the first 100 lines that made the reader pause and think after reading them?
2. The reader read lines 100 to 150 rather slowly. Why? What was it in lines 100 to 150 that was difficult to read?
3. Why did the reader go back from line 250 to line 150?
4. Why was it then so easy to read through from line 150 to the end?
If we explain that the first 100 lines were a simple introduction; the next 50 lines examined in detail the author's intentions; line 250 referred to an idea first dealt with in line 150; and the last 150 lines repeated the author's

intentions more elaborately, then we can begin to infer quite a lot from the reader's behaviour.

It is clear that discussion with students about their reading strategies for different kinds of text can prove useful, especially for remedial readers.

While many books on study skills have chapters or indeed exercises on reading, we feel that students are likely to make most progress if they attend well-run courses. Larkin and Reif (1976) describe one such course designed to teach a general skill for studying scientific text. More specifically the students were taught a skill for acquiring from a description of a quantitative relation (e.g. a definition or law) a generally specified set of abilities prerequisite to applying relations in problem-solving.

In the training procedure students answered questions about a text based on the list of abilities described by the authors; they obtained practice and feedback on performance by using systematically designed study material;

Figure 6.1   A simplified version of a record obtained with a reading recorder. (Reproduced with permission from Harri-Augstein et al. 1982)

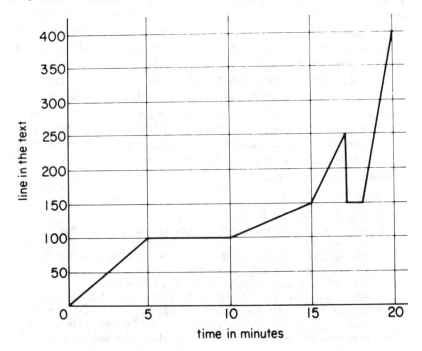

and they were tested with feedback, employing Keller-type format; that is, they had to pass the test before proceeding to the next section.

An evaluation of this course showed that (1) the students gained appreciably in ability to understand new relations in a text; (2) they continued to use the skills they acquired after training; (3) they became considerably less dependent on instruction; (4) they gained a general skill potentially useful in various quantitative subjects; and (5) they acquired a skill for learning from text which was retained for an average period of at least two weeks, and without conscious effort on the part of 70 percent of the students.

6.3   Using the library and obtaining information

As we saw in Chapter 3, activity on the part of the learner is essential in acquiring skills. Teachers and librarians who recognize this typically set exercises in using the library facilities for first-year students to complete. Crossley (1968) found that this led to a higher level of library inquiry and to an increased use of inter-library services.

Although it seems natural to place such activities early in the student's first year, courses with more specific purposes and more extensive objectives may come later. Steedman (1974), for instance, found that lectures on information sources resulted in a better start to final-year projects.

Glen et al. (1983) introduced an optional course for second-year physics students which was designed to give them experience of finding information in Birmingham University Library. One aspect of this course involved the students in completing sets of exercises, one of which is shown in *Figure* 6.2. The students attempted these exercises during a two-week period after the June examinations. Most of them completed a good proportion of the tasks set and some did them all.

McElroy and McNaughton (1979) described a library course which was designed for first-year HND students. The aim of the course was to increase the students' ability and willingness to read scientific literature – and ultimately to enable them to make their own contributions to the literature in an acceptable style and format. The course was integrated with the students' scientific work and was taught by a biologist and a librarian in cooperation. The students selected topics for study which were agreed with their teachers, and, having chosen a topic, they were required to identify and read appropriate literature and to write a paper. Every activity was set in its appropriate context. The students learned to use college and external library services, to identify the holdings of a library in a given subject, to

Figure 6.2   An example of a library exercise for physics students. (Reproduced with permission from Glen et al., 1983)

LOCATING REFERENCES IN THE LIBRARY

1. Locate reference (1) and answer the question.
2. Locate classic paper (2) and give its full reference.
3. Locate non-journal reference (3) and answer the question.
4. Use an abstract journal to find papers fitting description (4).
5. Use a citation index to locate recent work on subject (5).
6. Find paper (6) in current periodicals room and give its full reference.

(1) J.A.R. Griffith, G.R. Isaak, R. New, M.P. Ralls, C.P. van Zyl. Optical heterodyne spectroscopy using tunable dye lasers: hyperfine structure of sodium. *Journal of Physics* B, Vol. 10, No. 4, 1977, p. 91–95.

   Q: What is the quoted accuracy of the hyperfine splitting in terms of the optical transition frequency?

(2) F.W. Aston's paper on isotopes and atomic weights in *Nature*, Vol. 105.

(3) S.A. Durrani, K.A. Khazal, S.R. Malik, J.H. Fremlin, G.L. Hendry. Thermoluminescence and fission-track studies of the Oklo fossil reactor materials. In *The Oklo phenomenon. Proc. Symposium in Gabon, 1975*. Vienna, IAEA, 1975, p. 207–22.

   Q: What was peculiar about the materials from zone 2?

(4) Use Physics Abstracts to find papers between 1977 and 1980 on the temperature of the moon and its thermal history. List the references and their main results.

(5) Use the Science Citation Index for 1981 to find recent papers on the subject of (1) above and give the full reference to one of them.

(6) Find the recent review on high pressure studies in *Rev. Mod. Phys.* and give the full reference.

retrieve nominated documents from the library and to use bibliographical guides to the scientific literature.

In evaluating this course, the teachers noted that the work of these first-year students compared favourably with that of final-year ones. They developed a mature approach to literature which made it easier for them to tackle projects or to write essays. Of the 44 students who completed the course in 1978: 93 percent expressed confidence in their ability to read the research literature; 91 percent were making frequent use of the library (and 35 percent of other libraries); 82 percent said that they read selectively from books rather than reading from cover to cover; 82 percent undertook additional reading to supplement their lecture notes; 50 percent used citations to trace further reading; 36 percent were making frequent use of journal articles; 34 percent were making frequent use of review articles; and

71 percent provided a bibliography with their written work. Although there was no control group these percentages seem high in comparison with what is reported of most first-year students.

Many of the different attempts to provide instruction in library use can be classified in terms of two of the basic theoretical positions outlined in Chapter 3, that is, a behaviouristic approach or a cognitive one. Studies using a behaviouristic approach include those of Jewell (1982) and Surprenant (1982). Both these investigators compared the effectiveness of self-paced workbooks to lecture presentations on the same material, and both found a superiority for the workbooks. Aluri (1982) describes a computer-assisted program MEDLEARN, which fits more readily into the cognitive perspective. MEDLEARN provides on-line training in the use of the US National Library of Medicine's MEDLINE data base. Aluri describes how learners continuously interact with the program and receive continuous feedback on their performance. Quizzes are presented frequently to test the learners' immediate recall, comprehension and assimilation of the material presented, and these quizzes also require the learners to apply their knowledge in new and different contexts. In addition MEDLEARN is divided into three tracks: A for novices, B for people who have completed track A or who have equivalent experience, and C for experienced librarians and information specialists.

Finally in this section we may note a study by Hardesty et al. (1982), which was concerned with assessing the long-term effectiveness of instruction in library use. In this study various groups of students were tested (and retested) at different times over a three-year period so that comparisons could be made between students who had received instruction in library use and those who had not. The authors concluded that the long-term possession of library skills was more highly related to instruction in library use than it was to simply using the library for a period of three years.

6.4 Buying and using textbooks

Despite the widespread use of books by students and teachers alike there has been little systematic research into buying and using textbooks. Perhaps the most comprehensive account to date of book use in a British university has been provided by Mann (1974). *Figure* 6.3 indicates the main lines of communication that are involved in the provision of books for students. Each link in the diagram (e.g. lecturer – library) is clearly important, and most are discussed in detail by Mann. As *Figure* 6.3 shows, all the links are

Figure 6.3

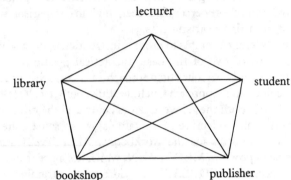

inter-related, and indeed can be considered in a wider framework (e.g. students – students, lecturers – lecturers).

Several commentators, including Mann, suggest how book use and purchase can be encouraged among students. Three fairly common, but valuable points are:

1. Booklists can be more carefully considered. (All the commentators produce horror stories of first-year reading lists containing streams of undifferentiated items.) Reading lists can indicate high priority items (and even annotate them) and clearer guidance can be given on what (and what *not*) to purchase.

2. Department heads (or their representatives) can coordinate such booklists, and make sure that libraries and bookshops are sent copies of the lists *in good time*. It may, of course, take several weeks, or even months, to obtain a book from overseas.

3. Careful thought can be given to which books and articles can be placed on the 'temporary reference' shelves in the library. Checks can be made on how often these books or articles are taken out, and each term the selection can be 'revitalized'.

Book use and purchase are affected to a large extent by the needs of different disciplines. Book use in the arts is 'extensive' whereas in the sciences it it 'intensive'. In a recent survey, MacDonald (1981) found that arts students claimed that the most useful books for them were likely to be paperbacks, to be thought-provoking, to have summaries and to suggest further reading. The arts students claimed they would buy books that were not expensive, but they would not buy books if the library had multiple copies or if they were difficult to obtain.

Science students, on the other hand, were particularly concerned that the layout of books should be attractive and that their books should have lots of pictures/diagrams. Science students bought books if they contained diagrams, were up to date, well written, and if material could be easily found in them. The scientists tended to buy books if lectures were based on them and if the books contained summaries and suggested further reading.

In discriminating between high and low spenders MacDonald found that high spenders looked for books with pictures and diagrams, an attractive layout and up-to-date information. She reports that such students were likely to buy books if they also had introductory guides, good bibliographies and if they were designed so that items could be easily found. While claiming to feel overloaded with work, high spenders tended to endorse statements that showed a general satisfaction with their courses.

Low spenders, perhaps as would be expected, were more concerned about the price of books and this was a major factor in their purchase. If books could readily be borrowed from other sources, they were unlikely to be purchased. Generally speaking low spenders expressed general disappointment with their courses.

6.5 Note-taking from lectures

A large proportion of the information acquired by students comes, of course, from lectures, and is retained in students' notes. In 1967, Hartley and Cameron published one of the first (and few) investigations to compare what students recorded in their notes with what the lecturer actually said. They found, for one particular lecture, that the students noted rather less than one-third of the total information transmitted. However, when the lecturer was asked to indicate which parts of his lecture he considered to be the most important, it was then found that the students had recorded approximately half of this information. The areas of agreement between what the lecturer and the students considered important varied quite sharply for different parts of the lecture: in some parts the agreement was very high (about 75 percent) and in some parts very low (20 percent). The items of information most frequently noted were definitions, names, technical words, references and, indeed, anything written on the blackboard. Items most frequently omitted were detailed accounts of the experiments which supported the thesis being maintained in the lecture. Similar findings were subsequently reported by Maddox and Hoole (1975).

In 1974 Hartley and Marshall replicated the Hartley and Cameron study with a different lecture topic, and a different group of students. In this investigation, however, when the lecture was over the students were tested on their immediate recall of the lecture, the test sheets were collected in, and the students were then allowed 10 minutes to revise from their notes for a subsequent test. Also in this experiment the investigators distinguished between 'good' note-takers and 'poor' note-takers (i.e. those who wrote down most and those who wrote down least). The test results showed that both groups of note-takers did equally well on the immediate test, that both improved following the revision period, but that the 'good' note-takers improved significantly more than the 'poor' ones following revision.

Why students take notes: process and product

These results indicate the importance of notes for revision, and they support the belief held by many students that 'good' notes are useful for revision at examination times. From discussions with students, and from other questionnaire studies, it appears that there are two main reasons why students take notes: one is concerned with the *process* of note-taking and one with the resulting *product*. Most students believe that the process of note-taking – writing things down in their own words – will somehow help their subsequent recall. Furthermore, most students believe that the product of their note-taking – their notes – will be useful for revision at a later date. Notes provide not only a record of 'what was covered', but also they enable the student to recall and to reconstruct the original instructional material.

Tables 6.1 and 6.2 attempt to summarize the evidence concerning these beliefs – evidence derived from over 50 studies on note-taking. The tables

Table 6.1 A survey of studies relevant to the question of whether the process of note-taking aids recall

	Studies saying note-taking helps learning	Studies saying note-taking has no effect	Studies saying note-taking hinders learning
Audio presentation	21	15	2
Text presentation	8	3	1
Video presentation	3	1	0
Film/filmstrip presentation	2	0	1
Total	34	19	4

Source: Hartley (1983).

Table 6.2   A survey of studies relevant to the question of whether reviewing notes aids recall

	Studies saying reviewing helps learning	Studies saying reviewing has no effect	Studies saying reviewing hinders learning
Audio presentation	13	4	0
Text presentation	9	2	0
Total	22	6	0

Source: Hartley (1983).

summarize the answers to two questions: Does the process of note-taking aid recall? Does reviewing one's notes aid recall? The answers given in *Tables* 6.1 and 6.2 are presented in accord with whether the learner is listening, reading or looking at a screen. Research into note-taking from text has increased in the past decade and, as can be seen from *Table* 6.1, it presents clearer results than does research into note-taking while listening. We assume that this is largely because note-taking from text takes longer and allows for deeper text processing. (In the few studies where the time of reading for the control group is equated with the time of reading and note-taking for the experimental group, most of the results show no significant effects.)

In addition to the experimental studies listed in *Tables* 6.1 and 6.2 Hartley and Davies (1978) reviewed studies which examined the relationships between what is noted and what is subsequently recalled. The results, reported over a 50-year period, seem to be remarkably consistent, and showed a clear correlation (often of the order of +0.50) between note-taking and recall.

The overall conclusions to be drawn from the research literature thus seem to be that (1) there is evidence to suggest that note-taking can aid the learning process in certain situations, (2) note-taking is related to recall and (3) reviewing one's notes is a useful procedure.

Improving note-taking

Questionnaire studies have indicated that many students wish they could improve their note-taking practices, and a number of authors have offered guidelines in this respect, for example Hartley and Davies (1978) and Brown (1979). Hartley and Davies (1978) presented guidelines for students, but added the following guidelines for teachers:

- Instruct learners in the skills of note-taking. Learners can be shown how different styles of note-taking seem appropriate to different aims and to different subject matters. Help can be given over the business of organizing and displaying notes so that the structure of the instructional material is more readily apparent.
- Make clear the organizing principle (of a lecture, or a chapter for a text, for example).
- Consider the different ways of making clearer to the learner what it is that follows. Lectures may be related to each other; if so, this relationship should be made explicit.
- Provide lecture handouts during lectures. Skeletal handouts allow the structure of a lecture to be easily displayed, make note-taking for personal reference easier, and ensure accuracy in recording names, dates, tabular materials, references for further reading, etc. The preparation of handouts also ensures that the lecturer has thought about what he wants to say before he says it. Handouts can be distributed just before the lecture, allowing a few minutes for overview.
- Use verbal signposts in a lecture or text so as to convey its structure, and in a lecture provide cues as to when note-taking is important. Use questions as headings in text or in lectures.
- Counteract fatigue by using these same devices, by humour and by the use of 'buzz' sessions, etc. Omitting key words in handouts – which then have to be filled in by students during the lecture – may also help them to maintain attention and focus on the key issues.
- Make arrangements for the tasks of listening and note-taking to be separated as these tasks interfere with one another. Time should be allowed for note-taking in lectures, particularly during the presentation of slides and overhead transparencies. Copies of lecture scripts and audio- or videotapes of lectures can be made available for students to work with at their leisure.
- When collecting lecture feedback from students ask specific questions about the lecture in terms of ease of note-taking.
- Encourage students to take notes, examine what they have written, and suggest to them how their note-taking products might be improved.

Hartley and Davies pointed out that their guidelines were only suggestions. which needed to be confirmed or rejected by further research.

A number of investigators have examined the efficiency of courses in general study skills, and many such courses contain a note-taking component (e.g. see Driskell, 1976; Garfield and McHugh, 1979). Some of these investigators have concluded that general study skills can be taught successfully (see, for example, Entwistle, 1960; Gadzella, 1982) but others have been less successful.

Gibbs (1981) takes the line that it is preferable to teach specific study skills in a particular context rather than attempt to teach general study skills which can be applied to different situations. Gibbs argues that successful learners (within the same discipline) do different things, and different techniques suit different people. The problem is to convey this plurality to the students. Gibbs' method of teaching study skills is to take a group of students within a specific discipline and to ask them to do certain tasks. In the context of note-taking, for example, Gibbs first asks them as individuals to take notes from a particular piece of text or lecture. He then asks them to work in pairs, examining each other's notes and trying to understand why they are written in the way they are. Following this the pairs form groups of four, and each student has to explain his or her partner's notes to the three other students. After this the four students are asked to consider the characteristics of their notes that make them either 'good', 'poor' or 'useless', and to indicate which strategies are useful and which should be avoided. These characteristics are written down so that they can be read out to the whole group of students in a final plenary session.

Gibbs' aim, therefore, is to make the students consider (and later practise) note-taking in a particular context, and see for themselves the advantages and disadvantages of particular styles of approach within different disciplines.

Using notes and handouts

One further way in which students can be helped in their note-taking is to reduce the difficulty of the task by supplying an appropriate handout. As will be observed in Chapter 8, handouts can serve several different functions. Students express a marked desire for handouts presumably because they allow more time for noting personally relevant material. Furthermore such handouts can be seen to be directly relevant to subsequent examinations.

Several studies of the usefulness (or otherwise) of handouts have been reported (see Hartley and Davies (1978) for a review). Many of these found no significant effects upon subsequent examination scores, but none of them actually examined how note-taking and lecture handouts interact, if at all. The five preliminary investigations reported by Hartley and his undergraduate students (Hartley, 1976) are, therefore, of interest in this respect. Hartley cited evidence to show that: (1) the presence of a handout reduced the amount of note-taking; (2) a handout led to improved recall; (3) opening up the spatial arrangement of the text led to increased note-taking; (4) students compensated for omitted details on a handout by taking more notes; (5) students filling in key words and phrases that had been omitted from the text did better on a subsequent recall test; and (6) this procedure did not reduce the amount of note-taking.

Studies such as these suggest that students adapt their note-taking practices to take into account the amount and nature of material that they require for future activities (e.g. follow-up, revision); and that handouts can be structured so as to affect what students actually do during and after lectures. This last point is particularly important, for some students, it seems, do not take notes if they think a handout is adequate. Many people suggest that in order to make note-taking and handouts more effective, teachers need to devise ways of making their students interact and use the materials presented to them in some way. In practice it appears that many students take notes and collect handouts but never refer to them again, or simply retrieve them for review purposes at examination time (Trueman and Hartley, 1979).

Is there any evidence that students who process their notes or who use their handouts in some way do better in examinations than those who do not? Norton (1981a) examined the use that 35 students had made of their notes taken in a lecture before a class test. She grouped the students into those who had made no use of their notes, those who had mainly reread their notes and those who had mainly rewritten their notes. She found that the latter two groups did better in the examination than the former.

Norton correlated scores on the class test with the amount of notes taken, attitudes towards note-taking and the use of notes. She found the following positive correlations:

    0.23 between a positive attitude to note-taking and test score;

    0.36 between the number of words noted and the test score;

    0.44 between attitude and use of notes;

    0.52 between the use of notes and test score;

    0.60 between use of notes, attitude and test score.

In other words, the best test performance came from the students who had taken full notes, who held positive attitudes to the value of note-taking and who used their notes after they had taken them.

Other approaches to note-taking

Two other approaches to using and making notes can be considered here. Both of these approaches focus on making learners reprocess their notes once they have taken them. Pauk (1974), for instance, recommends that students should take as many notes as possible in a lecture, using all of the shorthand abbreviations and devices that they find personally satisfying, but that they should leave a large margin on either the left- or the right-hand side of the page. Then, after the lecture is over, the students are recommended to go back and write in the margin the key ideas being expressed in the lecture, that is, to make sure that they have its main structure and ideas. This activity, of course, forces students to review and to reprocess the lecture content shortly after its delivery. In addition, rereading the marginal notes will aid revision at a later date.

A second activity, 'patterned note-taking', has been suggested by Buzan (1974). Buzan advocates that learners take notes in their usual way and then, after the lecture is over, they make a 'map' or 'pattern' of the key concepts. An example is given in *Figure* 6.4. Buzan is suggesting here the same idea as Pauk; namely, that making a pattern of the lecture content forces the learner to review and reprocess it, and such maps (Buzan argues) are easier to revise from than is continuous prose.

There is little evidence to support the assertions of Buzan or Pauk, and most people who have expressed interest in evaluating patterned note-taking have been concerned with comparing it with conventional methods. This, however, is to miss the point. What requires testing is the effectiveness of making learners reprocess their notes, and more research needs to be done with different procedures which require students to do just this.

6.6   Note-taking from text

In discussing the findings presented in *Table* 6.1 we commented that the results of studies of note-taking from text presented clearer evidence for the value of note-taking than did studies of note-taking from lectures. We suggested that this was probably because students, when they take notes from text, spend longer studying.

Note-taking from text differs from note-taking from lectures in this one rather obvious way. Because students have more time they can read the whole text (or chapter) in advance, they can stop to think about its structure and argument, and they can decide what are the important points. In

Figure 6.4   An example of patterned notes. (Reproduced from Norton, 1981b, with permission)

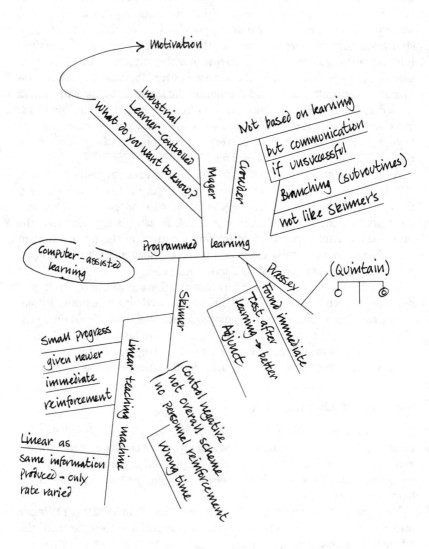

addition, the extra time allows students to plan the presentation of their notes more carefully, and to carry out in a more relaxed way many of the suggestions made about note-taking from lectures.

Some students prefer to underline sections in a text (or to highlight them) rather than make notes. The evidence for the effectiveness of underlining is equivocal (Hartley et al., 1980), and some commentators (e.g. Maddox, 1963; Rickards, 1980) suggest that students underline too much. Underlining may seem profitable (it is fast and it aids review), but it demands less processing time than taking notes. For this reason we think that note-taking might be more effective than underlining, especially if students recast material in their own words when taking notes, but this proposition has still to be adequately tested.

6.7 Summary

- Students need to develop effective study skills if they are to become effective independent learners.
- Speed-reading courses may improve reading speeds but it seems that only some students sustain this improvement. Courses can be designed to help students develop different reading strategies for different purposes and different kinds of text.
- It is valuable to practise using library skills both in the first year and later. Students can be helped to make a more effective use of books by teachers paying attention to some fairly obvious details.
- Note-taking can aid learning and recall in certain situations. Again, exercises which help students to develop different strategies for different kinds of task would seem to be worthwhile.

CHAPTER 7

DEVELOPING STUDY SKILLS: USING INFORMATION

In this chapter we turn from acquiring to using information. The topics covered are writing essays and reports, and preparing for examinations.

7.1 Writing essays and reports

Students spend a large part of their time writing essays and reports and tutors spend much time marking them. Why should this be so? What is the purpose of this writing?

Like many activities in higher education essay writing is multi-faceted. Some of the aims of essay writing overlap and some are contradictory, causing problems for students and tutors alike. Commentators suggest, however, that essay writing has three major functions:

1. It helps students to learn – about the subject matter and about their own personal development.
2. It helps students to practise the skills of written communication.
3. It helps tutors to assess the students' achievements in terms of (1) and (2).

Learning from essay writing

Writing things down for others to read requires the learner to make a commitment. Writing demands more than reading, listening or even speaking in tutorials because it forces the writer to express ideas in a particular way – a way that is less open to negotiation or retraction; writing 'involves putting learning on display' (Hounsell, 1982).

Essay writing is not free writing: there are constraints. The student has to produce an essay or a report for a tutor who probably knows more about the topic, could probably write it better and who will be required to assess it. The work has to be about a specified topic, to be within a prescribed length, to be completed by a specified date and to conform to certain canons of style and requirements which will differ for different disciplines. Students can rarely write about what they want and in a manner which suits them. Thus, for many, writing essays and reports is neither pleasant nor easy.

How do students go about such tasks? Recent studies by Branthwaite et al. (1980) and Hounsell (1982) suggest some answers. Branthwaite et al. administered a questionnaire to approximately 80 students who were required to write three essays – one per term – for a subsidiary course in psychology. The study found that:

1. Although they were writing essays for different disciplines, three-quarters of the sample (78 percent) always worked on one essay at a time. Half of the students (52 percent) allocated time in advance to do the psychology one. On average, the work for the essay was started four to seven days before handing it in but a quarter of the students (23 percent) started work less than three days before handing it in. Almost no one (4 percent) drew up a timetable on paper for doing this work.

2. Three-quarters of the sample (72 percent) used lecture notes in preparing for the essay. In addition, three-quarters (74 percent) used books and articles other than those recommended by the tutors or the course programme. On average, just over three books were read (at least in part) but only half a journal article.

3. Six percent of the sample used six or more books, while another 6 percent used only one book. Almost a quarter (22 percent) of the students looked around for existing essays on the same topic.

4. Half the students (52 percent) claimed that they left some time for reflection between finishing the reading and starting to write the essay.

5. Just over two-thirds (69 percent) made a written plan of the essay structure, and just over half (57 percent) made at least one draft before writing up the essay. One quarter of the sample (25 percent) discussed the plans for the essay with someone else, usually a student rather than a tutor. (These were not the same students who looked around for existing essays on the topic.) Only 5 percent discussed the essay with a tutor (on an individual basis).

6. Well over three-quarters (85 percent) said that they tried to present their own ideas and draw their own conclusions in the essay. Only 12 percent found it necessary to fill out the essay in order to make it longer. About 10 percent gave the essay to someone else to read before handing it in.

Two main differences emerged between first- and second-year students. Generally speaking, the first-year students worked on their own and followed diligently what they thought was a 'proper' course for writing essays. They allocated more time in advance to do the essays, they worked on only one essay at a time, they used the recommended books, and so on. The second-year students, however, were more 'product oriented': they were more aware of the variety of ways in which one could go about writing essays. They were more likely to use books and articles other than those recommended by the tutor, to look for existing essays on the topic, to discuss their plans with other students and to give their essays to someone else to read.

Branthwaite et al. (1980) were unable to find any relationships between the particular strategies used by individual students and the marks subsequently awarded to the essays. And, as we shall see later, they were unable to find any marked improvements between the first and the second essays completed by each student.

Hounsell (1982) used interviews rather than questionnaires and suggested a different line of attack. He distinguished between two main approaches to essay writing: in the first an institutional perspective is more dominant whereas in the second a personal perspective seems more obvious.

With the first approach students are not particularly involved in the essay topic: they see the task as a job to be done which can be best achieved by following through a set of more or less discrete procedures. For them the content is made up of bits and pieces (culled or copied from various sources) and stitched together to form a whole. Typical statements from students following this approach are as follows:

> Sometimes I find that my main objective, when turning out an essay, is just to get two-and-a-half thousand words and finish. Which I know is, it's not a good idea but when you've got a backlog of work in, you sometimes have to do these things.

> I was blowed if I was going to co-ordinate it all.

> I feel essays stamp out whatever individuality you have in writing, because you've got to write them to a format, which I haven't as of yet discovered although I know it exists somewhere. So as soon as I've found that I'm starting to say something that's me personally, I have to stop. But I always get my revenge at the end, where you can, you know, have a little flourish during the summary.

When the personal perspective is dominant, the student is personally involved in the topic and sees personal reflection as central to the essay: the content is organized by what the writer wants to say. The student is aware of the demands of the task, but is not so inhibited by them.

> I found the actual topic very enjoyable (. . .) I thought it was quite interesting, so I actually put a lot of thought into it . . . I usually . . . first make a very quick sort of plan of what should be in the essay . . . and then go and do the reading. I may change my mind during the reading.

Students and teachers, of course, will be intuitively aware that students use both approaches and that they adopt different strategies according to different circumstances. What may be required for one essay (say in the social sciences) may not be required for another (say in the natural sciences). Students learn to adapt their styles and methods of writing to the demands of the situation.

Hounsell maintains that students learn much more from the second approach than they do from the first. He points out that in essay writing there is a tension between the personal and the institutional. Hounsell sees this tension in two main areas: in the dual function of essays (for personal learning and for institutional assessment) and in the contrast between learning on the one hand and performance on the other – where the latter might simply demonstrate an ability to parrot certain conventional procedures. In order to learn from essay writing, Hounsell argues, the writer has to be personally involved.

Finally, in this section, we may note that Branthwaite and his colleagues (unpublished) have recently elaborated their views on how students go about writing essays. Using less-structured and more open-ended questionnaires, they found the process depicted in *Figure* 7.1. This is organized vertically to suggest that some activities have logical priority over others. However, this organization is not meant to imply that writing essays involves carrying out a fixed sequence of steps. Essay writing involves some or all of the activities shown in *Figure* 7.1 and many of them are carried out several times. Furthermore the strategies involved in each activity vary for different students. Some brief descriptions and elaborations are as follows:

Choosing a topic   Sometimes the topic is set for the student by the tutor, but often students are given some freedom of choice in this respect. Students generally choose a topic that interests them, but other strategies are apparent. For example, some students say that their choice is based upon how much information is readily available, or on how easy or difficult the topic is thought to be, or on how wide-ranging or narrowly focused they want their essays to be.

Figure 7.1 How students go about writing essays (after Branthwaite et al., unpublished)

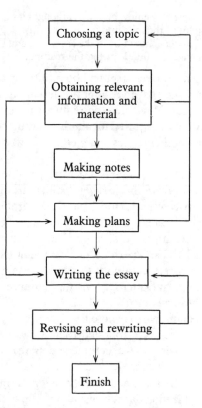

Obtaining information and material   For most students, having decided on a topic, the next and possibly the most difficult stage is to find useful and relevant material. Books seem to be the main source here, with lecture material playing a less prominent, but nonetheless important role. The over-riding aim at this stage seems to be to find *relevant* material. Students describe various strategies of using books; for example, choosing the simplest book available and making this the main source on which to add material, choosing short books, choosing books that are not on the reading list, etc.

Making notes   Two-thirds of the students questioned by Branthwaite et al. indicated that they made notes from the books that they obtained, but few commented on how they went about doing this. Sometimes parts of books were copied, or paraphrased, sometimes specific ideas were noted for a particular essay, and sometimes more general background observations were recorded.

Making plans   Again, two-thirds of the students reported drawing up a plan for an essay (with more women saying that they did this than men). As in Hounsell's study, two main approaches seemed discernible: some students simply arranged their notes and material into some sort of logical order; others predetermined the plan by the points they wished to raise. A few said that they revised their plans as they went along.

Writing the essay   Few students gave specific details about how they wrote particular essays. Some, however, mentioned strategies such as paraphrasing those parts of the books which seemed relevant; interpreting the book in their own words; always stating authorities and evidence for their assertions; trying to answer the question set – or trying to look as though they had. Several students commented on the particular problem of writing the introduction and conclusions, with the introduction causing particular difficulties. One said, 'From past experience it will probably take me several attempts before I find a satisfactory introduction'.

Finishing off the essay   One-third of the students (again more women than men) said that they first wrote out their essays in rough, and then made a fair copy. Similarly, only about one-third of the students claimed to read over their essays (to check for errors and mistakes in spelling, clarity and coherence). Very few students made more than one rough draft. An even smaller number said they left their essay for a day or two before coming back to complete it. A few specifically mentioned adding references and/or a bibliography at the end; as one said: 'Write a bibliography and hand it in'.

In considering these descriptions of what students *say* they do when they write essays we need to note (1) that what they actually *do* may be somewhat different, and (2) that essay writing is not the ordered process we have suggested here. Indeed we think it likely that students following a personal perspective, as described by Hounsell, would be more likely to move backwards and forwards through the stages shown in *Figure* 7.1 than would students following an institutional perspective.

Improving the skills of written communication

These descriptions of what students actually do when writing essays can be compared with the advice that students are given on this topic in current study manuals. Many textbooks on study habits contain advice on how to write essays and it is not our purpose to reiterate the advice here. Much of it is based upon tacit knowledge, that is to say that it is based upon experience, and (possibly because of this) it is sometimes contradictory. Students, therefore, might be well advised to read different authors on this topic to see, first, what seems most comfortable for them to practice, and, secondly, what seems most novel for them to experiment with.

The first thing that most study manuals advocate, although in varying degrees, is that students should plan their essays in advance. And, it will be recalled that in the studies by Branthwaite et al. approximately 70 percent of their students claimed to do this. There are, of course, degrees of planning. Each section, each paragraph and each sentence of any essay or report need planning – or thinking about – both before, during and after its construction. What the authors of the study manuals are suggesting is that it is sensible to clarify one's thoughts about what it is that one is trying to say, and to make some sort of outline of the subject matter before one begins. Maddox (1963) puts the issue rather well:

> Any large task needs to be broken into manageable units; and you need to think carefully about the order of presentation of these units and how they are to be linked together . . . Sub-headings and sub-divisions should always be used in essays and articles of any length, not only because they assist the reader, but also because they impose a useful discipline on the writer himself, and keep him from wandering away from the point.

Planning, however, is not without its critics. Some authors claim that many writers do not plan, and others have found no difference in the marks obtained on examination scripts prefaced with plans, and those without them (see Hartley, 1984). Nonetheless, it would seem that planning allows the student to form a structure, which may be externalized in an outline. The structure allows one to set about writing, although the resulting product need not necessarily stick to the initial plan.

The next thing that most study manuals advocate, in varying degrees, is that attention must be paid to stylistic points when writing essays and reports. Many suggest writing short unambiguous sentences with simple clear vocabulary, and they point out that it is easier to demonstrate that you have understood something if you can explain it to others in simple language. Such advice, while being helpful, does not help the writer to deal with the problem of trying to deal with several issues all at once – the basic problem of writing. It is difficult to pay attention to content, planning, style and legibility (and spelling) all at the same time. At this point, therefore, some authors suggest that some of the problems of essay writing can be separated. Thus, it is argued, one should first write quickly, getting down the main points of what needs to be said, and then go back later to work at the niceties of style. As Wason (1983) puts it, 'First say it, and *then* try to say it well'.

Finally, whether or not separating activities is advocated, most study manuals comment on the need for redrafting and rewriting. The argument is that new ideas occur while writing so that it will be necessary to read the text through in order to incorporate these, to excise extraneous details, and perhaps to resequence part of what has been written. Hardy (1974), for example, argues here that one should tidy up the first draft, and then leave it for a while (perhaps a week) before rereading and rewriting it. Such a process is of course time consuming, and many students avoid doing it (43 percent in the study by Branthwaite et al. (1980)). Nonetheless, as Rowntree (1976) argues, 'Just a few days can give you a new perspective on your work. You will come back to it fresh, able to look at it more objectively and you will see a great many obscurities and pomposities that were not apparent to you in the heat of creation.'

Rowntree provides the following checklists for students to use when rewriting their essays:

- Does the essay answer the question or deal with the topic that was set?
- Does it cover all the main aspects and in sufficient depth?
- Is the content accurate and relevant?
- Is the material logically arranged?
- Is each main point well supported by examples and argument?
- Is there a clear distinction between your ideas and those you have brought in from other authors?
- Do you acknowledge all sources and references?
- Is the length of the essay right for its purpose?
- Is it written plainly and simply, without clumsy or obscure phrasing? (A good test is to read it aloud.)
- Are the grammar, punctuation and spelling acceptable, and is it neatly and legibly written?

Learning from assessment

The checklist given by Rowntree also, of course, reflects what teachers look for when marking essays. When grading and assessing essays, tutors are aiming to help students to learn from their essay writing. Comments on details of grammar, style and organization should help students improve their writing skills. Comments on subject matter, which provide additional or contrasting material, can help students to learn more about the topic. It is generally assumed, therefore, that constructive comments provide useful feedback to students, and that students learn from such assessments. Is such an assumption justified?

The study of Branthwaite et al. described above produced some interesting findings in this respect. First, while the approach of the students was different in the different years, this approach did not seem to change much between the first and the second essays (which were completed in the first and the second terms respectively). In short, many students did not seem to benefit from the essay-writing process or from the feedback received from the tutors. Generally speaking, the mark each student got on the first essay was little changed on the second.

This was somewhat surprising in view of another finding. It appeared that the criteria that the students believed the tutors used when they assessed the essays were markedly different from the actual criteria used by the tutors involved in the study. The students placed high weight on originality, on the use of source materials, on clear expression and on understanding. The tutors, on the other hand, placed high weight on the use of source material and on clear expression but much less on understanding and originality. Indeed, none of the seven tutors involved mentioned originality.

Of course an assumption being made here is that the tutors' criteria were made clear to the students via written comments on the essays and spoken comments in tutorials and lectures. This assumption is probably not tenable. Branthwaite et al. suggested, because of the mismatch between the students' and the teachers' criteria, that the students were trying to fulfil course requirements which they did not fully comprehend.

Findings such as these suggest that it would be of value to conduct further research on how students and teachers perceive the aims of essay writing, and on how each believes the other can help him or her in this respect. In fact, surprisingly little attention has been paid by research workers to the role of written comments on essays and coursework but this is now being remedied.

MacKenzie (1974) observed the variety of comments made by tutors on 50 student assignments at the Open University. He found that some tutors went for 'overkill', that some had a relentless eye for grammar and that some relied excessively on ticks. He found that only about half the tutors commented on what was good in the essays, and that few attempted to explain or justify the grades they gave. Similarly Sommers (1982) found that many teachers' comments were not text specific (and thus helpful) but could be interchanged, or rubber-stamped from text to text.

Clanchy and Ballard (1983) analysed all the marginal, incidental and end comments added by tutors on over 300 essays written by arts and social science students. The aim of this research was to see if any common themes could be detected, and then to provide such themes, with exemplars, to students in order to help them interpret future comments. Clancy and Ballard's book, *How to Write Essays*, provides four such themes, each with copious examples of tutors' comments. These themes (with one or two examples only) are listed below.

A concern with relevance   It is expected that essays will be clearly focused on the set topic and will deal fully with its central concepts. Typical tutors' comments are:

> Good work. You've covered the topic well and put much thought into your essay.

> This is a perfectly reasonable essay but, unfortunately, rather off the track. The question asked for a discussion of the role of the *relationship* of X to Y, not of Y per se. There is certainly some overlap and you have, in an implicit way, touched on some of the issue pertinent to the topic, but in all of this you have not really dealt to any satisfactory degree with the X relationship. Did you misread the essay topic?

A concern with the effective use of source material   It is expected that essays will be the result of wide and critical reading. Typical tutors' comments are:

> What you say is all very well, but it is only *one* view. It happens to be the one I share but there is little evidence in this essay that you are aware of the objections which some writers have raised to it, or of some of the problems it raises.

> We are not interested in your opinion but in well-founded argument based on wide reading.

> Well done. Based on extensive and intensive research, and giving an independent response.

A concern with reasoned argument   It is expected that essays will present a reasoned argument, evaluating evidence and drawing appropriate conclusions. Typical tutors' comments are:

The main problem with this essay is linking the discussion in each section to the main theme. In general the examples you give are relevant to the five points raised by X. However, you cover so many social situations that it is hard to see any consistent thread in each section and impossible to find one in the essay as a whole. You should try to concentrate on a particular issue . . . to focus your theoretical ideas.

You have some real points, but your arrangement of them is disorderly.

Where is the thread on this page – in fact in this essay?

A concern with matters of presentation   It is expected that essays will be competently presented. Typical tutors' comments are:

This is a very impressive piece of *research* and a rather indifferent piece of *reporting*. Your writing is often obscure, clumsy and wordy. I don't feel sure how I should mark this but on balance I think I should give high marks for what you have discovered and a severe reprimand for your poor language.

Bibliography and footnotes are excellent. Apart from a few minor slips, you use scholarly apparatus well and it is gratifying to find a student who gives it careful treatment.

Too imprecise: what exactly do you mean?

What Clanchy and Ballard are saying is that the hidden message behind the hundreds of different comments that they observed is that tutors expect that essays should be relevant to the set topic, in both content and focus; that they should provide evidence of wide and critical reading; that they should present a reasoned argument based on valid evidence, which leads to appropriate conclusions; and that the essays should be presented in a competent manner. They argue in their book that although there is no one way to write an essay and there is no single set of skills or techniques for essay writing there are a number of useful guidelines that can be drawn from the experience of lecturers and students. These guidelines are presented in their text.

Improving feedback

Few students, it appears, discuss their essays with their tutors before or after receiving their assessments. Branthwaite et al., for instance, noted that only five percent of their students discussed their essays with their tutors on an individual basis. Hounsell (1982) observed for the psychology essays used in his inquiry that the students received no guidance on what the essay title meant, and they were expected to supplement their course textbooks and lecture notes with material that they tracked down on their own in the university library. The essays were returned to the students via 'pigeon-holes' and grades were accompanied by a few lines of comments (sometimes only a few words). The students were often invited to discuss their essay with their tutor if they wished, once it had been handed in, but few of them did so.

Thus, in practice, the dialogue between teacher and pupil which could help the students to improve their learning and their skills of written communication is sadly lacking. This need not necessarily be so, and there are some techniques which teachers can use to improve the situation.

First, teachers can increase the length and the quality of comments given on essays and reports. Despite the fact that there is some evidence that comments can be unreliable (that is to say that different tutors will comment in different ways upon the same work) (Morrow-Brown, 1978; Settle, 1981), there is some indication that students appreciate detailed and constructive comments from their tutors (see MacKenzie, 1976; Lewis and Tomlinson, 1977).

A second approach is for teachers to formalize their procedures for marking essays. One lecturer reported to a conference organized by the Society for Research into Higher Education in 1970 that he always wrote his comments on students' essays under the two headings 'good' and 'could be improved'. The lecturer concerned showed that a comparison between students treated in this way and those who received the usual uninformative grades indicated that the former improved steadily whereas the latter maintained almost unvarying standards of performance.

Other tutors have adopted similar systems, although often they are more complex. *Figure* 7.2 shows a checklist which is regularly used by a colleague at Keele for marking essays. This colleague has similar checklists for marking projects, laboratory reports and book reviews.

Many teachers of English circulate advisory checklists to their students in advance so that when they are writing their comments on essays they can say things like, 'Good work, but a lack of attention to points 5, 7 and 21 is causing difficulties'. Indeed, appropriate numbers can be written in the margin whenever a fault occurs. This approach, while typical in English departments, can be applied to other subjects. Settle (1981), for instance, suggests how it can be done in the teaching of mathematics. Checklists given in advance, of course, inform the students about what is expected.

Mullenger (1977) and Agutter (1979) have described rapid, simple methods for testing and improving students' ability to detect and to correct the misuse of scientific English. Mullenger presented students with essays

Figure 7.2 Sample checklist for marking essays

Name: _____ Year: _____ Option: _____

Essay title: _____

Essay title:	Zero	Poor	Fair	Good	Exc.	Comments
General points						
Examination of the actual question						
Relevance of material to question						
Essay structure and organization of material						
Coherence of essay/arguments						
Critical evaluation/arguments						
Comprehension						
Grasp of central concepts						
References to literature						
Adequacy of sources						
Use of quotations						
Clarity of expression						
Neatness						

General points	Zero	Poor	Fair	Good	Exc.	Comments
Legibility						
Spelling						
Originality						
Introduction						
Main thesis						
Discussion						
Conclusions						
Bibliography						

Overall comment

Assessment

0-34	35-44	45-54	55-64	65-74	75-84	85-100
E	D	C	B−	B+	A−	A+

Signed: ....

containing 50 deliberate mistakes of the kind normally found in under-graduate essays, and the students were required to identify and correct them. Agutter required students to detect errors in a succession of bio-logical statements, and to rewrite each statement correctly and precisely. Corrected versions were supplied (by both investigators) to enable students to mark their own work.

In evaluating his method Agutter found that the more tests that the students did the greater their improvement. Members of a control group showed no, or less improvement. In addition Agutter noted that:

1. students gained greater command of scientific language, specifically of biochemistry;

2. students appreciated, perhaps for the first time, the importance of clarity of writing in science;

3. students' performance in tests supplied feedback to those tutors who were then able to give extra time in tutorials to identifying and dealing with special difficulties;

4. students used textbooks which they would not otherwise have con-sulted in order to make corrections;

5. students learned to criticize their own work and that of fellow students, so gaining an increased understanding of scientific language;

6. students enjoyed criticizing each other's work, so perhaps increasing motivation and leading to better study habits.

Finally we may note an interesting technique used by McGlaughlin-Cook and his colleagues at Ulster Polytechnic. Students are provided with two essays, one good and one poor, and asked to write answers to the following questions: (1) which essay deserves the higher mark? (2) Why is one essay better than the other? (3) In what ways could the *better* essay be improved? The answers are then discussed in class, and finally a set of guidelines on essay writing is given to each student.

7.2 Preparing for examinations

Examinations come in different forms, and each has different require-ments. In this section we concentrate on how students might prepare for end-of-term or end-of-year examinations when the assessment for the term, the year or indeed the whole course is made.

Preparation

In such important circumstances it seems wise to advise students to ascertain how they are going to be examined. Copies of previous papers are usually available and they can be inspected to determine how many questions must be answered, what freedom of choice is allowed, whether there are a number of compulsory questions, whether different questions have different weights in the marking scheme, and what is the duration of the examination so that one can work out how much time to spend on each question. By inspecting a series of examination papers one can gauge whether certain issues get repeated (perhaps in various forms) or whether it is likely that if a topic is asked about one year then it will not be repeated the following year. Such 'question-spotting' is, of course, a risky business. Many experts consider it better to list what has been covered in the course and to decide which issues and topics are the most important.

Finding out how many questions have to be answered on each paper suggests that one can advise on the minimum number of topics to be reviewed, but caution is needed here, too. If students have to answer only three questions then preparing only three topics is a foolish strategy: five will be better and six perhaps safer. However, some commentators would question such selective review. Examiners can vary questions from year to year and, as James (1967) points out, 'theoretical questions may demand knowledge from different parts of the syllabus, and neglecting a portion may severely limit the number of questions one can answer'.

Organizing revision time

The next question that arises is what should one advise students about organizing their time for revision? If, for example, students are taking a series of six three-hour papers, two per day, and answering four questions on each, then over 30 topics will need revision. In cases such as these organization seems crucial, and students can be advised to draw up a revision timetable. If they start from the week before the examinations (to allow for extra revision on certain topics and last-minute uncertainties) and then work back to the period when they want to (or need to) start revision, then the number of days and the time periods available for revision may suddenly become startlingly apparent. Students need to be advised that they will need to plan for rest periods as well as for revision. If they revise in the morning and the afternoon, it may be wise to have the evening off. If they revise in the evenings and the mornings then perhaps they should do something different in the afternoons. In any event some writers suggest that each day of revision should be spent in revising topics from different areas and not just from one area at a time, as the former method will aid the integration of the material.

A perennial issue in the student's mind concerns the advantages of spacing out revision compared with cramming it together. Commentators in study manuals take a sanguine view of student life as, almost without exception, they recommend the spacing of revision. Some, indeed, advocate revision throughout the course. For example, Fontana (1981) suggests that 'a programme of phased revision throughout the duration of a course is of far more value than an attempt to cram everything in during the final weeks before an exam'. The arguments for this are that 'phased revision leads to a growing mastery of the whole course as students work their way through it, with each new piece of knowledge being placed in its proper context. When it comes to final examination preparation the student is therefore looking back over material that has already been overlearnt.' Gibbs (1981) has pointed out, however, that if much of the advice given about reviewing in many study manuals was actually carried out, then, after a certain period of time, the students would be doing nothing else but reviewing their previous work.

In point of fact a number of studies have been carried out which have examined the effects of massed versus spaced reviewing (Woodworth and Schlosberg, 1954). Many of the most relevant experiments (using prose materials) were carried out in the 1920s and 1930s, but some have been replicated in the 1970s and 1980s. The validity of the findings of these experiments is, of course, limited because they do not utilize 'real-life' examination conditions, and they often concentrate on low-level factual recall rather than higher-level integrative skills. Nonetheless, there is evidence to suggest that early reviewing and testing do help subsequent recall (e.g. see Duchastel, 1979, 1980; Duchastel and Nungester, 1981). The picture is less clear, however, when it comes to assessing the effects of differential spacing between the review periods. Some investigators have indeed found that the earlier the review the better the subsequent recall (e.g. Spitzer, 1939), but others have found that although a review period is important in helping recall, the position of the review within a given time-span has little or no effect (e.g. English et al., 1934; Peterson et al., 1935).

Cramming, of course, is usually condemned in study habit manuals. Maddox (1963), for instance, says, 'The common practice of cramming on the night before examinations may generate some memory traces which are fresh the next day. But it usually means a last despairing effort to tackle the work which should have been done long before. Cramming is likely to confuse the student, to dishearten him, and to leave him tired and below par on the day of the examination itself. And even if cramming enables the student to pass the examination, much of what he learns is very quickly forgotten and unlikely to be retained in the long run.' Similarly Pauk (1974) argues that students who learn under the pressure of cramming will be put off their stride in the examination by questions that require thinking beyond the facts, or thinking with different facts. Pauk concludes, 'it seems that studying under intense pressure precludes later flexibility in thinking and acting'.

James (1967), however, concedes that last-minute revision can be useful (especially if spaced reviewing has been practised) because: (1) 'ends' can be drawn together; (2) perspectives on the whole course can be obtained; (3) the final refreshing of the memory from notes is most efficient. However, he argues that spaced reviewing is best because: (1) it ensures complete coverage of the syllabus; (2) it makes a future task easier if previous work is thoroughly familiar; (3) it overcomes the problems of strain, ill health, etc., which may intensify or strike towards the end of the course.

Active revision

Whatever advice one gives about organizing one's time, when it actually comes to revising many writers of study manuals advise that this revision should be 'active'. What these writers mean by this is that students should utilize at least one or more of the following activities when they revise:

- Read notes from texts and lectures with particular examination questions in mind.
- Use colour coding when revising from notes to underline key concepts, or to mark relevant examples. (It may be useful to concentrate on marking less dramatic points or more significant *minor* points since it will be easy to recall the major ones.)
- Reorganize knowledge, form new connections, and look at things from different points of view.
- Revise two or three related topics at the same time. (This helps to illuminate common themes that link topics together.)
- Write outlines from notes, severely condensing the materials, and integrating across different sources.
- Answer previous examination questions in note form – noting down the main points.
- Recite (subvocally) the answer you would give to an examination question.

- Answer previous examination questions under examination conditions (i.e. without books or notes, in a quiet room, and in the time needed in the actual examinations).
- Self-test before and after revision sessions: such testing will indicate how successful the revision has been.
- Explain a topic to other people (e.g. fellow students) who are unfamiliar with it. Listen to and try to answer the questions that they ask.
- Work in groups of two or three, or in 'syndicates' as Rowntree (1976) calls them. Meet two or three times every week to review particular topics, to work out how to answer particular questions and to discuss prepared outlines on specific topics.

The argument for these strategies is, of course, the now familiar one: active processing aids recall. Whether or not students actually carry out many of these activities is a question to which we now turn.

Study habits and exam performance

As already noted in this chapter, much advice on study draws on experience and practice rather than on carefully controlled experimental data. There has, however, been some attempt to evaluate the contribution to exam performance of study habits of the kind we have been discussing throughout this chapter.

Three different ways of doing this have been tried: (1) investigators have drawn up study habits questionnaires and attempted to relate scores on such questionnaires to exam performance; (2) investigators have run courses on either specific or general study habits and attempted to evaluate their effects; and (3) investigators have asked students before their examinations what revision strategies they intended to pursue, and, similarly, they have asked them after their examinations what revision strategies they have employed.

Generally speaking, attempts to relate scores on study habits questionnaires to exam performance have not proved successful. The resulting correlations have often been very low – of the order of $+0.1$ or $+0.2$ – although one or two studies have provided correlations of the order of $+0.4$ (e.g. Brown and Holtzman, 1955). The items on questionnaires that correlate best with academic success are usually those which refer to the amount of time spent planning or organizing one's activities (Main, 1980). More recent studies suggest, however, that the matter is not as simple as this: as we saw in Chapter 4, ability, motivation and personality factors also affect student performance.

There is some evidence that taught courses on specific or general study skills can have some effect. Entwistle (1960) and Robinson (1961) reviewed over 30 studies that evaluated such study courses and concluded that many of them were effective. Most of these studies, however, were conducted in the 1950s and many of them were concerned with improving students' reading habits. Nonetheless, the criteria of effectiveness were often gains on examination scores. It would seem likely, therefore, that general courses might have some effect and it is unlikely that they would do any harm. We would agree with Gibbs (1981), however, that more specific courses, tailored to specific students with specific problems in specific disciplines, might be more effective.

Phillips (1981) carried out an inquiry into the intentions of students concerning revision. The study was designed to see if students changed their revision strategies when they revised for different examinations. A group of joint honours students were asked to complete a questionnaire indicating which strategies they intended to use for their forthcoming finals examinations in their two different disciplines. Three groups of students were established: those doing two social-science subjects, those doing one

Table 7.1 The percentage of students ($N = 64$) who indicated that they intended to follow out the revision strategies shown on preparation for finals (to be held in approx. 3 months' time)

% agreeing	During revision for finals I intend to:
83	Reread lecture notes on a particular topic
80	Systematically work out a revision timetable
80	Outline answers on paper to previous/possible exam questions
77	Roughly answer previous/possible exam questions in my mind
67	Write out new notes
63	Read any related papers (journals/articles)
58	Read any related books (not necessarily from cover to cover)
56	Systematically reread notes and condense them at each reading
53	Discuss with others taking the exam answers to possible/previous questions
45	Question spot on the basis of trends in previous exam questions and use this to decide on particular topics worth revising
39	Look at past exam papers
28	Take part in revision seminars with other examinees
22	Fully answer on paper previous/possible exam questions

Source: Phillips (1981).

social-science subject and one arts subject, and those doing one social-science subject and one natural-science subject. In the event the results showed that each student intended to use the *same* approach to revision for both of his or her subjects. *Table* 7.1 lists the general intentions of the students concerned.

Intentions, of course, differ from practice. However, it is hard to find any studies conducted in actual examination rooms on the study strategies of students. However, Forman (1972) did ask students when they had completed a biology examination, but before they left the examination hall, to indicate in a questionnaire which revision strategies they had employed in preparing for that particular exam. Forman then attempted to relate their strategies to the examination scores obtained. The results are shown in *Table* 7.2. Unfortunately this study was only a preliminary inquiry and not all of the data obtained were analysed or presented. Nonetheless, one can see that with the exception of 'writing out new notes', students who carried out a particular strategy did better (on average) than students who did not do so. More sophisticated analyses conducted with the data did not suggest that any one group of strategies was any more efficient than any other. The most that could be said, admittedly from this very limited study, was that any revision strategy was likely to be better than no revision strategy.

Table 7.2 The average marks obtained by students who adopted a particular strategy in preparation for a biology exam

Strategy	Strategies applied (N=34)		Mean exam mark (%)	
	Yes	No	Yes	No
Worked out a revision timetable	8	26	59	56
Allocated certain times for revision	13	21	64	52
Looked up past exam papers	22	12	60	52
Reread lecture notes	34	0	—	—
Read (parts) of related books	31	3	(data not given)	
Wrote out new notes	25	9	55	62
Mentally answered previous questions	20	14	(data not given)	
Wrote out answers to old exam questions	4	30	(data not given)	
Discussed the exam with fellow students	29	5	(data not given)	
Took part in revision seminars	3	31	68	?

Source: Forman (1972).

Taking the exam

Once in the examination room itself study manuals advise a number of precautions. *Table* 7.3 lists the guidelines provided by a colleague for a particularly anxious student. It seemed to us that such guidelines could be

Table 7.3 Notes on examination technique

---

1. Do not arrive more than 10 minutes before the start of the examination unless required to do so.
2. After arriving for the exam do not talk to friends about the revision you or they have done.
3. Check the instructions and then read *all* the questions on the paper twice, slowly and carefully before choosing those you will answer.
4. Work out how much time you have for writing each answer. For example, three questions in two hours gives you 40 minutes per question.
   Keep strictly to this time limit. If you have time left over after answering all your questions complete any you had to leave unfinished because of your time limit. If you finish all your questions early read over your answers checking them.
5. Make *sure* you answer any compulsory questions.
6. Check carefully what your selected questions require you to do. For example, if the question says 'Evaluate . . .' or 'Give a critical account of . . .' make sure your answer *does evaluate* or is a *critical* account. It is easy to give an answer which is not properly relevant to the question if you do not make sure *exactly* what is required of you.
7. To keep your answer relevant and coherent, and to make sure you say all that you can or want to say in your answer, make a list of important points *before you start to write the answer*. Number these in the order they are to be made and cross them off as you cover them in your answer.
8. Make *sure* you answer *all* your questions, i.e. if you have to do three questions mae *sure* you attempt three, not two or two and a half. Answering only two out of three questions gives you a maximum possible mark (for perfect answers) of 67 per cent.
9. If there is a choice between questions requiring specific knowledge and questions of a rather general sort, do the specific questions if you can. It is easier to keep your answers relevant on these.
10. If you become nervous or panicky calm yourself down with two or three minutes of relaxation practice.
11. After leaving the examination room do *not* discuss with your friends what questions you did or what answers you gave.

Source: Based on suggestions by A.B. Hill.

considered profitably by anyone taking an examination (anxious or not). Other, more or less lengthy guides can be found in most study manuals.

James (1967) suggests (for anxious students) that it is worthwhile revising the main points of main topics right up to the time that the examinations begin, even on the day of the examination. Others suggest that revision should be completed and seen as finished by at least the night before, and that one should concentrate on getting a good night's sleep (if possible).

Finally we should observe here that simply allowing students to practise examinations, or letting them know exactly what is expected of them on the day of the actual examination, can markedly improve their performance (Raaheim and Wankowski, 1981).

7.3 Summary

● This chapter focused on writing essays and reports and preparing for examinations.

● Essay writing allows students to learn, to practise writing skills and to be assessed.

● There are wide individual differences in how students go about essay writing, and also in the techniques they use for preparation, organization and revision for examinations. Teachers and staff need to be more aware of these differences and their implications.

● Studies of essay writing and examination strategies all suggest that a greater exchange of information between teachers and students can lead both to more successful outcomes and to greater personal growth.

PART FOUR

ON BEING A TEACHER

CHAPTER 8

THE LECTURE METHOD

In this chapter we discuss the place of the lecture method in teaching. We offer advice, based upon research and inquiries, to teachers concerning the preparations and presentation of lectures, the use of visual aids and the provision of handouts. Finally, some methods of evaluating lectures are considered.

8.1 The advantages and disadvantages of lecturing

Lecturing as a method of teaching has so frequently been attacked by educational psychologists and by students that some justification is needed to retain it. Critics believe that it results in passive methods of learning which, as we have seen, tend to be less effective than those which fully engage the learner. They also maintain that students have no opportunity to ask questions, that they must all receive the same content at the same pace, that they are exposed to only one teacher's interpretation of subject matter, which will inevitably be biased, and that, anyway, few lectures rise above dullness.

Nevertheless, in a number of inquiries (e.g. Bliss and Ogborn, 1977; Beard and Senior, 1980) this pessimistic assessment of lecturing as a teaching method proves not to be general among students although they do fairly often comment on poor lecturing technique. Students praise lectures which are clear, orderly synopses in which basic principles are emphasized, but they dislike too numerous digressions or lectures which consist in part of the contents of a textbook. Students of science subjects consider that a lecture is a good way to introduce a new subject, putting it in its context, or to present material not yet included in books. They also appreciate its value as a period of discussion of problems and possible solutions with their lecturer. They do not look for inspiration – this is more commonly mentioned by teachers – but arts students look for originality in lectures (Marris, 1964; University Grants Committee, 1964).

Predictably, the views of most university teachers are favourable to lecturing as a method. Teachers of science consider that lecturing is the best method to open up difficult topics which students cannot undertake unaided and that, where subject matter is quickly outmoded, lecturing is the most economical method to make new topics available. Many teachers, in any case, believe that students are too immature to study independently (University Grants Committee, 1964).

Despite students' criticisms, nearly all teachers claim to cover the syllabus in broad scope and principle, using only sufficient illustrations for the principles to be understood. They claim also that in lecturing they can respond to students in a way that teaching aids cannot do, that they are able to show their students how to build up a complex argument or diagram, sharing their enthusiasms for the subject while making reference to recent developments or indicating topics for further inquiry. Australian lecturers express similar views, but in one investigation (Schonell et al., 1962) 15 percent of students were relying exclusively on lecture notes while the majority depended primarily on notes with little further study. Thus, there is a danger that students will learn entirely, or largely, at second hand.

One aspect of lecturing that is rarely, if ever, mentioned by its critics is its efficiency. With the aid of microphones and closed-circuit television it is possible to teach large audiences within one building; and, as we know from national television, lectures of great interest, employing expensive visual aids and a high standard of preparation, can be made available to millions. Moreover, video-tapes may enable other audiences to see and discuss the same programmes at convenient times in their own courses. Had there been little else to say in their favour, these advantages of economy and availability would certainly ensure their continuation, but, even without the aid of television, lecturing is still an economical method.

8.2 Styles and objectives in lecturing

One might suppose from students' comments on lecturing that clarity in presentation was not the greatest but the only virtue that they looked for. Perhaps this is because lack of clarity is so disastrous. However, if one observes a large number of lecturers it is clear that a variety of styles, stressing different skills in presentation and organization of subject matter, is possible. Thus, in observing short lectures in courses for university teachers at the Institute of Education, London, many have fallen into the category of well-organized and clearly expressed expositions; but, in addition, we have heard lecturers outstandingly good in handling evidence, in dramatizing a situation, in evoking a mood or in arousing interest in a problem. A teacher of medicine had his class (on this occasion of university lecturers) thinking with him as he produced evidence for and against successive theories. He spoke as though thinking aloud, while including his audience, and by this method demonstrated how to weigh evidence and ask questions. It would have been impossible to describe such a lecture as didactic or to criticize the lecturer for advancing a biased point of view. This lacked the finality of a 'clear exposition' which may enumerate points for and against a question without inciting students to think for themselves, but left the audience prepared to discuss the matter further and to seek new evidence.

In their 1983 monograph *Styles of Lecturing*, Brown and Bakhtar describe how they designed and administered a questionnaire on lecturing (based on observations of the kind we have been discussing) to 400 lecturers at the Universities of Nottingham and Loughborough. From the 258 responses received they were able to categorize lecturers into five different types, and these are summarized briefly in *Table 8.1*.

The respondents were also asked what advice they would give to a young lecturer in their subject on preparing lecture material and on giving lectures. The most popular responses to this question are given in *Table 8.2*. Brown and Bakhtar conclude by discussing their findings in terms of lecturers in the arts, the sciences and the social and biomedical sciences.

In his book *What's the Use of Lectures?* Bligh (1971) presents fairly extensive evidence which shows that lecturing as we know it is effective mainly for imparting information. He found little evidence that students learned to think as a result of listening to lectures. To do so they need to use information and to discover any inadequacies in their thinking in the course of some relevant activity. For this reason, and because it maintains or revives interest, Bligh suggests mixed methods of teaching during what is normally a lecture period.

Nevertheless, the traditional method of teaching by lectures and note-taking may still have its advocates. A clear, well-planned lecture can contribute very effectively to understanding.

Table 8.1   A simplified account of styles of lecturing

Oral lecturers   (17 per cent of the respondents)
These lecturers rarely use any means of communicating other than talk. They do not use blackboards or overhead transparencies to outline main points or provide full notes, nor do they use diagrams to show relationships, structures or processes. They use technical language sparsely.

They are less likely to write down full lecture notes or scripts, more likely to write down headings, subheadings and brief notes, and less likely to rely on one text for preparing lectures.

Visual lecturers   (26 per cent of the respondents)
These lecturers are essentially confident visual information providers. They use the blackboard or overhead projector to provide full notes to their students, they use diagrams to show relationships and processes, and they usually give students time to copy down complex diagrams. Of all the groups they are most likely to write down full notes when preparing their lectures and least likely to use only headings and brief notes.

Exemplary lecturers   (25 per cent of the respondents)
Exemplary lecturers are confident, well-structured and able presenters who use a wide variety of oral and visual techniques of presentation. When preparing lectures they are the group who are most likely to write down headings, subheadings and brief notes rather than whole lectures. They do not have difficulty in selecting or structuring materials for their lectures. They think about and write down their objectives and they tell the students the objectives of the lecture. They inform students, in advance, of the topics of their lectures. They rarely use the blackboard to provide full notes for students but almost all exemplaries use the blackboard or overhead projector to outline main points. The exemplaries provide more handouts, but this difference is not significant.

Amorphous lecturers   (23 per cent of the respondents)
These lecturers may be characterized as confident but ill-prepared and vague. Of all the groups they are least likely to think out or write down their objectives or to tell the students the objectives of each lecture. They are least likely to tell students at the beginning of the term on which topics they will be examined or to tell students in advance the topics of their lectures. Despite these characteristics they are as confident as the visual, oral and exemplary lecturers that they achieve their objectives.

Eclectic lecturers   (9 per cent of the respondents)
Eclectic lecturers are lecturers who use a variety of techniques, including humour, but who lack confidence in their lecturing prowess. When preparing lectures, this group admit to having difficulty in selecting and structuring materials. They tend to write down headings, subheadings and brief notes rather than detailed lecture notes and they are likely to use more than one text as a source for their lectures. However, of all the groups they are most likely to digress from the content of their notes.

Source: After Brown and Bakhtar (1983), reproduced with permission.

Table 8.2   Advice to young lecturers

---

1. Speak loudly and clearly, do not mumble, do use change in tone, use pauses, don't go too fast.
2. Plan, prepare, structure every lecture to give a clear, simple and original perspective to the subject.
3. Make it understandable – explain, emphasize, recap, repeat and summarize main points and relate to current examples and applications. Don't confuse with unnecessary long statements, be clear and simple, clarify key points, stress the particular with the overall.
4. Watch out for reaction and feedback, invite questions and ask questions, encourage participation, involve your audience.
5. Be adequate, do not try to cover everything and give too much factual information, speak round a maximum of four or five points.
6. Read widely round the subject area from different sources, know your subject, and understand your materials.
7. Keep time, don't rush, don't arrive late, don't worry about finishing before time but don't let it happen every lecture.
8. Look at your audience, meet their eyes, do not talk just to the first row, do not talk when you are writing or facing away from your audience, do not distance yourself.
9. Assemble, as much as possible, materials to which the students won't have easy access (up-to-date material from journals and scientific meetings, etc.).
10. Don't read from your notes or dictate or transcribe notes.
11. Project your enthusiasm for a topic, don't look bored, enjoy it. Be interesting and humorous but not too much.
12. Prepare handouts for the students.

Source: Reproduced, with permission, from Brown and Bakhtar (1983).

> He started off, and did it well. He gave an historical background, showing where thermodynamics came into it. He talked about it – he didn't immediately start writing formulae, and giving you an unreal sense of 'Well, here are the formulae; learn them; they do something but I'll tell you about that later'. He told us what they did; he explained what thermodynamics was about and why it had come about, which is quite fascinating. Then he started to go from the basic concepts, and the people who developed it . . . he was explaining it in human terms . . . That is what physics is about, it's a process of thought, and this is the way he was putting it across. (Ogborn, 1977a)

A lecturer such as this has mastered the art of exposition. He knows how to obtain attention and to organize material meaningfully so that it will be readily memorized. In addition, he responds so well to his audience that his difficult subject is found fascinating.

While some lecturers seem to have a natural gift for explaining interestingly and clearly, the majority need to learn the skills involved. Brown (1978) has written a book *Lecturing and Explaining*, which is designed in workshop style, interspersing exposition with practical activities to improve the skills of lecturers. Since the text is clearly presented and the activities are sensibly chosen this could be used with advantage by colleagues in any department. Brown has also contributed to an excellent article for medical teachers entitled: 'How to . . . improve lecturing' (Brown and Tomlinson, 1979). This would certainly be helpful to teachers of any science subject, and could well be of assistance to arts teachers also.

8.3   Preparing a lecture

Defining its purpose

The first essential in preparing a lecture is to state clearly what its purpose is. Although this seems so elementary as to be hardly worth mentioning, criticisms by students suggest that this necessary step in preparation does not always receive the attention it requires. Since one purpose of a lecture, as in all teaching, is that students should learn something, the first step is to state what the students may be expected to know or be able to do as a result of it. Curiously, some university teachers seem to think of 'good teaching' as though it is unrelated to students' learning! Possibly this arises from the tradition that it is up to the students to teach themselves, for it is then a short step to say that meeting them at their own level is 'spoon-feeding'. Yet, if their needs are not to be considered, there seems little justification in taking their time for an hour when they might study more profitably in their own way.

Some of the most common failings are to prepare far more material than can be covered comfortably in the time, or to go at a pace too rapid for the class – or both may be combined. Haste and 'inability' to pause are often justified on the grounds that it is necessary to get through the syllabus; so the lecturer writes at a speed which makes a fair copy difficult and thought impossible, rubbing the board clean immediately he or she has reached the bottom, starting again, and so on. A visitor might suppose that the purpose was that students should obtain a copy of an inaccessible or unwritten text. Yet in the absence of a text for the students to consult it is essential that they should understand at the time, while should a text exist, it is difficult to justify the use of their entire time in writing.

Content

What evidence there is suggests that too much detail, or a lecture too condensed in content, militates against sound learning. Erskine and O'Morchoe (1961) compared a class that was taught essential principles with little detail with one in which considerable detail was presented, and they found that the former did better. Similarly, in experiments with programmed texts, students following a version containing only essentials tend to do as well, or better, than those who are given many more examples or illustrations (Wallis et al., 1966). However, if the material is already partly familiar, good organization may enable students to comprehend and remember subject matter from an entire field. It is in the early stages of learning that the pace should be slowest to give students time to take in and relate to basic concepts and principles.

A second recommendation which has general application, regardless of subject matter, is that the content of the lecture should not be too abstract. In the investigation by Trenaman (1967) of broadcasting media and reading, comprehension increased markedly for concrete subjects which were understood well even if they were initially felt to be uninteresting. Beginners especially require illustrations and applications which relate a new subject to their prior knowledge and experience.

A matter which is usually inadequately considered is the presentation of material to a class of mixed abilities and backgrounds. This is likely to be the problem of a teacher required to give a series of lectures to a class from outside his or her department on such topics as statistics, computational metods, economics for engineers, etc. For example, a class of adults attended 10 lectures in elementary statistics which were given with a view to helping them to comprehend statistical data when reading and, perhaps, to use simple statistics in research projects. They reported that they found the lectures amusing; yet, when one member added: 'But I didn't understand a word of it after the second lecture', others immediately agreed that this had been their case also. Since the range of ability and knowledge within the class was very great one might question the wisdom of grouping all of them in a single class; but even so, had the lecturer considered his task from the point of view of what each student should learn, he might have arranged group work in each session or have sought programmed books to meet their different needs. By any standards, giving a series of lectures to them all was unrealistic.

Organization

When objectives and content are clear it remains to plan and organize the lecture itself. The beginning deserves careful thought and, perhaps, rehearsal. There are a number of opening gambits according to subject matter and objectives. Thus, if the purpose is to direct attention to a particular problem the introduction may take the form of a question, an arresting quotation or slides showing consequences of failure in development or construction. In this way, the attention of the audience is captured. If, however, the lecture is one of a series a brief reminder of previous material and how the next lecture fits into the course may be helpful; or a question relating to the last lecture or work arising from it may be discussed. If the subject is a unit in itself a very brief summary of what is to follow will help the audience to organize the content and give advance warning of topics which are of special interest.

Next, organization needs careful attention. It would be tempting to say that some subjects organize themselves had one not listened to a few lectures in mathematics which were far from lucid and which were represented by a chaotic collection of data on the board in place of the orderly exposition a class should expect. Perhaps the only answer for a lecturer who cannot organize data logically in front of the class is to prepare it in advance either for presentation on an overhead projector or in the form of duplicated notes. In most subjects where a selection of data and illustrations must be made, the lecturer needs at least a list of headings and main points; and in a small class of up to 15, say, where the lecture may in fact become in part a response to questions, or even develop into discussion, he or she may need little more. For a large group, however, the lecturer needs careful preparation of points under section headings, and it may be wise to keep each section together with relevant subheadings and illustrations on separate pages or cards.

Five different methods of organizing lectures have been described by Bligh (1971) and Brown and Bakhtar (1983). These, briefly, are as follows:

1. The classical – in which a topic is divided into broad areas and then further subdivided.

2. The problem centred – in which a problem is posed and then alternative solutions with their attendant advantages and disadvantages are provided.

3. The sequential – in which an extended argument or chain of reasoning leading to a conclusion is used.

4. The comparative – a comparison of two or more processes, terms, literary works, etc.

5. The thesis – begins with a statement or assertion and proceeds to justify it.

The preparation of the lecturer's own notes is an individual matter and may well vary somewhat with subject. Some lecturers make continuous notes but rarely refer to them; others keep collections of notes in files under headings and draw on these, adding new material or further examples and illustrations as required. Sometimes separate sheets are most convenient, provided that they are numbered. The lecturer who reads his lecture must have the complete script available (whether one approves of the method or not); in this case, a roll-backed notebook is useful. Although this method is usually regarded as reprehensible there are a few lecturers capable of reading very effectively. Other lecturers favour loose-leaf files which make the addition or substitution of pages a simple matter, and still others use cards. If the lecture extends to more than four or five pages or separate sheets of illustrations it is almost certainly wise to have them linked together in order within a file.

Handouts and visual aids

Whether students should be given handouts is still a matter of controversy. It depends, in part, on the subject matter of the lecture. Where a lecturer discusses the interpretation of a poem, for example, the poem itself may suffice to recall what was said; or, if the lecturer's purpose is to discuss data which he provides on a duplicated sheet, this with a few explanatory remarks may be all that is needed. If, however, the subject matter is difficult to follow and contains considerable detail, there is no doubt that students prefer to have a more detailed handout. In a report of an inquiry among students by the National Union of Students (1969a), the statement: 'The opportunity to grasp basic ideas is hindered by the necessity to take notes', was rated as a major criticism of lecturing as a method by more than 63 percent of students. At that time a very small proportion of teachers supplied duplicated notes to their students. The arguments usually advanced against the practice almost invariably were that it was 'spoon-feeding' or that, if given notes, students would not attend lectures. But a loss of 12 hours a week taking down notes without understanding, as many students reported, seems to require more justification than this.

Since memory for detail is generally rather poor, fairly comprehensive notes are needed where the purpose of the lecture is to provide information, particularly if no text books exist for students' references. Arguments for expecting students themselves to make the notes are that they should learn how to make notes and that some people find that kinaesthetic, muscular and visual sensations are an aid to memory. On the other hand the students' view that 'The opportunity to grasp basic ideas is hindered by the necessity to take notes' is confirmed in a study by Aiken et al. (1975) who found that, after two days, retention of information was superior if note-taking was separated from listening.

In a study of the effects of three different kinds of notes in electronics, Collingwood and Hughes (1978) found that overall, duplication of the lecturers' notes proved most effective. Partial notes containing copies of headings, key points, diagram outlines, tables and references from the lecturer, with spaces for students to add notes as appropriate, were almost as effective. Students who made their own notes remembered least in a delayed achievement test. However, students' preferences interacted with method. Those who liked full notes did best when given full notes, whereas students who preferred partial notes or making their own notes did better when given partial notes. This may confirm what students sometimes say, that making additions to notes helps to keep them alert, and it obviously draws their attention to the important points which have been deliberately omitted.

At Keele University, Trueman and Hartley (1979) investigated the use by psychology students of lecture handouts. These were unusually designed. On the left-hand side there was space for note-taking; on the right, main points of lectures were supplied, with all slides and blackboard diagrams and spaces for the addition of key words from the text. These students said that they liked the handouts because they were useful as an aid to comprehension and revision. However, most students made few notes during the lecture and did not add to them subsequently. They simply filed the notes away for revision and relied heavily on them when revising to the exclusion of other material. This, presumably, could have been prevented if tasks requiring further reading had been set prior to the examinations.

The teachers' reasons for giving these handouts were that they wished to make it easier for students to follow, to present details without need for lengthy dictation of definitions, etc., to reduce note-taking since it would be likely to interfere with attention, and to present all the diagrams used in lectures in order to prevent loss of important points during hasty reproduction of graphs or drawings. A further and crucial argument was that in order to produce the handouts, the teachers had to consider carefully what it was that they were going to say in the lectures themselves.

Visual and auditory aids need similar careful preparation and should be tried out in advance. Illustrations that are too small and/or text that is unreadable are inexcusable. Drawings should be bold and simple with few and brief labels and, above all, letters should be large enough to read. Far too often typewritten data suitable for showing to a small class are used in a hall where they are illegible for the majority of the audience. A duplicated paper or a specially prepared slide or sheet with larger printed letters would be greatly superior. In any case, it is wise to have a blackboard available in the event of aids failing to work. Some automatic slide projectors, for example, jam if a change of slides is a trifle too rapid, or the class may find the noise from an overhead projector so distracting that they prefer imperfect hand-drawn illustrations in order to hear the lecturer clearly. Cassette tapes or film loops are, perhaps, easiest to handle; and, since audio-tapes and video-tapes can now be used with inexpensive players, their many uses may be more fully exploited.

Three-dimensional illustrations have become much easier now that closed-circuit television is fairly commonly used in universities. Where it is not available, either large models or sufficient models for several students to share are required. It is important in the latter case that teachers should make certain that both they and the students are observing the same things, perhaps with the aid of diagrams. Lack of a model, or of a verbal exposition while pointing to parts of a small model, may render a lecture incomprehensible to most of the audience. This tends to happen when the lecturers are themselves very familiar with three-dimensional illustrations and fail to realize that their students are not yet capable of visualizing these unaided.

8.4   Presenting the lecture

When presenting lectures speakers should remember that it is their responsibility to keep the level of arousal of the audiences high. Evidence from studies of lecturing suggests that if the lecturers present their subjects verbally, with little illustration, the initially high level of arousal falls steadily until just before the end, when it rises somewhat, only to fall finally with the concluding remarks (Lloyd, 1968; Stuart and Rutherford, 1978).

In a study of 90 lectures given by 12 lecturers, Johnstone and Percival (1976) noted periods of inattention. These differed with subject, delivery rate, legibility of blackboard work and lecturer personality. Some lecturers commanded a better attention span pattern from the class by deliberate variations which had the effect of postponing or even eliminating the occurrence of an attention break. In 50-minute lectures without variation in style, however, there was usually a period of non-attention initially, followed by another some 10–18 minutes later and, as the lecture proceeded, attention spans became shorter, falling to three to four minutes before the end.

The lecture plan should therefore include various methods of stimulating attention. Good lecturers use illustrative stories and examples or visual illustrations, or build an outline on the board to enable members of the audience to keep track of the argument; they also vary their pace, pausing before important names or statements, raising their voices or speaking more deliberately to give emphasis. In these ways they keep the arousal of the audience at a high level. Despite this, the audience will still experience micro-sleeps which result in temporary losses of attention (Bligh, 1971). For this reason, a written record is needed, or repetition by presenting the subject matter in a number of different ways, to enable the audience to follow an argument without missing points, or, if they are making their own notes, to do so without serious omissions.

A brief account of the main faults perpetrated by lecturers at courses for university teachers will serve to illustrate the requirements for satisfactory presentation. The first, most disastrous, error is for lecturers to put their notes on a low table or a lectern and talk to them, never glancing at their audience. A lecture given in this way is almost certainly inaudible to the majority and irritating to the remainder, for there is a lack of rapport with the speaker as well as difficulty in hearing him or her.

The second most serious error is poor organization. It is rarely so poor that the lecture is meaningless but it may be so ill-planned that it is difficult to tell what the lecturer hopes the audience will get from it. Similarly, it is a result of poor organization when lecturers pay so little regard to time that they have to speed up at the end, stop before their exposition is completed, or run over time, to the irritation of both their audience and any subsequent incoming class.

A third error, somewhat less serious but responsible for much distraction, is that of wandering about the room, rocking back and forth, from foot to foot, or, as a new university teacher commented, 'One of your lecturers danced'. Since the offenders inevitably move their heads in these cases, possibly even turning away from the audience, the difficulty in following what they say may be very great.

Other serious errors may occur in speaking. A habit of addressing the board, with back to audience, is, perhaps, one of the most exasperating of these since it makes the speakers inaudible and simultaneously indicates that they have less regard for the class than the subject matter. Another common and irritating error is to become inaudible at the end of every sentence. In the latter case, expert advice may be required since it is possibly a matter of incorrect breathing; this may also apply when the delivery is utterly monotonous, a fault which can render a lecture tedious to the point where it becomes unendurable. One might suppose that this could happen only if the lecturers felt bored or uninterested but, surprisingly, they may look interested. Again, it is desirable that such faults should be detected before lecturers begin 'unaccountably' to lose their audiences. However, less dull speakers may keep the attention of their audiences by the use of illustrations, whether visual or on tape, or by pausing from time to time to invite or ask questions.

From this variety of errors we may deduce that it would be desirable for all lecturers to attend a course prior to taking up their posts and, if necessary, to attend subsequent classes in effective speaking. In the case of minor errors, a friendly arrangement with another new lecturer to sit in and criticize might well be sufficient. Failing all else, the use of a well-placed microphone will at least solve the problem of poor audibility.

Errors of a different kind occur when lecturers obscure their own visual aids by poor positioning or by absent-mindedly interposing themselves between them and the audience. For this reason it is advisable to use a pointer and to practise using visual aids with a friendly critic present. It is also wise to invite audiences to say if they are unable to see since all too often they suffer without complaint.

Aspects of communication which are rarely considered are the non-verbal ones. Studies by Argyle (1983) suggest that these have important consequences. They consist of facial expression, eye contact, tone of voice, posture and gesture. Through these means it is possible to convey the impression of superiority, of friendly concern, rejection and so on. It is, therefore, of interest to recall an occasion when the sound failed to operate in playing some short lectures on video tape, so that we observed non-verbal communication alone. The lecturer who had been most successful was looking around his class, smiling from time to time, using his hand to make gestures, digressing to tell a story and so on, whereas those who were less successful were comparatively wooden. Indeed, in one case a lecturer who seemed to lack rapport due to timidity proved to have been looking either at the board, his notes or to one side of the front row of seats.

Since non-verbal communication is evidently important it is, perhaps, desirable that all lecturers should have the opportunity to see themselves in action and to be provided with a list of points to check, enabling them to rate different aspects of their performance. And they should see themselves as the class sees them, and not only in close-up, for close-ups tend to maximize the effect of even slight facial movement and so may misguide dull lecturers into supposing that they are really quite interesting to watch whereas, in fact, their non-verbal communication is minimal. Useful advice on voice production and the art of speaking may be found in Colson (1963) and Gohdin et al. (1970). Falus and McAleese (1975) have prepared an extensive bibliography of studies of micro-teaching.

Courses in speaking may remedy lack of confidence also; but should this be deep seated, therapy is possible. Stanton (1978) describes group treatment consisting of relaxation training, positive suggestion and success imagery. As a consequence, members of the group felt that they had gained in confidence and their students subsequently evaluated them more highly in relation to a control group.

8.5 Modified forms of the lecture and teaching large classes

Modified forms of the lecture can be particularly well suited to large classes where there is little opportunity for students to question the lecturer. They can also be more effective in small classes in ensuring that students understand concepts or principles and their applications. For, if students use the subject matter immediately to answer questions, or to solve problems, they discover what they misunderstood, and so can correct errors before leaving the class. Or if they understand correctly in the first place, their learning is reinforced. For example, buzz sessions may be used in which small groups of two to five students discuss a point for a few minutes, or larger groups of six to ten students may discuss a problem, presenting their solutions to the entire class, prior to concluding remarks by the lecturer. Both of these methods have been used successfully with classes of up to 90 students.

Other very successful approaches have been devised in university schools and, although they were used initially in medical sciences, it is not difficult to think of suitable applications of the methods in other subjects, including the arts. One method is to give a somewhat shortened version of the usual lecture followed by questions, either on duplicated papers or projected onto a screen for students to answer. Correct responses are immediately read out and errors are discussed. This technique has been used in teaching anaesthetics (Davies, 1968) where the introduction of problem sheets has made progress so much more rapid that additional topics are now included in the syllabus.

A more carefully planned approach is to give a short, highly organized lecture outlining main principles and a few applications, followed by two or three questions for students to answer briefly. The answers can be immediately discussed by pairs or trios of students and any outstanding points finally raised with the lecturer. This method proved so effective in a course of clinical medicine that almost all the students gained full marks in an end-of-term test (Mosel, 1964). Other similar methods are described by Bligh et al. (1975).

Trickey (1974) describes an experiment in which various ways of modifying lectures were compared: lecture plus buzz session; lecture plus multiple-choice questions; lecture plus duplicated notes with spaces (deliberate omission of key phrases, etc. for students to fill in). In addition a traditional lecture was used and a lectureless method in which students wrote their own notes from supplied references and answered a self-checking test. Students liked the traditional lecture least. The style involving note-writing and a test proved most effective, although unpopular with some students. A different approach is that favoured chiefly by students, namely the 'teach-in', which consists of a series of short talks followed by discussion; this, too, has the advantage of allowing immediate clarification which facilitates understanding before proceeding to the next topic.

Another method designed for a large audience is that of Betts and Walton (1970) who cooperated in preparing lectures in basic science for 600 first-year students. Betts provided the straight exposition while Walton interposed questions, entertaining illustrations or demonstrations. Discourse of this kind, or indeed any method which offers more than one point of view – a succession of speakers perhaps – is too little used; it is likely to stimulate interest and may arouse the more passive students to undertake some genuine thinking. Nevertheless, with so large an audience, it seems improbable that questions from a second teacher could simultaneously meet the needs of the most advanced students and of those having a weak scientific background. It is hard to justify such large classes unless all the students begin from an equal state of ignorance so that division on the basis of past performance is impossible.

8.6   Evaluating lectures

Evaluation of learning by questioning and discussion will provide only part of the information lecturers require to make their teaching as effective as possible. There are some things that students will hesitate to tell them; for example, that their voice does not carry, or that they speak too rapidly. Yet it is necessary to know these things, or carefully prepared and otherwise well-presented material may not be appreciated to the full. For this reason a group of lecturers in the sciences from nine of the colleges in London University cooperated in preparing a questionnaire which students could fill in anonymously early in a course. It covers the information which they wished to have but leaves space for comments to enable students to add points or to elaborate criticisms they make. The lecturers give out copies of the questionnaire, probably at the second or third lecture, explaining that they would appreciate the cooperation of the students in telling them how, in the students' opinion, the course could be improved. Lecturers who have done this report that students are pleased to be consulted and take the matter very seriously. They say, for example, that the lecturer spoke too fast or ignored the audience, that they would welcome more illustrations and applications or better notes. All of the lecturers report that one result of using the questionnaire has been improved relations with their students (even if they were already good) as well as increased interest. Students have also made some very helpful suggestions under the heading 'Advice for the future'.

One lecturer who wrote a detailed report commented on the value of the different items in the questionnaire. He found items which required merely a tick among five choices were easy to interpret (McVey, 1968). Possibly this was because different behaviours were described and were fairly easy to identify. On the other hand, some items seemed irrelevant to his classes and could possibly be omitted when using the questionnaire in that department in future; but as this is likely to vary for different individuals, it is as well to use the questionnaire in its entirety at first and to modify it in the light of experience. A point of considerable importance is that the items used should be as specific as possible. To ask students to rate the general ability of a teacher, for example, could mean such a variety of things to different students that it would be difficult to interpret; and knowledge of the students' response to this would be as unhelpful to the teacher as is a literal grade on an essay. What the teacher needs to know is in what ways he can help the students to learn more effectively.

In America a great variety of evaluating techniques have been tried. Some of these are summarized by Nadeau (1977) and may be of interest to any teacher who wishes to devise methods most suited to the evaluation of his or her own courses. (Further discussion is also provided in Chapter 14.)

When running courses for new lecturers in London, we issued in advance a list of points to bear in mind when criticizing a lecture. Since this is equally useful in the preparation of a lecture or a short course, it is reproduced here in the appendix to this chapter, followed by the questionnaire which the scientists devised.

8.7   Summary

- Lectures have been widely criticized but are still widely used as a teaching method.
- There are several different styles of lecturing and several different ways of organizing lectures.
- In *preparing* lectures, teachers need to pay attention to their purpose, content, organization and to appropriate aids. In *presenting* lectures thought needs to be given not only to the clarity of the exposition but also to the effects of non-verbal communication.
- Lecture techniques can be modified (e.g. by the use of buzz sessions) to break up monotony, to arouse students' interest and to get learners more actively involved.
- Lectures can be improved by feedback – from students and other colleagues. Some ways of doing this are illustrated in the appendix to this chapter.

Appendix

Points to bear in mind when criticizing a lecture or evaluating a short course of lectures

Timing   Did the lecture begin promptly? End promptly? How long did it last? Was any section of the lecture too drawn out, passed over too quickly?

Content   Could the subject matter have been followed more quickly, and profitably, in a book (or books)? Was it descriptive? If so, was it interesting? Was it explanatory? If so, did everyone follow? Was it inspirational? Was

Questionnaire to evaluate lectures

Surroundings and other factors   Please comment on any of the following (e.g. excessive, good, slight, poor . . .)

Noise	Ventilation	Seating	Fatigue
Light	Space	Temperature	Hunger

The lecturer

Voice

Audibility: very clearly audible	easily heard	just audible	sometimes audible	almost entirely inaudible
Quality: lively varied tone and pace	fairly lively	satisfactory	rather dull	very monotonous
Speed: spoke much too fast	spoke rather quickly	about right	spoke rather slowly	tediously slow

Comments, if any

Appearance and grooming

very good – a pleasure to look at	good – a pleasing appearance on the whole	satisfactory	rather poor	poor disagreeable/distracting

Manner very agreeable	pleasant	satisfactory	rather disagreeable	unpleasant

Rapport with class

excellent	good	satisfactory	fair	poor

Comments, if any

Amount of material:	far too much	rather too much	satisfactory	rather little content thin	practically nothing worth saying
Clarity and organization:	very clear and easy to follow	clear	only fairly clear	rather difficult to follow – somewhat muddling	could not understand. Less clear than before
Use:	will help me greatly in the future	helpful	of some use	practically no use	absolutely no help
Stimulus and interest:	I shall certainly follow this up (by reading/practice . . .)	I shall probably follow this up	may follow this up	uninterested, would have been better occupied elsewhere	very bored, shall avoid subject whenever possible; less interested than before
Comments, if any					

Audiovisual materials

Blackboard:	material very clearly and attractively presented	material well presented	satisfactory	untidy, rather crowded, partly illegible	far too crowded, illegible
Slides or other visual illustration:	very clear and attractive	well presented	satisfactory	lettering too small, slides rather crowded	almost illegible
Sound:	very clear and agreeable	clear	satisfactory	not entirely audible	almost inaudible
Comments, if any					

there too much/too little content? Was part irrelevant? If so, was it valuable nevertheless?

Organization   Did the lecture have a perceptible form or structure (e.g. an introduction, examination of a case or problem, elaboration of principles, and a survey or conclusion)? Or was it rambling and rather incoherent? Did the lecturer state clearly what he or she intended to do – and did he or she do it? Was it easy to follow?

References and notes   Did the lecturer dictate notes? Did he or she go slowly enough for notes to be taken? Did he or she pause while note-takers caught up? Did the lecturer distribute notes or a summary beforehand? If so, did he or she make use of them in class? Did the lecturer indicate precise references to printed material?

Visual aids
   a. The blackboard: Did the lecturer use the blackboard to put up names which were not well known? formulae? skeleton notes? outlines of a proof? stages in the solution of a problem? illustrative diagrams? If so, were they clearly visible? well arranged? Were they rubbed off too soon?
   b. Charts, flannel graphs, magnetic board, slides, film strips, film loops and films, TV pictures on monitor: Were they clearly visible to all the class? Interesting? Informative? Relevant? Were they awkward to handle so distracting the audience? Were they used or merely displayed?
   c. Specimens or models: Was there one big enough for all to see? Or were they distributed to all the class? If so, could the lecturer and students be cartain that they were talking about the same thing?

Other illustrative material   Did the lecturer mention case history material; an industrial application; examples from his or her experience or students' experience; similar experiences met before, etc.? Did the lecturer use tapes of interviews, of a previous lecture? If so, was it relevant, interesting, useful? If irrelevant, was it nevertheless valuable?

Delivery   Did the lecturer appear to speak spontaneously, without notes? With few notes? Or did he or she read from a prepared manuscript? Was the lecturer's manner stilted, nervous, rhetorical, conversational? Did he or she speak clearly? Mumble? Drop his or her voice at the end of each sentence? Shout? Had the lecturer an accent difficult to understand? Were the pace and tone varied? Did he or she speak too fast or too slowly?

Rapport with audience   Did the lecturer appear aware of the audience? Did he or she react to it in any way, e.g. by jokes, humorous asides, examples from experience, ask questions of the audience or invite questions? Was the audience afraid to ask questions? If questions were asked was the lecturer welcoming, sarcastic, indifferent, cold? Did the answers appear to satisfy the questioners? If not, did they give up? Did the lecturer make certain that he or she had answered the question which the student meant to ask?

Did you understand what the lecturer said?   Did most of the audience? Did the lecturer have a pleasing appearance? An agreeable manner?

Evaluation   What means, if any, did the lecturer take to ensure that the purpose of the lecture had been achieved, e.g. asking questions of students, a class, setting homework, setting a test (e.g. multiple-choice), etc.?

What would you advise this lecturer to do on future occasions (i.e. suggestions rather than pure criticisms)?

CHAPTER 9

THE ROLE OF DISCUSSION IN
TEACHING AND LEARNING

In the first half of this chapter we outline the objectives of teaching by group discussion, and we consider the causes of some common problems met by group leaders. In the second half we discuss a variety of group discussion methods and the role of the leader in each.

In this chapter we deliberately avoid the difficulty of defining 'tutorial' and 'seminar' by using the term 'group discussion' throughout. 'Tutorial' is commonly used for discussion of a student's work with his or her tutor or, possibly, with one or two other students as well as the tutor, whereas 'seminar' is normally used to denote a question-and-answer session directed by the tutor with 6–12 students. However, since some teachers use these terms interchangeably, or reverse the meanings, it seems clearer to employ 'group discussion' for either, or for any oral method involving discussion, and to specify the purpose and corresponding organization in each case.

9.1 The objectives of group discussion

Group discussion methods have been used increasingly since the 1950s. In part, no doubt, this has been due to the increase in class sizes which has added greatly to teachers' problems in identifying students' difficulties and helping to resolve them. In part, too, it has been due to the greater demands made of students by the rapid growth in many subject areas, by new requirements in relating differing disciplines in interdisciplinary courses, or in mastering concepts drawn from several different fields in new specialities. The evidence from a large number of comparative studies of lectures with other methods, which showed that these methods, in particular discussion, were often more effective than lectures in promoting thinking (Bligh, 1971), may have convinced teachers in the sciences that teaching through lectures was no longer sufficient. Since discussion has always played a part in teaching in the humanities, and in tutorials in all subjects at Oxbridge, this was a new requirement primarily in departments of science or applied science at other universities and in the polytechnics.

An inquiry made by Beard (1967) among teachers of mathematics, chemistry and biology in London University showed that group discussion was in common use, the most popular size of group being six students. In a few instances, smaller groups of two or three first-year students met with a member of staff to discuss students' problems in adjusting to university life. Larger groups of 10 or 12 students, or exceptionally up to 25, were held mainly to discuss the content of lectures, to identify and discuss difficulties or to assist students in learning specific skills. A small number of teachers admitted to finding group discussion a difficult method, and a few were uncertain what sessions of discussion were intended to achieve.

The objectives of group discussion range widely. The objective which outweighs all others in importance (although this varies from subject to subject) is that students should be helped to discuss and to clarify difficulties arising from lectures or other teaching sessions. This appears in various guises: 'to provide opportunities for questions', 'to help understanding of lecture material', 'to ensure that students are not getting lost in lecture courses', 'to answer any problems arising from lectures and practical classes', 'to search for areas of ignorance and to direct attention to these', 'to promote understanding of concepts and principles', and so on. Another objective mentioned by a sizeable proportion of teachers in all subjects is to obtain more intimate and personal contact with students than is possible in lectures, which many still consider to be one of the greatest advantages in holding group discussions. Then, with varying emphases in different subjects, follow more specific objectives such as: to promote critical and logical thinking; to aid students in solving problems or making applications of theory; to give practice in oral presentation of reports; to discuss students' work such as essays, designs and plans, experimental results, etc.; to extend studies to topics beyond those covered in lectures; to survey literature relating to one field or one topic; to widen interests; to change attitudes – an important aim in a field such as social studies; and to provide feedback to staff on (1) students' progress and attitudes and (2) the effectiveness of their teaching.

On the whole, therefore, teachers see discussion as an extension of instruction given during lectures. The view of Abercrombie (1960, 1979), that discussion should assist students in changing from a state of dependence on authority to that of full acceptance of adult responsibility, is not often mentioned and, perhaps, is not shared. Many teachers see themselves as always in authority. The possibility that students need to work through their confusions, and will not outgrow them if someone always supplies 'right answers', seems not to be universally appreciated. Certainly, the role of the teacher varies in differing kinds of group discussion and, whereas it is fairly easy for any teacher to maintain the role of an authority, it presents some difficulties to play a facilitating role which allows students to learn from each other.

Jean Ruddock (1978), in *Learning Through Small Group Discussion*, discusses some of the problems which arise in discussion groups due to the tutors' inability to relinquish their role as an authority, or the unwillingness of students to allow them to do so. The book is based on problems described by teachers in universities and colleges and is illuminated by transcripts of group discussions and of interviews with teachers and students. Ruddock has concentrated on the kind of group in which discussion rather than instruction is the main mode of learning and this involves participation by students. Her aim is to increase the self-awareness of participants in group discussion.

Similarly, the book by Abercrombie and Terry (1978), *Talking to Learn*, is based on selections from taped group discussions held at London University. The discussions are about learning how to work better in groups and sometimes include parts of tutorials with comments on them. In this way they raise a range of problems experienced in discussion by tutors and students.

Abercrombie's *Aims and Techniques of Group Teaching* (1979) is well suited to teachers who have engaged in very little group discussion. The book describes a range of methods which may be used, with their different purposes, before considering how to evaluate group work and how to lead it. In Abercrombie's view:

> The group system aims to emancipate the student from the authority–dependency relationship, and to help him to develop intellectual independence and maturity through interaction with peers, by glimpsing not only 'the context in which a more experienced scholar sees his problem, but the various contexts in which several equals see the problem'.

Other texts which readers may find useful are Ogborn's *Small Group*

Teaching in Undergraduate Science (1977a) and Bligh et al.'s *Teaching Students* (1975) (see Chapter 5).

9.2   Encouraging students to talk

One of the most commonly reported problems in group discussion is that students do not participate. Accordingly it is essential to consider how to promote and to sustain discussion.

Getting the group going

Teachers acknowledge that the environment in which the group is held, the arrangement within the group itself, the placing of the tutor and the role he or she assumes, all influence a group's performance. It is easier to talk in a small common room which is already associated with friendly conversation than it is in a corner of a lecture room. But if the discussion is held in tutors' rooms and they sit in the customary position behind the desk, then they have already assumed a position of authority unsuited to the less directed kinds of groups. Seating arrangements are important: students will not talk to those they cannot see, the physical distance may suggest intimacy if the group is crowded together, or an individual may withdraw, choosing to be both physically and psychologically remote (Abercrombie, 1960).

In a review of research on seating arrangements Hawkins et al. (1981) found that:

1. When communication was free:

   a. The maximum number of communications was made between people sitting opposite one another.

   b. The minimum number of communications was made between people sitting side by side.

2. The most centrally placed member of a group was likely to emerge as the group leader.

3. Leaders were most likely to emerge on that side of the table which had the fewest people.

Bligh et al. (1975) suggest that if group members are beginners in the use of discussion as a method of learning, then the rule is 'start with simple tasks, with small groups for short periods. Then gradually increase them.' They suggest further: 'Some students think that discussion periods are occasion for general relaxation and "chit-chat". If the tone of the course is set by making them work on a problem on the first day, teaching is easier later on.'

Bligh et al. stress the need to promote confidence at this stage and to foster curiosity by the use of problems which apply the principles of a subject in a practical way, or by talks involving the acquisition of facts and their interpretation. Alternatively students may be asked to solve a problem and to discuss their methods when the first one or two have reached a solution. In this way everyone has something to contribute. Meanwhile if the teacher circulates among several subgroups, or withdraws and listens if the group is working as a whole, he or she may learn a great deal about the students' capacities and thinking.

As group size and task difficulty increase so does the problem of keeping the group active. It is essential that the teacher should withdraw so far as possible from a dominant position. Tutors may use eye contact to bring in members who appear to have something to contribute and thus avoid the danger of speaking again and being left to continue. Bligh et al. suggest the following prohibitions: (1) 'Don't correct or reject the first contributions' – even if they are wildly wrong; (2) 'Don't state an opinion rigidly' – it may inhibit students (even if the opinion is an outrageous statement intended to arouse disagreement); (3) 'Don't answer questions that could be answered by another member of the class'.

Silent members of a group may be induced to contribute by pausing occasionally for a buzz session during which neighbours discuss points more fully. In this way students who are too shy to address the whole group have an opportunity to contribute indirectly through a question or comment to their neighbour. Indeed, if each student is at intervals asked to introduce a topic and to answer questions, all but the most persistently silent are likely to make worthwhile contributions.

If more mature groups will not participate the difficulty may lie in unsuitable topics, lack of preparation or in unconscious inhibition of discussion by the tutor. The last is easily diagnosed by introducing the topic and withdrawing for a time on some pretext such as a telephone call. If the group is talking fluently on the tutor's return 10 minutes later, then the tutor's presence is inhibiting. One solution to this problem is to divide the group into two and to alternate between them. This allows the leaderless group to become animated before the tutor joins in. Other roles for tutors and students are listed in *Table 9.1*.

Avoiding habits which inhibit discussion

In a study of 10 tutorials, Beattie (1982) found that the tutor spoke much of the time and was involved in a disproportionate number of exchanges. The

Table 9.1   Some possible roles for teachers and students in group discussions

Initiating	Starting things off, suggesting new ideas or new ways of looking at what you're discussing.
Seeking information	Asking for relevant facts or authoritative information on a subject.
Giving information	Supplying relevant facts or relating personal experiences.
Giving opinions	Stating an opinion about something the class is considering: perhaps challenging consensus or complacency.
Clarifying	Restating something that someone has said. Translating a poorly worded statement into a clear one.
Elaborating	Building on previous comments, giving examples.
Controlling	Making sure that everyone who wants to gets a chance to speak.
Encouraging	Being receptive and responsive to comments.
Setting standards	Supplying and asking for criteria to judge the different ideas that are discussed.
Harmonizing	Reducing tension: getting pupils to explore their differences.
Relieving tension	Diagnosing what causes frustration during discussions and trying various remedies.
Coordinating	Extracting the key ideas from what's been said and integrating them: helping the group to use and to build on each other's ideas.
Orientating	Defining where you think the class is in their discussion and where you think they have to go.
Testing	Checking with your class as to where they feel the discussion should be going.
Consensus testing	Checking with the group to see how much agreement has been reached: protecting the divergence of views.
Summarizing	Reviewing what's been said, pulling together ideas and comments.

Source: Based on Schmuck and Schmuck (1971), reproduced with permission.

average probability of the tutor speaking next after each of the five students in five groups ranged between 0.74 and 0.88, but the probability of any pair of students following each other was only 0.04. In other words, a student was considerably less likely to be followed in discussion by another student than by the tutor. In fact, the talk was mainly channelled through the tutor. Beattie suggests that seating arrangements were partly responsible for this. When the tutor was persuaded to sit in the middle of a line of students with a student in the tutor's chair, this student started taking on some of the pivotal role of the tutor. Beattie adds that 'the tutor in the meantime was desperately trying to interrupt to regain control of the discussion!' Evidently, it is not easy to relinquish this role.

In attempting to explain further the poor contribution by students Beattie noted two other bad habits in leading discussion. First, the tutor tended to follow on students' contributions with minimal delay, so leaving little opportunity for the other students to organize their thoughts. Second, the tutor commonly interrupted the students by cutting in when they were nearing a possible completion point. The latter occurred in about a quarter of all instances when the tutor gained the floor. And, it is noteworthy that the groups experiencing the highest rate of tutor interruption had the lowest rates of student-to-student contributions. While this might be due to the tutor's desire to maintain the 'momentum' of the discussion, Beattie points out that it may need to be sacrificed to allow more opportunity for the students to speak.

Allowing for personality differences

Whether group discussion goes well, particularly if it is of the free, less directed kind, also depends to some extent on the personality characteristics of the students and the tutor. A number of tutors complain that some group discussions tend to be monopolized by students seeking to impress the others or by those who persistently argue. In this case it may be worthwhile to rearrange the group on one pretext or another so that persistent talkers are adjacent to each other or on either side of the tutor and opposite to the least talkative members. If this fails more positive measures should be tried, such as thanking the most persistent speaker for his interesting comments and inviting the views of other members, individually, on the same topic. As a last resort the persistent speaker may be asked to take notes of the discussion for the group's use or to write a brief account of his helpful observations.

Perhaps it would also be beneficial to acquaint the students with research findings concerning the status of talkative and taciturn group members. It seems that the most frequent speakers (with a few exceptions) tend to be popular and are almost universally perceived as being more influential in getting a solution, or view, accepted than the least frequent speakers (Riecken, 1958; Klein, 1965). Even with the best solution to a problem, infrequent speakers fail to get it accepted unless they gain the support of a talkative member. Ability to influence the group results from gaining their attention, so infrequent speakers tend to be ignored and any contribution they do make is undervalued.

A student writing about discussion groups (Seale, 1977) noted antagonism between 'noisy' and silent members. The latter were silent because they feared that the 'noisy' members would 'trample over their ideas'. They commented that the 'noisy' members were insensitive and too full of themselves; but the silent members were seen as stupid and lacking in initiative by the 'noisy' ones. In groups so unfortunately mixed, good leadership is essential, or separation into two groups might be better.

Indeed, in one attempt to make the taciturn speak, talkative and untalkative students were separated (Knutson, 1960). The untalkative groups proved even quieter than anticipated and tended to dislike their groups, whereas vocal groups were well satisfied. However, the untalkative groups presented better organized and inter-related reports of their proceedings. Thus taciturn members may make efficient group secretaries or prepare good reports to present to the group and, in the latter event, they must inevitably give answers to questions.

Encouraging students to prepare for discussion groups

There seem to be three main reasons why students do not prepare for discussion: (1) the subject chosen is not sufficiently controversial; (2) they are under pressure to achieve more than can reasonably be expected of them in the time; and (3) they have learned from experience that if they arrive unprepared, the tutor will give another lecture.

If the topics are not suitable for discussion and all that is required is that students should learn some fairly straightforward information, then this is better learned through reading, or by following a lecture with questions, or by self-teaching techniques. In this case it is wiser to change the method or to choose topics which raise problems that can be profitably discussed.

Where students have, or believe they have, too much to do in the time, the tutor may ask two or three of them to follow up limited aspects of the subject to be discussed. It is usually possible to provide each student with a brief paper or xeroxed chapter; and if these are written from different points of view, the group will be provided with a basis for discussion. Since presentations can be made by different students on successive occasions this also ensures that each makes a contribution and leads some of the discussion.

Where the tutor has been depended on to speak at length when students arrive unprepared, it may be best to give them substantially more responsibility. Black (1971) reports that degeneration into sporadic staff monologues led to student reaction and the formation of a student committee which asked to be allowed to run the discussions – a request which was readily granted. Subsequent discussion was more brisk because at least some students felt responsible and came prepared.

Contributions may increase, of course, if they are assessed. The effect of assessing students' contributions to seminars in the English department at York has been entirely good. Jones (1969) reports that the work is more thoroughly prepared than ever before and, as he says, the 'high quality of discussion led to our forgetting all about the examination'. Jones claims that this method recognizes that a student's activity is to a large extent a collaborative one, and that sustaining informed discussion is a central and essential function of a university. The difficulties of assessing participation in group discussion are explored in more detail by Armstrong and Boud (1983).

In student-led discussion, achievement of a wider range of objectives becomes possible than in most teacher-led groups. Students not only acquire information in an active way which enables them to assimilate it more readily into their store of knowledge; they are also able to develop skills in explanation and questioning, in commenting on and criticizing differing views expressed by their peers and in summarizing contributions to discussion. Generally such methods foster cooperation rather than competition. These methods, therefore, assist students in developing the skills of communication and cooperation required in the modern world.

One way to get students involved is to use the syndicate method (Collier, 1983). Initially a common task or area of study, or a group of related problems is introduced by the tutor. Students are then assigned to small groups to work on clearly defined tasks which may involve collecting information and working out possible solutions to a problem. They come together in a self-directed group, appoint a chairperson and a secretary, and work together on a report on the solution, or solutions to the problem, referring any outstanding difficulties to the tutor. In a plenary session, individuals from the groups present reports which are then discussed by the other groups and the tutor.

Newton and Seville (1977) report on use of this method in a multi-disciplinary systems and management course. Since their main aim was to produce graduates able to reconcile social, economic, scientific and political aspects of problems they used topics such as: 'the history of tunnelling', 'low impact technology' and 'social implications of nuclear technology'.

Students' participation was inevitable. Following two introductory lectures and the assignment of tasks, all the students were expected to spend three weeks reading prior to reporting to the group and deciding on any changes in approach. In the second term, students completed fieldwork (if any) and gave talks to the entire group, supplying written summaries and documentation and finally a two-hour survey was chaired by a member of staff. Each student was expected to hand in a report of some 4000 words.

Evans (1980), in a stimulating report on the use of student-led groups in French literature courses, supplies an extract from the course programme (e.g. Sartre and biography), a list of handouts on group work describing the role of the leader, the role of the group secretary and the role of a group member. The last of these lists advises students to be prepared; be audible; listen actively; state views, opinions, ideas, interpretations, problems; give information, evidence, proof, explanation; seek information, evidence, proof, explanation; express support; express and justify disagreement; build on others' ideas; comment on the group's progress and process; direct or redirect progress; sum up or rephrase or clarify; link each contribution to what has preceded; use the board when appropriate; be aware of time constraints.

The probability of a silent or quiet group after this seems slight. Evans' inquiry showed that contributions in student-led as opposed to a tutor-led group discussion were both substantially more numerous and more varied. A brief transcript from a video-recording of a student-led seminar concludes his article.

9.3   Varieties of group discussion

The use of discussion to overcome difficulties
It is of interest that one of the objectives teachers most commonly mention about discussion – that it should help the students with their difficulties – is also the least clearly defined. The uncertainty lies in the meaning of 'difficulty'. Should the tutor verify that the students know the principles and theories or that they have as much information as possible? Should they ensure that their students learn to solve certain kinds of problems or assist them in developing an approach to solving problems in general? Or, as common sense at first dictates, should they perhaps ask the students what their difficulties are?

Many teachers say that they do in fact do this, but experience shows that it can be in the nature of a difficulty that the students cannot identify it. For example, if they too readily accept assumptions without questioning them, or if they are illogical, this must be demonstrated to them to make them aware of it. Thus, to say that an objective in holding group discussions is to meet students' difficulties is inadequate without further elaboration, unless the teacher already knows the kinds of difficulties students have or is knowledgeable about ways of discovering and overcoming them. However, this is unlikely to be the case if the tutors are young and inexperienced or if they have neither analysed the difficulties of weaker students nor experimented to see how they can be helped.

In the great majority of cases eliciting difficulties involves setting problems in the form of written exercises or questions to which answers must be thought out and at least jotted down. Such methods will expose ignorance or misunderstanding. A comparison of students' answers may be sufficient to demonstrate to each individual his or her own omissions, unjustified assumptions and errors. Discussion then arises naturally between the students and tutor, provided that the latter resists any temptation to give an additional short lecture and has sufficient confidence not to wish to appear as an infallible authority.

Thus if group discussion is to be used to elicit students' difficulties it should be based on some activity on their part. This may be simply listening to a lecture and thinking about it, or reading, but is more likely to be some common experience such as a visit, listening to discussion of a case-study, or viewing a film; or it may be based on solutions to problems which the students have already attempted or answers to questions set in the first 10 minutes or so of the discussion period. In the case of oral work such as making a report, or in chairing a meeting, tapes of the students' own efforts make a stimulating introduction to discussion of their performance; these may be supplemented by tapes of other groups at work. Video-tape should be used if at all possible, since the non-verbal elements in effective communication, or in interactions within a group, then become apparent.

A second point which seems not to be generally appreciated is that the way in which the group is conducted, and the role the tutor plays, also depend on the objectives. These may reflect differences in subject matter or in personality; for instance, the accounts of social scientists seem to assume that discussion is necessarily of a free kind in which the tutor plays a minimal part, whereas physical scientists are more likely to see themselves as authorities to whom questions should be directed by the students.

Some examples will serve to show how the tutor's role may change in pursuing different objectives. We will begin by considering those in which the degree of direction on the part of the tutor is usually greatest and proceed to those in which the aim is maximum freedom of discussion between the students themselves. However, it is inadvisable to conclude that each tutor should proceed in the same way with every group: the personalities of tutors and the needs of groups of students differ so greatly that the methods used to attain the same objectives may vary appreciably.

Development of cognitive abilities and skills

Promoting understanding   This objective is so broad that one might say it is an essential ingredient in most discussion. Nevertheless, it appears that when teachers mention this as a main objective, scientists' aims are to ascertain that students know new concepts and principles in the field, that they can interpret graphical, visual and statistical data or, perhaps, that they obtain a grasp of relationships within the subject; whereas in the arts the purpose may be to ensure that students gain a knowledge of the social and political setting of a text, learn to appreciate the originality of a writer in relation to his or her time, to recognize differences between discursive and dramatic writing, and so on.

In teaching biology, and subsequently economics and chemistry, Epstein's (1970) method of discussing research papers with students proved particularly effective in promoting understanding. Epstein developed his method initially to interest a group of intelligent 17-year-old non-scientists in the advances of modern biology. The students learned about a subject, for example photosynthetic organisms, through discussion of recent research papers from teachers working in the field. They discussed how a biologist went about solving a problem, considered definitions of words and concepts which they then classified, 30 terms being clarified in this way on the first day of the course, since the original terms chosen required the clarification of other terms. Each concept was explained in fairly simple experimental terms whenever possible. If that took too long, it was explained superficially but with as little misleading information as possible. By the end of one week Epstein could comment, 'As I pondered the events of the first week . . . it occurred to me that the students had gone through the definitions and explanations of perhaps seventy-five terms. This began to look like a considerable accomplishment . . . ' During successive discussions an increasing number of students 'caught on' and became 'enthralled with both the science and their ability to understand it'. A later course of a similar kind with science specialists took longer as they were so eager to obtain detailed information. Some of these students were able to follow graduate colloquia after only seven weeks in college, having reached the frontiers of insight and knowledge as well as the ability to read journals. Few courses lead to so much initial enthusiasm or to such considerable advances in understanding. The method has now had successful trials in economics, chemistry and philosophy (Epstein, 1972).

Another method, recommended by the British Medical Students' Association (1965), is the CORLAB. In this method, which originated in Canada, a printed booklet is issued to each student in advance of the discussion; this contains a detailed clinical history and questions to indicate profitable areas of inquiry. During a series of discussions, students make additions to the booklet and teachers trained in a number of specialities are present to answer questions and to take part in discussion. At the end of the session, mimeographed abstracts of recent relevant papers are distributed. An advantage of this method for the teaching staff is that they hear the views of different specialists in the field and they see a number of approaches in discussion with students. The students gain in a number of ways: a wide field is covered in a short time, all students participate by the prior reading and by making additions to the booklet, and all have a permanent record of the discussion. But, above all, many aspects of the subject can be raised simultaneously, instead of considering different aspects at intervals during the course; in this way, the students are provided with a coherent body of knowledge which is easier to remember and they spend less time on the topic. This seems to be a method suited to any subject matter where the cooperation between experts is important.

Where the teacher does most of the talking it is, of course, essential that students should follow up the discussion with further activities – in writing, interpreting graphs or whatever the task may be. In the case of statistical data it seems likely that teaching by programmed text would be at least as effective since each student would then be fully occupied and free to work at his or her own pace. But students enjoy question-and-answer sessions with a teacher capable of making them entertaining, and the opportunity to learn from other people's errors without embarrassment to themselves!

Developing intellectual skills through discussion of essays, designs, experimental findings, etc.   Discussion groups, or tutorials, to evaluate students' essays are most usual in the older universities but designs or plans are frequently criticized in the course of discussion in some schools of architecture or engineering, and discussions of reports on projects or experimental work are not uncommon in departments of science or engineering. Despite provision of time for these purposes, complaints by some students that time intended for discussion of their work is used as an opportunity for another monologue by the tutor suggest that even where the tutorial system is well established its purpose is not always fully appreciated. It is intended, of course, that the student should receive the maximum of criticism while defending his views, conclusions or prepared design.

In a group this works admirably when a student displays a design, briefly reminds his audience of the purpose it was intended to fulfil and explains how, in his or her view, it does so. A tutor and students of comparable standing are then in a position to ask many leading questions and to offer criticism. The whole group is likely to be fully engaged, their interest being greater if the students are comparing a number of their own different solutions to the same problem. There may be some difficulty in objectively evaluating the students' contribution but there is none in providing the criticism they need from which to learn.

In the case of written work, however, students' complaints suggest that the situation is often very different. One student's essay, which is not accessible to the rest of the group, may be discussed while the others sit uninterested and unable to take part. A solution might be to duplicate one or more essays, giving the writer an opportunity to speak on it briefly before all the group joins in questioning or commenting on it. A list of points could be given to serve firstly as a guide to the writers, if they required it, and subsequently to assist the students and tutor in framing criticisms of an indifferent piece of work. The essay chosen for discussion should not be of such outstanding merit as to discourage the group and might well be selected for an unusual point of view or for its illustration of errors that many students are currently making.

Reporting on a project may be dealt with similarly, except that one or more students are likely to report at some length and there may be other groups of students and several tutors present to ask questions and to offer criticisms.

Abercrombie (1979) describes a method devised on the spur of the moment, by Felicity Baker, in which students each read and comment on a translation of an English passage into French made by a fellow student. This allowed them to form and exchange opinions, instead of listening to orderly and numerous comments from the tutor which, she felt, had gone in one ear and out the other. She comments that real work is always done in that hour, that the social atmosphere and group morale are unusually good and that quieter students join increasingly in the discussion.

Teaching problem-solving   The teaching of problem-solving to less able students seems often to be ineffectual although, we must assume, they were reasonably successful in solving problems at school. Comments such as 'they are not able to think' do nothing to explain their disability nor do they suggest remedies for it. Two main explanations are possible for the increasing weakness of some students in this respect. The first is that they have been drilled in solving specific kinds of problems without learning a problem-solving strategy. In this case, they may get by in examinations which are of a highly predictable kind. The second possible explanation for failure is simply that less able, or less well-prepared students are hurried too much by class teaching and need provision to work at their own pace.

In the former case, students may be led to develop a strategy by approaching the solution to problems through well-defined steps. These involve: clarification of the question by asking students to explain exactly what is required (they should not be told); discussion of principles which could be used in such a problem and why (this should lead to consideration of several possible approaches to the solution); and, as each of these is explored, a quick review of formulae, standard integrals, techniques, etc. which may be useful. Finally, when a solution is obtained, it should be discussed to see whether it can be improved in method, brevity or lucidity of expression. If the tutor feels that the more able students in the group will be bored by this treatment they may be invited to solve the problem independently, checking subsequently to see whether their solution was superior or not to the class solution, and a list of other problems should be available to keep them occupied. A student who obtains an unusual solution to the problem can be invited to present this to the group for discussion and comparison.

An alternative approach is simply to present students with an assortment of hard problems without a guide as to which principles may solve them. Hammersley (1968) reports that in teaching problem-solving in pure mathematics at Oxford, about half the students attended problem-solving classes and were set very difficult problems while the remaining half continued to attend tutorials. In subsequent examinations the performance of students attending the classes was significantly superior, at all levels of ability, to that of students attending tutorials. But in applied mathematics, where easy examples were set, this was not the case. Presumably a combination of the stimulus of difficulty, discussion with other students and the necessity to find a way into a hard problem results in development of problem-solving strategies; but these may not be needed if a tutor is at hand, or if problems are known to be soluble from information in a particular section of a textbook.

Even these methods may work indifferently for less able students where most of the group is superior to them. For this reason, a number of departments 'stream' students by ability. However, since a really weak group tends to become seriously discouraged it seems advisable to stream very roughly, if at all. If this also fails, problem-solving sessions in which students work independently, or occasionally in pairs, while staff circulate to discuss any difficulties with them, are said to be a satisfactory method and are fairly commonly in use. Surprisingly, the amount of discussion encouraged between students seems to be slight; yet this can be a valuable step in becoming independent of the teacher's aid, for each student then sometimes plays the role of adviser and will discuss difficulties more openly than he or she would do in a group.

Procedures in solving problems in the social sciences are basically the same for they also require the capacity to discern the nature of the problem, knowledge of resources and ability to organize available resources and techniques to a satisfactory solution. However, they are more likely to require good personal relations in cooperating with, or helping, other people, and the emphasis in such courses can be on changing students' attitudes. In this case, free discussion in which attitudes can be exposed and discussed is preferable to discussion in which the tutor plays a large part. There is also the difference that there may be no one best solution, or even a good solution, and that, indeed, no two problems are quite alike. Thus there is little danger that students will be drilled in specific types of solutions, but rather that they will find problems too nebulous and ill-defined for confident action. This is one reason for the introduction of 'games' or simulated problems involving fewer complications, for in these ways the problems students meet can be limited to make them more readily comprehensible and thus easier to solve.

Passivity and inactivity on the part of students are thus partly, or largely, due to the organization of the group within itself, but they may also be due to the attitude of the tutor. The tutor's role should essentially be to inspire confidence, to incite students to action by questioning or by praising them for making contributions. Students' suggestions, however poor, need to be treated with respect; if tutors make even a single caustic comment it will diminish the response of the group except, possibly, undesirable responses from aggressive members.

Making decisions and diagnosis   In some practical fields such as medicine and social work, engineering or management, skill must be developed in summing up a situation, perhaps before full information is available, and in making decisions on the basis of probabilities. Wherever possible this is best learned by practice but 'games', simulation systems and related methods or role-playing are being introduced in an increasing number of fields as an intermediate stage in learning. If the decisions by a beginner could be disastrous, or if it is too time consuming to wait for their consequences, or if suitable situations cannot be found at will, a 'game' provides a model of the real situation or certain relationships within it. Exercises follow prescribed rules which, together with the model itself, give a structure to the participant's decision-making. In this way, 'players' or participants are placed in roles which simulate those they would play in the corresponding real-life situations such as planning an advertising campaign, making decisions as to land uses, diagnosing an illness or injury and treating the patient, etc. We discuss these issues further in Chapter 11.

The role of the teacher in this kind of group work is to prepare, or to provide, a suitable activity. Discussion between participants consists largely in cooperative planning initially but subsequently in criticizing the way in which players have fulfilled their roles or in analysing causes for unsuccessful interactions. The tutor's presence is, therefore, not essential, although his or her greater experience and objectivity are likely to result in the group inviting the tutor's criticism.

Developing critical thinking   One of the major objectives of teaching in higher education is usually said to be to train students to think in a disciplined rational fashion. However, the evidence suggests that teaching students the basics of logic or expounding rational argument has little effect since their difficulties lie largely in preconceptions and misconceptions in their thinking of which they are unaware. It is, therefore, essential that they should state their views, whether in writing or in discussion, and discover through criticisms made by their teacher or fellows the faults in their argument. Abercrombie (1960), in a most interesting account of an experiment in group discussion in which students of biology were asked to define words such as 'normal' or 'average', to read a controversial passage and to comment on it, and to describe two X-rays, etc., showed that it was only through fairly prolonged discussion among themselves that students eventually became aware of their own errors in thinking. Intervention by the teacher had little effect.

> One or two might listen as though they understood what I said, but most were quiet only to save their breath and reverted back into their own confusions as soon as they could without being obviously rude. It seemed as though the associations that each person had to the word were extensive and tangled; the teacher could make it possible for the student to recognize that there was a muddle, but could not do much to help tidy up. That a long struggle is necessary to do this is indicated by the fact that students went on discussing the subject long afterwards.

Abercrombie observes that the kind of change which has to be effected is the reassessing and rearranging of what is already in the mind, rather than the receiving of new 'facts' and this is a change which has to be made by the students for themselves. In this process the role of the teacher is a modest one – that of arranging conditions to facilitate the change.

In Abercrombie's experiment a subsequent test showed that students who had attended eight such periods of discussion, as compared with those attending the usual anatomy classes, made fewer false inferences and fewer inferences unaccompanied by descriptions. More of them considered two hypotheses instead of one only and a smaller number of them were inappropriately biased by one test item in dealing with the succeeding one. Since all these differences were highly significant (that is to say, such large differences would have been extremely unlikely to occur by chance) it is reasonable to infer that discussion of this kind is an effective method of promoting reflection by students on their own modes of thinking and so facilitates criticism of argument and experimental evidence in what they read. Continuing use of this method confirms the results of the experiments that Abercrombie carried out in the 1950s (Barnett, 1958; Beard, 1967).

Some of the virtues of this method are reflected in a use of group discussion in teaching French in a college of London University (Uren, 1968). Group discussion is employed here to discourage too great an eagerness on the part of students to give their own opinions on views of an author before ascertaining what they really are. The work is designed in three stages so that students are confronted with each others' assumptions. First, they clarify the meaning of words (*éclaircissement*); second, they study what sentences mean or imply in the particular context (interpretation); and third, they make personal judgements (evaluation). This leads naturally to précis writing or 'critical' essays.

Tutors using discussion for the first time need to be warned, first, of the possibility that some students will resent their apparent withdrawal from the role of teacher to that of observer, and, secondly, that students who prefer to be given information to memorize will dislike the apparent aimlessness of the discussion. For these reasons it is advisable to explain something of the purpose of discussion of this kind: that it helps to uncover assumptions, misconceptions and errors in argument and so makes for improved performance. Tutors might also agree to warn students in advance that discussion may prove upsetting and frustrating, and to point out that if the tutor takes notes, it will be only in order to draw attention at the end to good contributions which were neglected or to questionable statements which were received uncritically. The truth is that learning to think is not painless and that students, or teachers, who have come to feel that they should never be detected in an error and who find themselves obliged to give up this or other cherished belief, tend to suffer in the process.

Using discussion to change attitudes   Since change in attitudes requires that students should become aware of and examine their existing attitudes, one might infer from the previous consideration of the development of critical thinking in discussion that similar methods would be appropriate. Evidence tends to confirm this view. It seems that participation by students, exposure to views different from their own and to criticism from their fellows, together with some withdrawal of the teachers' authority, are needed if attitudes are to be changed. Thus in a medical course devised to develop in students a concern for the social and psychological aspects of patients' illnesses it was direct contact with their own patients' homes which led to changes in attitude about social aspects of care, while comprehensive case conferences encouraged them to coordinate their knowledge of social, psychological and medical aspects of illness (Hammond and Kern, 1959). This evidence suggests, therefore, that a new experience combined with free discussion is crucial in changing attitudes where a breaking-down of prejudices and misconceptions or an increase in awareness of factors which have been habitually ignored is desired.

A third factor which may well be important is that individuals should commit themselves to a new mode of behaviour as well as being prepared to admit to earlier misconceptions, prejudices and so on. During the war years, Lewin (1947) found that about one-third of housewives who had been persuaded by discussion to commit themselves to try new kinds of food, did in fact do so whereas lecturers without commitment had practically no effect.

Discussion of a fairly free kind, but with a tutor present, is also effective in changing attitudes towards others in the group. Several experimenters report that group members learned from their fellows' criticisms to be less aggressive or less voluble and that some participants remarked a change in themselves towards the end of a series of discussions.

In all of these methods designed to influence attitudes the role of the teacher is to plan the right kind of experience for the group and to elicit contributions from them. For example, the teacher can show a film of committee meetings, play a tape of a patient's interview with a doctor, or of a class getting out of hand with a student teacher. The aim is not to offer an interpretation but to invite this from the group members. If they fail to observe critical incidents the teacher can replay the events and ask further questions until they see the significance for themselves.

The positive effect of discussion on attitudes in a small group of teachers meeting regularly is described by Abercrombie and Terry (1978). This they attribute to the supportive nature of the group as its members work together over a period of time, and to the opportunities it provides for increasing awareness of one's own behaviour. Teachers taking part in these groups comment:

> I've seen big changes in other group members (of both long-term and short-term membership) – eyes opening to aspects of teaching that previously were mysteries, new perception of themselves as teachers, deepening capacity to think out teaching problems. There's a relational dimension to this too, an increased mutual appreciation and respect as we watch one another change and develop in the professional context.

> Instead of viewing a group as an opportunity for students to understand clearly my thinking on some topic, I now regard group meetings as opportunities for students to clarify, communicate and to understand their own ideas about a topic. I am therefore much more silent in groups of students and try, with varying degrees of success, to behave less didactically than I used to do.

> I think, probably, if you're going to try to establish some sort of discussion then the very last thing you want to do in your first seminar is to appear effortlessly knowledgeable, with all the answers just quivering at your finger tips.

9.4 Summary

● Teachers tend to view discussion as an extension of traditional instruction when they say that the objectives of discussion are to clarify difficulties that arise from lectures or other teaching sessions. However, group discussion can be used to develop independent skills of problem-solving, decision-making and critical thinking, and this too is a major aim.

- One of the most difficult problems of group discussion is getting all of the students to contribute equally. Students can be encouraged to talk by a variety of methods, ranging from manipulating seating plans to avoiding habits which inhibit discussion.

- For group discussion to work effectively, in addition to knowing their subject matter, teachers need considerable understanding of their students and themselves as well as being aware of the range of methods available to them.

CHAPTER 10

PRACTICAL AND LABORATORY TEACHING

In this chapter we first survey views of the objectives of laboratory work for students. We comment briefly on the organization of laboratories and of experimental work, we discuss the role of postgraduate demonstrators and we describe a variety of laboratory courses. Finally we consider methods of teaching problem-solving skills and the role of field trips.

10.1 Objectives in laboratory teaching

Hofstein and Lunetta (1982) present a brief review of the goals of laboratory teaching which indicates that its main purposes are to some extent agreed. The objectives of laboratory teaching, stressed by pure and applied scientists alike, are: the acquisition of practical skills; learning about apparatus and measuring techniques; the development of observational skills; learning to interpret data; the development of ability to write clear reports; appreciation of the practical significance of theory and its applications; the acquisition of skills of inquiry; a critical approach to experimentation including an ability to recognize telling questions, the development of problem-solving strategies and, depending on past experience and on knowledge, responsibility of the students for their own learning.

A report on physics practical work (Ogborn, 1977b) describes how a research team of ten physicists visited eight university physics departments to study first- and second-year laboratory work, and a further eight universities to study third-year project work in physics. The staff and graduates of these universities agreed fairly closely about their aims (*Table* 10.1). Similar results have been reported by Boud et al. (1980).

Short and Tomlinson (1979) provide an interesting example in the area of

Table 10.1 The average ranking given to different aims in laboratory and project work in physics by staff and graduates

Aims	Rankings by staff	Rankings by graduates
To foster 'critical awareness' (e.g. extraction of all information from data; avoidance of systematic error)	1.0	1.0
To stimulate and maintain interest in physics	2.0	5.0
To familiarize with important instruments, devices, techniques (e.g. CRO transistors, vacuum techniques)	3.0	2.5
To train in handling data	4.5	2.5
To train in writing reports	4.5	5.0
To train in keeping a day-to-day notebook	6.0	8.5
To enable staff and students to meet and talk informally	7.0	11.0
To illustrate and drive home material taught in lectures	8.5	8.5
To train in simple aspects of experimental design	8.5	5.0
To teach some 'theoretical' material not taught in lectures	10.5	8.5
To impart manipulative skills (e.g. glasswork, soldering)	10.5	8.5

Source: Based on Ogborn (1977b).

physiology and pharmacology where general aims were translated into more specific objectives and these were translated in turn into teaching methods. Their scheme is summarized on pages 39–40. In this example, as noted in Chapter 2, the aims and objectives served to guide the learner and supply a basis for evaluating both the students' learning and the success of the course.

10.2 Teaching in laboratories

Although the aims of teaching and learning in laboratories have come under scrutiny in Britain during the past 10 years, and numerous innovations have been introduced, some teachers and students still question the value of practical work. For example, Johnstone and Wham (1979) comment:

The value of practical courses for undergraduates has been questioned on grounds of both cost and effective learning for some time. Not only is the ability of practical work to transmit the intentions of teachers to their students not as strong as might be assumed but investigations have shown that there are at least two weaknesses which militate against effective learning:

(i) there is insufficient emphasis on mastery of skills to a high level;

(ii) the student is 'programmed' too much and takes too little responsibility for his own learning.

Similarly, in the USA Kyle et al. (1979) and Shymansky and Penick (1979) comment on mechanical basic laboratory classes and cookbook-like laboratories for college-level students. One reason for this mechanistic approach appears to be that some teachers think of laboratory work simply as a means of developing manual skills and faculties of observation, or of acquiring familiarity with equipment through the performance of set experiments. They do not consider the need of students to learn to apply scientific methods, nor do they ask, in the case of students who will never employ laboratory skills in their professions, whether it is worthwhile for them to spend many hours verifying results in the laboratory.

At the University of Keele arts students are still required to do some science in their courses (and vice versa). Clearly it is believed that students need to be aware of the problems and methods of different disciplines. The question which arises at Keele (and elsewhere) is whether or not arts students need to carry out laboratory experiments in order to appreciate scientific methods. Macdonald-Ross (1971), in discussing Epstein's work (see Chapter 9), raises the question of whether or not many important aims could still be attained even if practicals were abolished. He suggests that this depends partly on our view of science – whether we see it as established human knowledge, a problem-solving activity, a concern with the relation between theory and specific instances or experiments, and so on.

The argument for practical work is that it gives students direct experience of the basic material of the subject and of complex apparatus; it is important, too, since science rests on complex and varied links between theory and empirical tests. The value of direct experience was felt by a student who said:

> I think the tedium was broken by being able to get up and have a look at little experiments – and that didn't really prove a lot of anything – but I think in your own mind you got a clearer picture . . . It showed me that things in the physics course weren't just things out of a textbook . . . You can see it happening, you know that it really exists the way they say it does.
>
> (Ogborn, 1977b, p.8)

Renner and Paske (1977) demonstrated the beneficial effect of practical experience on learning when they compared two methods of teaching. One depended on lectures, visual aids and demonstrations only, while the other included practical work. The students who experienced the practicals did better in examinations, in particular in problem-solving. The students were also happier with some practical work than with wholly teacher-directed modes of instruction.

Some authors, however, have suggested that the value of direct experience might be gained as effectively by devoting some of the practical time to other things, such as discussion or demonstrations or experiments done on a bigger and grander scale by the teachers. And it is of course possible to provide students with a choice, allowing those who enjoy laboratory work to do more of it and those who do not to spend more time in tutorials.

A different way of looking at laboratory work is suggested by Hegarty (1978). Hegarty distinguishes between four different levels of scientific inquiry in university science laboratory courses as follows:

Level 0: the students are given the materials and employ a given method to achieve a given answer.

Level 1: the students are given the aims, methods and materials, but not told the answer in advance.

Level 2A: the students are given the aims (and probably the materials) but are not told the method (or at least not in full).

Level 2B: the students are given the aims only.

Level 3: the students must define the problem before proceeding to experimentation.

When levels are specified in this way, it seems clear that level 0 is pre-scientific, since it consists of copying and so involves neither conscious application of principles nor scientific thinking. Some activities of this kind, however, may be necessary before students can proceed to real science. Level 1 is a little more demanding. Yet a survey of laboratory manuals for final-year students of micro-biology in two Australian universities showed that over 70 percent of experimental work in one, and 97 percent in the other, was at these two levels.

From observation of work done at all levels, Hegarty found that inquiry-related behaviours of both students and teachers were most noticeable at level 2A. At level 2B a greater proportion of staff time was taken up with management activities, such as finding apparatus, and with laboratory organization. There was also a marked increase in the proportion of students' time spent on talk and other activities apparently unrelated to class work.

Thus, while Hegarty recognizes that experimental work may legitimately be set at different levels depending on objectives, the proportion set at the lower levels in the two departments studied seemed high. And, at the higher levels, an increasing proportion of the activity of both the staff and the students seemed to be unproductive. As Hegarty says, more work along similar lines is needed before general conclusions can be drawn.

10.3   Organizing laboratories and experimental work

Most teachers consider that ideally students should work independently, and there is considerable improvement in their understanding when this is possible. However, large numbers and limited space usually make group work in laboratories inevitable. Some teachers turn this to advantage by using discussion within the group prior to and subsequent to the experimental work, or before the writing of reports, or commonly, in the case of medical work and psychology, by requiring students to conduct experiments on one another.

The circulation of individual students or small groups to a succession of experiments – the circus – is common in the UK. In this way, one set of bulky or expensive equipment may suffice for all. A modification of the 'circus' occurs where groups from a large class are sent one at a time to a sequence of 'unit laboratory' classes, each with its own room which is organized by two or three members of staff, and each with its own subject area and its own pattern of work. Students spend all their laboratory time in one unit laboratory for a period of several weeks and then move to another unit. Ogborn (1977) reported that this framework brought 'rapid and visible benefits to both staff and students' when applied to physics teaching at Birmingham University.

A possible disadvantage of the 'circus' for first-year students is that some come to an experiment too early and others too late. For this reason, the 'circus' may be preceded by introductory laboratories in which the students acquire essential basic skills before proceeding to more demanding experimental work. Alternatively, 'preparation laboratories' may precede each major experiment or group of experiments (Johnston and Fiel, 1967). The purpose of preparation laboratories is that complex equipment and intricate procedures can be mastered before the students undertake a difficult experiment. This avoids loss of time and attention in the process of familiarizing oneself with new equipment, becoming proficient with surgical procedures, and so on. The research suggests that preparation laboratories are well worthwhile for most students since they lead to savings in time and improved performance.

Where courses are more tightly structured, as in PSI and Keller plan courses (see below), these difficulties do not arise since students are taken through experimental work step by step. However, these courses seem best suited for introductory work and may need supplementing by projects or by other open-ended and more demanding work.

A 'learning-aids' laboratory may act as a resource room and include a diversity of methods. Poller and Seeley (1977), for example, describe a first-year chemistry laboratory set up in 1973 in a large room with sufficient space to seat 25 students and with 12 carrels. A committee was set up with one representative from each branch of chemistry, and a full-time supervisor. For a modest outlay they were able to supply large numbers of audio-tapes of lectures and talks, film loops and filmstrips, models, transparencies for overhead projectors, television facilities, film shows, programmed texts, lecture notes and reprints, and books. Initially the staff found it necessary to sell the idea to the students that their course would not be completed until certain items in the learning aids laboratory had been worked through. Predictably, the most highly used materials were those specially prepared by staff members for specific courses. The laboratory has been used increasingly and has proved to be a new source of feedback to teachers. It helps to detect, at an early stage, problems likely to arise in individual courses. Remedial aids can then be supplied for the less gifted or less motivated students to help with 'difficult' parts of a course.

10.4   Advising students on practical work and reports

The problem of providing instructions for students is to avoid telling them so much that interest is lost or telling them so little that they do not know what is expected of them. The advice required falls under three headings: organization of work within the laboratory, laboratory sheets or questions to guide specific experiments, and points to note in the writing of reports. Even this may be insufficient. As one student said:

> I know when I felt completely lost, and that's in the labs here . . . We were given a piece of paper telling us what to do, and then they just put us in front of the apparatus and said 'carry on' . . . and we'd no idea how to start . . . they had three demonstrators between about 30 of us . . . and they just came round every half an hour and asked us how we were getting on.

The role of postgraduate demonstrators is clearly important. Ogborn

(1977b) reported that demonstrators felt that their special and positive contribution was their closeness to the students because they themselves had recently been undergraduates. It seemed that the general view was that the demonstrator's task could not be taught – 'you just have to pick it up'. One felt that there would be no point in discussing the marking of reports with examples, even though he had considerable doubts about his own marking ability. The only instance we have found of systematic training of postgraduate demonstrators was at Sussex where a new course served by the laboratory required the immediate availability of about 40 demonstrators to cope with large numbers of students.

Although Ogborn and his fellow contributors were concerned about some demonstrators' lack of confidence and staff doubted their effectiveness, the demonstrators did not do noticeably badly. However, the research team felt that more discussion between postgraduate demonstrators and teachers would be helpful, to convey relevant information about what students should already know and to provide standards in marking, with examples, so that students could be told why they received the marks they did. It seemed possible, too, that teachers and demonstrators, having a feeling for students and their problems, might convey this to colleagues during discussion.

Davies (1978) argues that it is unreasonable for members of staff to go to great lengths to devise and 'debug' experiments and perhaps to write detailed handouts for them, if the aims are not clear to the demonstrators. If this happens then all the work invested may be wasted because of faulty teaching. Davies therefore supplies notes specifically for demonstrators, giving clear and detailed information about the aims and the experiments, the slot in the curriculum into which the laboratory work fits, precautions which should be taken, and hints and reminders about theory. The notes are supplemented by day-to-day discussion between staff and demonstrators in which problems can be raised and suggestions made for possible improvements to the laboratory work.

Macdonald-Ross (1971) gives further examples of faulty communication in practical schedules and suggests techniques to improve them. He mentions David Rees' use of a programmed text to guide students in the use of complex apparatus, and suggests that network diagrams should be used to ensure that vital information about the timing of experiments receives due prominence. Instead of often lengthy instructions written in prose, he recommends algorithms to do the job better. He also suggests that students should be advised to construct their own algorithms to guide them in designing and carrying through their own experiments.

Many students complain that writing reports takes too long, and some writers comment on their excessive requirements. Perhaps some teachers need to reconsider why reports are required. In a manual for engineering instructors, Morris (1950) mentioned weekly report writing which developed into a tedious mechanical operation. He suggested that printed forms were useful for computations, since they can teach order and procedure, and that it would be helpful to include suggestions on report writing and a list of approved reference books on the subjects, in a set of laboratory sheets. In some courses detailed reports are only required once a term, and a brief report, or discussion and comparison of results, suffices on other occasions (e.g. Prosser, 1967; Elton, 1968). Teachers wishing to prepare directives for their students on writing reports, or for their research students writing theses, will find Cooper's (1964) *Writing Technical Reports* useful and comprehensive (see also Chapter 13).

10.5   Varieties of laboratory courses

The recent re-evaluation of objectives in teaching practical work has led to a wide variety of new laboratory teaching methods being introduced. Where classes are large or where students need to learn basic laboratory skills, structured, individual courses have often proved effective, including computer-assisted learning. If classes are small and students are more advanced, open-ended experiments or laboratory projects may be undertaken by groups or individuals. Between these extremes, courses have been devised combining structured, individualized activities with discussion in groups, so enabling students to learn not only from study guides and teachers, but also from peers. Structured courses may also include options or be supplemented by more open-ended work.

Individualized, structured laboratory courses

Some people argue that the number of individualized courses will increase as staff–student ratios become less favourable whereas others consider that organizing and managing individualized courses can be very time consuming. Bowden (1980) argues the case for individualized programmes in tertiary education to teach basic laboratory techniques in Australia. He explains that these have been developed in response to a situation in which the number of graduates enrolling for higher degrees has declined and the number of full-time demonstrating staff has fallen due to financial stringencies. In addition, the greater variety of experience and background among students entering courses demands methods which take these differences into account.

Self-instructional programmes have therefore been developed to teach basic chemical laboratory techniques and procedures such as, for instance, the use of the pipette and burette, or the weighing of chemicals. Each programme is a self-contained unit, using diagrams for steps which cannot be adequately explained verbally. Bowden considers that video-tape is less effective than printed guides since, when students come to use a pipette, for example, they need time to position their hands and to compare their performance with the model.

In Britain, as part of a laboratory physics course at Bath, quasi-programmed instruction is used to teach techniques and in demonstrations. Small duplicated booklets of instructions and questions are provided to lead the students step by step through an experiment, for example to teach the use of an oscilloscope, or to demonstrate, say, the use of resistive paper to plot exponentials and field lines (Squires, 1974). Written instruction used like this can relieve staff of the need to repeat the same routine instructions to many students individually, and while there is little scope for originality, the questions may require considerable thought and understanding.

Cryer and Rider (1977) have prepared a 'do-it-yourself' demonstration laboratory. Their aim is to let first-year students see physical phenomena which they did not meet at school. Following questions to discover what they have missed, the students can perform any of about 15 demonstrations with apparatus laid out and available at all times in proper working order. A programmed script lists apparatus, outlines a minimum of theory and gives step-by-step guidance, with questions at strategic intervals. A technician is present to help and the scripts may be taken home.

Garland et al. (1977) at Dundee have devised a method using audio-tutorial aids to reduce the time spent in teaching practical work in bio-chemistry. Teachers are able to specialize in different aspects of preparation or teaching. Topics are prepared by those who are specially authoritative and imaginative in the field, while practical classes are supervised by a teacher who is patient and sympathetic with students, and perhaps not distracted by commitments to advanced teaching and research. The teachers who prepare the topics may also attend the practicals when they choose. Students are supplied with a list of objectives, study notes, audio-tapes, tape/slide sequences and a choice of reprints and demonstration materials. Consequently, the interactions between teachers and students are now more personal and constructive, and the students offer helpful criticisms of each other's work.

Gaunt (1978) describes how greater efficiency has been achieved in a laboratory by use of cassette recorders with headphones and with colour prints designed to instruct students and to give background information before they undertake experiments. Whereas formerly the teacher took up to 40 minutes to get all the students started on the right lines, the students can now start work immediately. In addition, more students can be supervised by one member of staff. Gaunt reports that the students keep better lab. books, and that there is a notable increase in attention to secondary aspects of experiments. The 40 percent increase in marking is catered for by using lower-grade staff as markers.

These examples and others (e.g. Ferguson et al., 1976; Cryer and Rider, 1977) show the advantages of structured methods in efficiency and predictability. It is clear what the student will learn, and their teachers will know what they have learned. However, the level of thinking involved is not usually high.

Some more open-ended methods

The reorganization of entire courses to encourage creative thinking, or more initiative at least, began in the 1960s and continues. Methods which allow a measure of choice and which provide opportunity for some originality are used to help students develop scientific ways of thinking. For example, comprehensive changes have been made in the Civil Engineering Department at Heriot-Watt University where new methods are now used to direct students away from dependence on teachers towards a student-centred education. Learning sessions replace technological lectures and supporting tutorials. The objectives include the development of skill in writing and reading, in answering questions and solving problems, in making observations and inquiries and in writing reports of observations and deductions. Students make experiments of their own choice and open tutorials are used to deal with unanswered queries (Cowan et al., 1969–70).

Other teachers have developed different ways of fostering interest and understanding. Tubbs (1968) worked with groups of about eight students to help them to learn more about experimentation. A problem was outlined by the tutor, suggestions were invited from students and these were discussed in some detail. The students then chose their apparatus and spent three or four hours in making measurements, each in different ways.

Finally they discussed reasons for differences in their results and sources of experimental error. Tubbs reported that first-year students could profitably spend up to 20 percent of laboratory time in this way, and that the method proved economical of staff time, and usually of apparatus.

Johnstone and Wham (1979) provide experiments which allow students to plan their own work. A team of four students decides how each experiment should be done and how the workload should be shared. For example, to start with students might be given 15 samples of each of four juices and be asked to determine the concentration of nitric acid in each. They would be provided with normal volumetric apparatus, a range of indicators, molar NaOH and a number of hints: Is nitric acid weak or strong? Will colour changes be visible against the colour of the juices? Do the juices themselves change colour with pH? Does the alkali need to be diluted? Will the titration, using molar base, be large enough, or is dilution necessary? If so, by what factor? What equipment should be used for measurements? Most students find this approach enjoyable and nearly all agree that it forces them to plan procedures in advance. The method also has the advantage that it can be used with large classes.

Finally we may note that in order to give students more time for analytical and interpretative skills, investigators have prepared home experiments (e.g. Adamson et al., 1979).

10.6 Comparisons of laboratory teaching methods

Since there are few extensive studies comparing the effects of more with less structured laboratory teaching methods, findings must be accepted with caution, for it is difficult to control all the variables in social science experiments. Most experiments are made with small, or fairly small samples in a single subject and involve testing limited aspects of achievement, often without reference to personality factors, and practically never with reference to the teacher or teachers involved – although their influence could be crucial. And, as we have seen, structured and open-ended methods tend to be used with different populations of students.

The most common claims for structured courses, as compared with open-ended ones, are that they save time for students and staff, that students learn more effectively as measured by quizzes or tests, that attrition from such courses is less, and that students enjoy the courses more, possibly because they are more successful (e.g. see Postlethwaite 1972; Keller, 1968; Case, 1980). In one study, for example, the authors concluded that, 'The structured laboratory provided examples of the activities of scientists and, as a result, caused the students to learn better the process of science'. They added: 'This result seems consistent with our present understanding of the intellectual development of college students . . . We would not expect a student who is not at the formal operational stage in his approach to physics to devise his own procedures which would help him understand a formal process''(Spears and Zollman, 1977).

The evidence suggests that structured courses can be used to direct students' attention to more effective procedures (Moreira, 1980), and that personality factors might be important (Freeman et al., 1978; Kozma, 1982). In general, it would appear that less able and less well-prepared students gain more from structured courses, whereas more able and more advanced students profit more from open-ended methods.

10.7   Projects and open-ended experiments

As a result of reconsidering their objectives, many departments of pure and applied science have redirected some part of their laboratory courses to 'open-ended' experiments and to research projects. Fifteen years ago, most project work in the United Kingdom occurred in the final year of degree courses and occupied about half that year; but, even then, some science and engineering departments introduced projects at an earlier stage. At the University of Bath, projects found a place in the second term of the first-year physics course, along with quasi-programmed instruction in techniques and demonstrations and some supporting lectures and problem classes. By the third term most of the students' time was, and is still, given to projects (Ogborn, 1977b).

Projects have an obvious validity in the training of a scientist. They offer opportunities to study chosen topics in depth; and also demand exercise of skill in every stage of the work: in obtaining information, defining questions or clarifying problems, setting up hypotheses, finding or developing techniques to make an independent investigation, testing different possibilities in solving problems, synthesizing materials from various sources and writing a full report. Thus they require learning which is not developed by other activities in science courses.

In addition, if projects are undertaken by groups of students who examine different aspects of a problem and discuss their results together, then they foster skills in cooperation (Black et al., 1968). And, if students accept design problems from industrial firms, to be completed within given limits of time and costs, they must exercise tenacity when difficulties are encountered and accept the full responsibility of mature applied scientists (Goodlad, 1975). Of course, students, like all research workers, experience not only the intense interest of studying a problem in depth and the excitement of discovery, but also suffer the frustration when apparatus fails to arrive and when ideas and experiments fail to work.

An important consideration in subjects such as engineering and architecture may be that students should learn to cope with interdisciplinary problems. As Goodlad (1977) says, in writing about sociotechnical projects, students have the opportunity to combine technical competence with social concern. If students work with experts or students in other fields, the objectives of communication and cooperation become important. Brancher (1975) suggests that open-ended projects can help prepare engineering students to understand and reflect on some of the changing values of society and to develop autonomous learning habits.

The project supervisor's role is an important one. The supervisor must (1) direct the choice of problem that can be tackled in the time available, and (2) direct the student on how to organize the time available, how to obtain or make apparatus, when to start writing and so on. Supervisors differ in their styles as do students in their needs; a problem is to match them to their best advantage.

The ways in which projects and researches are introduced differ widely. Some teachers expect each student to seek his or her own topic, others give their students a list of suitable subjects but will consider any likely alternative, while still others choose the topics for their students but allow those who are dissatisfied with the topic they are assigned to choose a different one. Which method is followed depends primarily on whether tutors feel that it is an essential part of the training that students should read widely initially and explore new lines of development, but it also depends partly on the availability of equipment and resources.

A questionnaire given in a school of engineering showed that most students were in favour of group projects (Beard et al., 1974). A popular kind of topic was one requiring a specific answer, such as 'Recommend a suitable transport system for use between Central London and London Airport'. Many of the students were enthusiastic about working in groups of four to six, but 85 percent of them felt that it would be desirable for groups to meet from time to time without a member of staff being present. Indeed 74 percent were in favour of a student acting as chairperson, with members of staff as observers available for consultation. Among the techniques and general matters that the students said that they learned from working on group projects were:

● Sources of information, library services, etc. (57 percent).
● The problems of coordination between bodies working on different aspects of the same problem (52 percent).
● What makes for effective oral reporting to a group (39 percent).
● What best way to collect and classify information (35 percent).
● The internal organization of industrial or governmental bodies (20 percent).

Often studies of project work (e.g. Allen, 1968; Black et al., 1968; Wakeford, 1968a, b; Wright, 1968) show that such projects arouse considerable interest and enthusiasm and give students opportunities to solve unfamiliar problems and to exercise a measure of creative thinking.

10.8   Further work on the development of problem-solving skills

Two main teaching methods have been developed to promote problem-solving skills. Like the work on laboratory teaching the first is highly structured and involves analysing a method of problem-solving into constituent steps. This method seems well suited to students beginning a subject such as law, or to less able students at an early stage in structured subjects like mathematics and physical sciences. The second method is more open-ended, ranging from the provision of limited structure and guidance for students who already have some background in a subject, to the provision of difficult problems for able and experienced students who have a good background and ability. Open-ended methods also seem more suited to subjects where there may be a range of alternative good solutions to a problem.

Structured methods

Algorithms are an approach to decision-making which arose from psychologists' preparation of 'flow charts' of instructions which enable the reader to arrive at decisions simply by making a succession of single alternative choices.

An interesting attempt to use this method to train students to solve legal problems was made in Holland (Crombag et al., 1972). Initially, with a view to developing the method, these investigators asked legal teachers how they solved problems. However, this approach elicited replies that it was 'an art', vague advice or suggestions ill-suited to inexperienced students. Next, they invited skilled problem-solvers to 'think aloud'. This tended to leave a chaotic and unsystematic impression as the experts often worked on several lines simultaneously, oscillating between them, or produced provisional solutions at an early stage. Such methods are unsuitable for beginners, since they lack the experience to think of reasonable hypothetical solutions. Crombag et al. were therefore driven to devising a step-by-step working programme. To do this they placed themselves in the position of a beginning student and considered what would be the most 'logical and economical' way to solve a particular legal problem, listing the operations which had to be carried out.

Seven such operations were defined and tested on other problems for general application. These were:

1. Mapping the problem, i.e. rearranging the facts, chronologically or diagrammatically.

2. Translation of the problem into legal terms, allowing for all alternatives.

3. Selection of relevant principles from the total body of legal doctrine.

4. Analysis and interpretation of statutory material.

5. Application of principles to the case in hand.

6. Evaluation of alternative constructions, derived from alternatives in (2), against each other.

7. Formulation of a decision and a presentation of the decision, or possible decisions, supported by arguments.

A later version recognized the need to return to earlier stages as successive steps were considered. A third version was prescribed in the form of an algorithm (*Figure* 10.1) – designed for application to somewhat more difficult problems. Students began with the second version, and progressed to the third and fourth amplified versions, guided by corresponding manuals prepared in the law school. In this way they learned to ask the right questions and to develop a habit of consulting source books in order to clarify a problem or progress towards a decision – a habit needed for future professional practice.

Lowe (1982) describes a structured method of teaching problem-solving to undergraduate engineering students. This makes use of a loop-type model developed at Lancaster Polytechnic which draws attention to successive activities in problem-solving (*Figure* 10.2). It also provides a vocabulary to use in communication with other students or teachers. Informal monitoring and evaluation activities indicate that the model seems to promote effective student learning both by forming a basis for group

Figure 10.1   An algorithmic approach to decision making

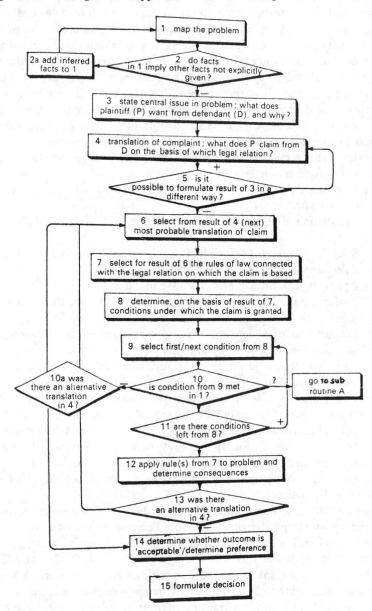

Figure 10.2 Successive activities in problem-solving

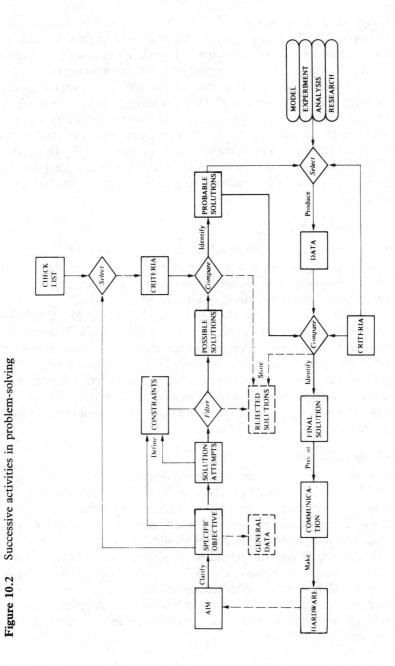

communication and as a form for teaching methods. Although the model was originally prepared for specific use in teaching engineering design, it has been found suitable as it stands for use in a wider range of problem-solving situations and is readily adaptable for use in other cases.

Systematic approaches like these are suitable for computer-managed learning. Van Humbeeck et al. (1982) describe a large-scale computer-managed training programme in problem-solving in applied mathematics, which involves a four-step strategy of which the main features are: analysing the problem; planning; execution; evaluation and help. Information about most frequent errors, and key steps to the solution are also supplied. The authors claim that students learn better problem-solving strategies with this method.

Semi-structured methods

An example of what might be called a semi-structured method is supplied by Elstein et al. (1979), who analysed problem-solving in teaching clinical medicine into four more elementary processes: cue acquisition; hypothesis generation; cue interpretation; and hypothesis evaluation.

Another semi-structured method, devised by Brewer (1979), combined self-instructional modules in plant anatomy with discussion in groups. The method was evaluated by group quizzes and final examination results – which allowed comparisons to be made between successive years. These analyses showed that there was a highly significant improvement in the capacity to answer problem-solving questions in the final examinations, and a correlation between this improvement and the strategies used in small-group teaching.

Open-ended methods

A somewhat more open-ended method is described by Moss and McMillen (1980), for teaching problem-solving in the social sciences. Students were given a group project in which they studied, for example, the future of Australia, and considered how this should relate to contacts with Asia. Six objectives were listed: The students should:

1. Appreciate and understand ways in which the concepts and techniques of the social sciences can be applied to analysis of complex problems.

2. Develop an ability to analyse complex social problems by breaking them down into smaller, 'logical' and 'researchable' components so as to facilitate individual research, and then to reassemble these subproblems into an overall solution.

3. Increase their ability to function as a group by undertaking an interdisciplinary approach to problem-solving.

4. Develop an ability to define and defend their ideas and to criticize colleagues' ideas constructively in an open-ended forum situation where there are no 'right' answers.

5. Develop their knowledge of Asia and of the various relationships between Asia and the rest of the world.

6. Identify areas of study that they may wish to pursue in their main study programme.

By programming the resources carefully, this method was successfully used with four groups of 25 students, each with four tutors. The students decided how to divide the task between groups of four to six students, following two keynote lectures and preliminary meetings with tutors. Subsequently the individual work and the group sessions alternated with the group evaluating and coordinating the individual contributions.

A completely open-ended approach *for able and advanced students* would be simply to supply them with an assortment of difficult problems and to leave them to it, except for discussion between students and occasional consultations with tutors. In the late 1960s some engineering and physics departments at London University introduced final-year students to experimental work in this way.

10.9   Preparation for inspection and field trips

Inspection and field trips are usually closely related to work in the laboratory. They depend for their success on careful preparation and on full information to the students, and need to be timed so that students will understand and appreciate what they see. If the time cannot be carefully chosen, students must be pre-prepared so that they can ask intelligent questions and benefit from the answers. Instruction can be given so that they know what they are to observe and how to use the time available. If a schedule of instructions exists from previous years it can be carefully examined and brought up to date if necessary.

Where the time of the trip is optional it may be wise to discuss the most suitable time for the visit. For example, Morris (1950) recommended that student engineers should visit a plant when it is disassembled for inspection and maintenance, since a better knowledge of internal parts is then possible. He found that plant managers were usually glad to notify instructors in engineering schools when such a disassembly was to be carried out.

Before the visit, the teacher needs to consider exactly what the students should see, or do, in order to clarify and give meaning to the theory they are studying in their department. The details of observations or investigations should therefore be considered, preferably on the spot, and students should be consulted for any relevant questions they would like answered. From this information a schedule can be prepared and issued to each student a few days before the visit. In this way students can become largely independent of the teacher except to return to him or her for essential information and final discussion.

10.10   Summary

- The argument for laboratory teaching is that it gives students direct experience of practical situations and it fosters 'critical awareness'. Some commentators suggest, however, that laboratory classes are often low level, and are not necessary for non-specialists.
- Limitations on space and facilities often mean that laboratory work involves group teaching. Group work, however, can be exploited by using appropriate methods.
- Laboratory classes and project work can be highly structured – which seems helpful for less able, more conforming and possibly overseas students – or it can be more open-ended – which seems to suit the more able and motivated students.

CHAPTER 11

INSTRUCTION WITHOUT TEACHERS: SOME NEWER TECHNIQUES IN TEACHING

In this chapter we review several different approaches to learning without teachers. We examine Keller's personalized system of instruction and structured methods of teaching languages. We consider the advantages and disadvantages of computer-assisted and computer-managed learning. We describe new developments in audiovisual methods (such as tape/slide instruction) and we consider the benefits (or otherwise) of learning through games and simulations.

11.1 Introduction

In Chapter 3 we noted that various theories of learning had certain educational implications, and that modern teaching methods had their roots in these early theories. In the 1950s in particular much interest centred on the possibility of carrying out systematic instruction without the actual physical presence of teachers. The best known of these methods – Skinner's linear programmed instruction – was derived originally from behaviouristic psychology although even in the context of programmed instruction there was research inspired by cognitive theories of learning (e.g. see Hartley and Davies, 1977).

These systematic methods of instruction extended in the 1960s: schemes such as the audio-tutorial approach (Postlethwaite, 1972) and the Keller plan (Keller, 1968) proliferated under the general title of 'behavioural instruction' (Robin, 1976). Computer-assisted instruction was introduced and systematic exercises, based on a careful analysis of the subject matter, were devised for teaching languages by audio-tapes and computers (Lunt, 1976).

New methods based on more cognitive and social theories were those of 'games', originally played to teach military or managerial tactics, and 'simulations' for teaching in medicine and the social sciences. These methods did not entirely dispense with the need for the teachers' presence for they were still required as critics and, in addition, sometimes to lead or direct the games.

Since the 1960s, the main growth areas have been the use of television and video-tape, the development of materials for self-instruction, and computer-managed or computer-assisted learning. Theoretically, perhaps the most interesting development has been the rapid evolution of 'educational technology'. During the 1970s, this term has been used increasingly to cover all aspects of the organization of educational systems and processes (Hawkridge, 1981).

In this chapter we consider several different approaches to learning without teachers: behavioural instruction; structured methods of teaching languages; computer-assisted and computer-managed learning; audiovisual methods; and games and simulations.

11.2   Behavioural instruction

Programmed learning

One model of instruction familiar since the late 1950s and early 1960s is that introduced by Skinner through his programmed texts. This is a rational 'objectives, methods, content, evaluation' model as described in Chapter 2 and it underlies most systematic methods of individualized learning.

For example, when writing a linear programme, the programmer first specifies his objectives very carefully in terms of what the student should be able to do by the time he has completed the programme. The programmer then lists the information, concepts and principles which must be learned to achieve these objectives. Thirdly, the programmer develops a test, or two parallel tests, which the students will take before and after completing the programme. The results from these tests will tell both the students and the programmer what they have gained from the programme. Next, the programmer writes the items or frames (sentences or brief paragraphs with words or figures omitted, to which the student is to respond) making sure that the responses correspond with the most important facts, etc., to be learned, and avoiding the many pitfalls described in such books as Markle's *Good Frames and Bad* (1969).

The completed programme is then first tried out with a small group of students (one at a time) who are comparable with those for whom it is intended. Those frames which are judged unsatisfactory are revised, and the programme is retested until it is thought that most students will respond with the correct answer without undue difficulty. Finally, the corrected programme is tested with a larger group of relevant students, and their achievement is recorded for both the pre- and the post-test. If this achievement is insufficient (many programmers aim at 90 percent of their students achieving 90 percent on the final test), the programme is revised again – the revisions now being based mainly upon the errors made in the post-test. Finally, a test of retention may be made by repeating the post-test some weeks or months later. In short, the programme is tested and revised until satisfactory results are obtained.

The reader will begin to appreciate how much care goes into the development of a good programme. It might take up to 80 hours' preparatory work for a programme which students, on average, complete in three hours. One way to overcome the problem of the time needed for preparation is to share the work. In London, for example, groups of chemists combined to write new programmes which were then tested in their own and other departments (Beard, 1971).

Experimental studies of programmed learning

The evidence from experimental studies suggests that many programmes are at least as effective as expert teachers and that often it takes as little as two-thirds of the time for average students to cover the same ground (Teather, 1968). There is some indication, however, that the best approach is to use a combination of the expert teacher and the programme. Hartley (1972b), for instance, reported that of 12 studies known to him which had compared teacher and programme with the teacher alone, or the programme alone, the teacher and the programme working together came out best on 11 occasions.

Hartley (1974) reviewed much of the research that had been carried out into the principles of learning advocated by Skinner and used in linear programmes. He concluded that there was some support for most of them in certain situations, but that the picture was more complex than that initially suggested by Skinner. Hartley pointed to certain successful variations on the principles: he suggested that students could work in pairs, or small groups – they do not always have to work alone; he indicated that the amount of information to be presented per frame, and the need for an active response, depended on the difficulty of the subject matter, the learner's prior knowledge, ability and confidence, the need for learning technical vocabulary, and so on. Hartley suggested that immediate knowledge of results (given after the student has responded) may be superfluous, or even detrimental if the learner is contiuously responding, but that it could be helpful when responses were required less frequently, when the learner was motivated, when the knowledge of results was informative, and when the learner knew (or was told what to do) in order to correct errors.

Many people fear that learning from programmed instruction will in some way reduce the flexibility of students' learning, or that students will cease to think for themselves. This possibility does not seem to be a real one. Good programmes, if used for purposes for which they are well suited, result in sounder and more rapid acquisition of basic knowledge, providing groundwork and leaving a greater part of the course for more advanced forms of study. And, it might be argued, students who are better prepared or better taught should be able to develop their thinking skills further.

Many studies have shown that students respond favourably to good programmes (see Hartley, 1972b). For example, an inquiry into students' reactions to programmed learning in chemistry showed that most students liked them (Hogg, 1973): only 0.64 percent thought them a waste of time, 6.24 percent of the sample of some 1300 students found them not very useful, 33.23 percent found them satisfactory, while 51.04 and 8.85 percent respectively rated them very useful or extremely valuable. Neidt and Sjogren (1968) showed that such favourable attitudes declined with time, but that this was true for other methods too.

Reviewing the literature concerning the relation between students' personality characteristics and programmed learning, Dallos (1975) found that students and adults scoring low in anxiety tests did best in learning from programmed texts. He quotes research studies by Leith and his colleagues showing that adults scoring low in neuroticism, or high in introversion, achieved more with a highly structured and guided programme than with a 'discovery' type of programme, and that there was a positive correlation between 'need for achievement' scores and success in linear programmes. Morris et al. (1978) also found that students with high need for achievement worked faster and made more errors, and, perhaps surprisingly, these authors found a positive correlation between achievement in programmed learning and tests of creativity.

The Keller plan

Perhaps the most famous extension of programmed learning into large-group teaching and full-length courses was that provided by Keller, which became known simply as the Keller plan or PSI (personalized system of instruction). As noted in Chapter 3, the key elements in the use of these methods are individualized self-paced learning, independent study, frequent reinforcement or feedback, and enhanced social learning because of the student–proctor relationship. However, the Keller plan has often been modified and adapted to meet various needs. Student proctors are not always employed, examinations may be included following groups of units or all units, and occasionally the requirement of high-level mastery is lowered (Freemantle, 1976). In the USA the students' final grades usually depend on their passing a specified number of units, whereas in the UK the number of units passed is often related to coursework marks, and final examinations may be set on the whole course.

Surveys suggest that the Keller plan and other audio-tutorial methods are at least as effective as the lecture method of teaching (see Chapter 3). In general, students respond favourably to such courses (Hereford, 1979). Some authors comment, however, that whereas early reports are 'glowingly favourable', later reports are less so (Freemantle and Blackler, 1975). Rosati (1973) found a significant improvement in students' performance in engineering during the first year of instruction by Keller plan, but this declined later to a standard similar to their performance before the experimental course was introduced. There are several possibilities in such cases: the novelty of the method may wear off, teachers may lose interest and play a less active role, students may use the time they save to study other subjects which are taught less efficiently, or the proctors may not be receiving the advice and supervision which they require.

Modified forms of PSI

A number of innovations in PSI add opportunity for choice or for increase of understanding through discussion. Brewer (1977) and Brewer and Tomlinson (1981) describe the SIMIG course in which 'Self-Instructional Modules' in a course on plant biology are combined with 'Interactive Groups'.

> Participants in the SIMIG course seem able to develop or improve their own particular intellectual skills by alternating independent study with work in interactive groups. They develop autonomy by finding their own answers to

the given paper, defending these in open discussion, and sometimes later abandoning one or more in favour of a more valid contribution. By verbalising the thought processes which have led to a particular written answer, one student may suggest an entirely new approach to another member of the group. The sharing of answers, ideas and strategies appears to promote a more critical mode of thinking.   (Brewer, 1977, p.50)

The value of discussion groups in systematic courses is also mentioned by Stewart (1980) in an advanced financial accounting course, and by Pearlmutter and Pearlmutter (1977) in an introductory biochemistry course for medical students.

Gabb (1978) tested students' awareness of the effectiveness of different components in a self-instructional course on animal structure and function. The course included a package consisting of audio-cassettes, a document file, skeleton notes, and exercises together with tutorials, which allowed the students to manage their learning far more than in lecture courses. The results showed that students could differentiate between course components as regards both enjoyment and effectiveness. Multimedia components were rated most highly for effectiveness. Perhaps, therefore, November's finding (1978) that more able students liked a modified Keller plan system better than their less able peers, should be seen as reflecting on the course rather than the students.

Imrie et al. (1980) have reported on PSI and Keller mathematics courses in Australia and New Zealand. Where the aim is for students to acquire skills in problem-solving, they find the principle of mastery, stated explicitly in objectives, too limiting. Nevertheless, they consider that the principle of mastery offers useful guidelines for teachers which may be used with conventional timetables, lecture-paced teaching methods.

11.3   Structured courses in language teaching

The development of carefully planned oral courses in languages using tapes or the full facilities of a language laboratory began during the Second World War with intensive language teaching in the United States. Since then it has continued in order to meet the needs of executives, scientists and tourists as well as to supplement language teaching to specialists.

Several courses have been devised for those who may have little background in learning languages and who desire only to use the language during short visits to a foreign country. Such elementary courses are based on simple conditioning methods, with repetition of learned phrases, and there is no attempt to teach any appreciation of the foreign literature. The courses depend on analyses of the frequency of use of various phrases and common structures in the language; students are trained to build up associations between pictures and phrases, or between situations and phrases, repeating them until they are 'overlearned'. Meaning is maximized by presenting the basic structures and linguistic items of the language in structural contexts in dialogues. In this way a number of special patterns appropriate to the situations in which the students may find themselves are provided as naturally as possible. The idea is that these patterns are likely to be recalled when similar situations are encountered.

The first edition of the *Register of Research* prepared at the Centre for Information on Language Teaching and Research (CILTR) listed numerous such courses for beginners, including courses in French, German, Spanish, Russian, Bengali, Marati, Shona, Tamil, Welsh and Latin (Lunt, 1973).

Foreign language programmes for scientists are devised by using specialist vocabulary from highly specific fields. In one of the earliest programmes at Essex, Du Feu (1968) concentrated on teaching groups of low-temperature physicists. He invited specialists to provide him with a suitable range of texts and he used a computer to establish frequencies of words and constructions prior to devising ways of teaching the required material. This approach prevents the learner from wasting time on unnecessary vocabulary and any consequent loss of motivation.

Later reports by CILTR (Lunt, 1976, 1978, 1983) show a reduction in the number of specialist language courses since the mid-70s, particularly in languages other than French. However, there has been steady growth in the study of languages by non-specialists, either in combined courses or in elements of courses in other subjects. There is also a growing volume of independent study courses for undergraduates, and during the late 1970s and early 1980s, there have been more independent courses for mature students. The need to teach mature students who have a wide range of different backgrounds and experiences in learning has led in turn to studies of individual differences in language learning (Gardner and Winslow, 1982).

At more advanced levels the elementary visual/oral or aural/oral drills practised in the language laboratory are inappropriate because (1) they are needlessly time consuming and (2) they do not make use of the conceptual frameworks which students have already acquired. At this level there is practically no completed research to assist one in devising graded exercises for students and there are few highly structured courses. Indeed, many people think that graded exercises at this level would be unsuitable.

The CILTR *Registers of Research* show considerable activity in the field of language learning. The *Third Register* (Lunt, 1978) lists and briefly outlines 730 projects in progress. The *Fourth Register* (Lunt, 1983) includes references to research and development in Europe.

11.4 Computers in teaching and learning

During the 1970s, the accelerating development of computer hardware together with input of funds, notably from the National Development Programme in Computer Assisted Learning, led to considerable increases in the use of computer programmes in teaching in the UK. Computer-assisted methods were extended to pure sciences, applied sciences, mathematics, social sciences, business studies, languages, architecture and design (Hooper, 1977). The main developments in the UK were in the use of computer-assisted learning in the various subject areas; computer projects in which materials and expertise are shared between institutions; and instruction-centred projects where the staff of the computer unit promote computer methods in many subjects throughout a single institution.

Since 1980, the emphasis has been on the development of micro-computers which have the advantages of low cost, small size and weight, graphics, audio facilities and reliability. As their cost falls so the importance of computers in education is rapidly growing. In future we may well expect students to have their own microprocessors in much the same way as they now have pocket calculators.

In the USA progress has been rapid. In reviewing development in 1978, Zinn commented that too much was happening to list it all. The familiar definitions of computer-assisted learning (CAL) and computer-managed learning (CML) were therefore extended, using the headings prepared by a committee for a conference of the National Association of Users of Computer Aids to Learning in 1977. CAL here includes learning *about*, *through* and *with* computers, while CML is translated into 'learning support systems'.

1. Learning *about* the computer involves: a. computer literacy; b. data processing; c. computer science; d. professional development; e. in-service training; f. personal computing.

2. Learning *through* the computer involves: a. drill and practice; b. diagnostic testing; c. tutorial.

3. Learning *with* the computer involves: a. simulation and gaming; b. problem-solving; c. creative activities.

4. Learning *support systems* involve: a. computer-managed instruction; b. information management; c. guidance; d. generating instructive materials.

Thus the meaning of CAL is extended from learning through the computer, to include, first, learning with the computer, largely since the introduction of microcomputers, and second, learning about the computer. In the case of CML, this may now include the computer generation of learning and testing materials as well as aids to students with their information needs.

Zinn's optimistic account of developments in computer use in the USA must be balanced with the findings of Sugarman (1978) concerning developments in higher education. He comments that the major user of PLATO (Program Logic for Automated Teaching Operations) is the University of Illinois where it was developed; that there is considerable market resistance; and that to establish large networks would require an army of authors working at 50 hours' writing to produce one hour's courseware.

Advantages and limitations of computer-based learning

A few examples of CAL and CML serve to show some of their advantages and limitations. In describing CAL units for first-year undergraduate maths, for example, Daly and Dunn (1980) show how it is possible to make good deficiencies in students' prior knowledge, so enabling them to tackle topics in calculus that are normally poorly understood and incorrectly applied. This is achieved by analysing the prior intellectual skills required to master the problem-solving procedures taught in the programme, and developing branches in the programme to deal with students' deficiencies. The authors comment that students will seek help much more readily at the computer terminal, than admit their deficiencies to teachers.

Clavering (1980) has used an analysis of language by computer to assist students in achieving appropriate styles in non-literary writing in French, such as business letters. The aim is for students to learn how to analyse a piece of writing and to be able to judge for themselves how closely their own efforts approximate to some defined target. In the early stages of learning the computer contributes to motivation; but once the students are convinced that style is analysable and that they can analyse and imitate it, then the use of the computer becomes less essential.

In describing undergraduate computer-assisted learning in biology, chemistry and physics, McKenzie (1977) cites eight advantages and four criticisms of the method. The advantages of CAL are:

1. The immediate feedback provided by interactive terminals keeps students interested and eager to keep trying.

2. Weaker students are obliged to participate actively; they often remain passive in lectures.

3. The computer will wait patiently for an answer and will not express annoyance with a wrong response.

4. The graphics facility is a powerful aid in enhancing intuition, especially in giving insight into mathematical formulae.

5. Interactive graphics make it possible to sample many more illustrations than could easily be shown in a textbook.

6. Mathematical calculations can be done as readily for realistic examples as for artificially simple cases that can be solved analytically.

7. Large volumes of data can be handled with accuracy and without drudgery.

8. The novel techniques provide enrichment of a course through added variety.

The limitations and disadvantages of CAL are:

1. A programmer cannot cater for every possible response and may give unexpected and unhelpful responses to unusual input.

2. A few students are intimidated by the strangeness of a computer terminal (less likely for physics and chemistry students).

3. Packages can become boring if a student is alone at a terminal for too long; most packages should run for an hour or so.

4. A package will not be appreciated unless it has a perceived goal, and will not be considered important unless it is integrated into a course to the extent of being assessed by the teacher.

Garland and Munn (1983) point particularly to the advantages of animated graphics in the teaching of biology. Static diagrams, they claim, are often difficult to follow in this context. Modern computers have the capability to animate the graphics, which means they can be used, like a film, to show sequential changes and to build up understanding step by step. In addition, unlike a film, a computer program can be run at various speeds and is capable of revision and modification to suit individual needs.

J.R. Hartley (1978), writing more generally about computer-assisted learning, notes that the computer can cope with a class of widely differing ability whereas, in lecturing, a teacher tends to address mainly the students of average ability; the computer can use different modes of response to students according to their needs; records of students' performances are available for feedback or guidance to them, and these records also enable the teacher to monitor the course and to pick out those students who require remedial work.

Most computer-managed learning (CML) systems have the features of assessing students' performance, advising students on their routes through structured courses, keeping records of performance and progress and reporting these to the students, teachers and educational management (in the computer unit). In addition, after use by sizeable numbers of students, summary data can be presented on the quality of tests used. However, few CML systems have been developed in the UK.

In surveying computer-managed learning in the USA, Mitzel (1974) found three levels of use. The first of these he saw as only a high-grade clerical service; the second is typical of most CML programmes – having the features described above; while the third genuinely establishes interaction between learner and computer, using a diagnostic–prescriptive logic to manage students' learning. Since most producers of CML programmes aspire to reach this third level, possibly the distinction between CAL and CML will gradually disappear.

Some experimental findings about computer-based learning

Experiments with computer-based learning indicate that more organized courses may be more effective, that some kinds of feedback to the learner are more effective than others, and that student attitudes have a bearing on success in learning from computer programs. However, it should be borne in mind that results obtained from a limited number of small experiments are rarely generalizable and that it will only be safe to draw conclusions when a larger number of studies and results are available.

A number of studies have compared computer-assisted learning with other methods of instruction, and shown it to be highly effective in certain situations. Grubb and Selfridge (1964), for instance, found that a statistical course was taught more effectively by computer in half the time used for conventional instruction. Similarly, Abboud and Bunderson (1971) found massive gains in learning efficiency in the teaching of Arabic writing by computer. The time taken, compared with two other methods, was reduced by 40 percent, and test scores were higher (particularly those of low-ability students). Tsai and Pohl (1978) compared the effect of lectures, CAL and both of them together in learning a computer programming language. CAL and CAL with lectures proved superior to lectures alone on interim tests and in the final examination, but there were no differences for homework assignments or for the term project.

Jamison et al. (1974), after reviewing a dozen such studies in the context of higher education, concluded that computer-assisted instruction was usually as effective, or more so, than traditional instruction, and that often this success was achieved in a shorter time. However, in all of these studies it is likely that students' attitudes towards the new methods could have been an important uncontrolled variable.

Mahon (1977) carried out an experiment which took personality differences into account using a computer-managed course on curriculum theory. Students who saw themselves as responsible for their own achievement achieved better results than those who saw the system as responsible for their progress. Students who were more tolerant of ambiguity made less use of the system and achieved less, but they compensated for their low achievement by doing better in subsequent group activity.

There are, to date, a number of useful books and articles about CAL and CML, including checklists for choosing microcomputers and so on. Useful references include Tawney (1979), Andriesson and Kroon (1980), Reed (1981), Rushby (1981) and Davies and Higgins (1982). However, those wishing to learn more about computer methods in education are advised that 'No amount of description of CAL is a satisfactory substitute for actual trials by teachers and students' (Ayscough, 1976).

11.5   Audiovisual techniques in learning

In discussing individualized teaching we have already mentioned the use of audio-tapes and slides in science courses. Extended library services now commonly include not only these simple aids, but also a range of overhead projector sheets, film loops, films, video-cassettes and some materials for use with computers. Perhaps the simplest aids are slides for use by individual students or lecturers, yet for some reason teachers constantly need to be reminded to avoid slides that are too verbal, too comprehensive, too complex, too crowded and too colourless (Davies, 1981).

Graphics and other kinds of display may also be provided in audiovisual centres so that their advantages and limitations may be seen or even discovered by use. For example, it may be possible to compare and use different kinds of boards: a white board with coloured pens may be expensive compared with a blackboard and chalk, but it may be more legible; felt and magnetic boards are cheap and useful for demonstrating changes in a process but using overlays with overhead projectors may achieve the same results in an easier way, and so on. Again, teachers need to be reminded that although it may be easy to build up an argument by using a series of overlays, it may not be so easy for the students to record this information without some additional help (such as copies on a handout of each stage of the argument).

The use of audio-cassettes has increased dramatically in the past few years, particularly in courses designed for off-campus students. Such tapes are normally used by individual students although Teather (1976) described how groups of students organized themselves to hear them together. In an Australian study of home-based students, McDonald and Knights (1979) found that most only listened to a tape once, and that the majority of them did not listen to the whole tape. Nearly all treated the tape rather like a lecture, and took notes, and three-quarters of them used the tape material in their assignments. The students also proffered advice for the lecturers. They indicated that it would be helpful if they spelled out unusual names or words, that the talks needed to be presented more systematically to overcome the lack of visual clues, and that it would be helpful if the lecturers could spend some time on the point of the lecture before launching straight into it.

Tapes, whether audio or video, can of course be integrated into other methods of instruction, particularly workbooks. Tapes presented with workbooks have several advantages: the students can pace their own learning, they can wind the tapes forward or backward for revision purposes, their hands are free to carry out practical work, or to make notes, etc., and the workbook is useful for future reference and review. Tapes and workbooks are of course easily portable, and can be produced relatively cheaply. Studies of courses using tapes integrated with workbooks are described by Gale et al. (1976), Long and Povey (1982) and Winfield (1982).

It is but a short step from tapes integrated with workbooks to tapes integrated with slides (and booklets). Graves (1976) discusses many different uses of tape/slide programmes (e.g. preparative, basic, remedial, and programmed). Tape/slide programmes are presumably more expensive than tapes with workbooks but more economical than tapes with filmstrips, but the latter too have certain advantages (Pilkington, 1976).

Another development, in addition to the use of cassettes for distance learning, is that of tutoring by telephone. The telephone was first used in this way in 1939 to assist homebound and hospitalized students but it was not until the mid-'60s that the idea burgeoned in the field of continuing education. Today, in the UK tutoring by telephone is one of the many techniques used by the Open University.

Tele-conferencing is an extension of the basic idea of tutoring by telephone. Becker (1978) defines tele-conferencing as any type of long-distance discussion by two or more separate groups that are joined together by a telephone system. Becker's review of teaching by telephone comments in detail on the important studies conducted in this field, and gives a brief account of some of the more successful courses. Syrett (1982) expands this discussion to include the concept of videotex, where computers, data bases and visual display units are all connected by the telephone system.

Another area of massive growth in instructional technology has been in the use of television in instruction, particularly closed-circuit television and video-cassettes. Closed-circuit television programmes are commonly used to extend the students' experience and to encourage discussion. In medical schools they may be used to show a doctor's examination of a patient, an operation in progress or an autopsy. In schools and colleges, students may view lessons, watch themselves learning to carry out certain skills and compare their performance with that of experts.

The usefulness of audiovisual methods is an important consideration for students. Brown et al. (1982) report that at the Open University student control over the material also affects their attitudes. In an evaluation of teaching materials by the students, video-cassettes were received with enthusiasm, whereas radio broadcasts were far less popular. A pilot study currently being carried out aims to transform the text, television programme and video-cassettes associated with one particular course into a single interactive video package linked to a microcomputer. This will be evaluated by a small group of students who will work through it in their homes. Packages of this kind, which enable students to study at home, could help solve the problem of queuing for materials in libraries or resource centres, and seem a likely development in the near future. Useful texts on audiovisual instruction are provided by Flood-Page (1971), Romiszowski (1974) and Pitcher (1978).

11.6 Learning through games, simulations and case-studies

Although the use of computer games is a popular source of entertainment and learning in the home, the use of games and simulations has made less progress in higher education. The value of simulations and games as a serious contribution to adult training was originally recognized by the German Army in the First World War and later by Foreign Office officials in 1929 when games were used to study crises in a military-political exercise. However, it was not until the 1950s that games spread to business management training where they were introduced to assist with the development of skills in decision-making. In the 1960s, simulations and games were introduced in teaching pure and applied economics, planning land uses, stock market operations, political sciences, the making of medical diagnoses and in the study of international relations. By the 1970s, the use of games had been extended to teaching in pure and applied sciences, although in these subjects games tend to be used to reinforce basic facts and principles.

In simulation methods the participants can gain some experience of the problems facing real decision-makers. The advantages of simulated situations are that inexperienced students can make decisions without disastrous consequences. In addition, the results may be evident far sooner than is the case in the real world. Hunches can be tried out, and it is also possible to test decisions in hypothetical situations where, as in war or politics, there is no possibility of genuine experimentation.

In a game described by Taylor (1971), for example, students experience conflicts of interest in planning land uses when they operate as two groups – 'planners' and 'owners' with opposing interests. The planners, representing the professional advisers of a small community, attempt to ensure good planning while incidentally keeping their office in existence; the owners aim to make fruitful speculative dealings and to prevent the adoption of land-use regulations which are contrary to their own interests. Both sides are supplied with a list of strategies which may be used in designated areas and specified situations, and an arbitrator, representing the Planning Commission, makes known to the planners the consequences of their selected strategies. Since monetary values are assigned to specific outcomes it is possible to measure the success for planners or property owners in financial terms.

In teaching economics, Robinson (1977) uses a game to disabuse new students of the idea that the subject is straightforward and that it can suggest clearcut solutions to problems. Students are put into the position of the government of a country and asked to introduce budgets setting values for policy instruments, such as tax rates. As a result, the participants become more aware of the nature of economics and of the problems faced by economists.

One interesting development in medical education has been the use of live simulated patients. A simulated patient is 'a person who has been trained to completely simulate a patient or any aspect of a patient's illness'. Jolly (1972) lists the reasons for using simulated patients in medical training:

1. Real patients vary so much within and between themselves, that they make exceedingly inappropriate subjects for any controlled evaluation of teaching.

2. Simulation allows any learner to learn a complex or 'risky' skill and still be actively involved in the learning process.

3. Simulation patients can be used for focusing attention on any particular problem, therefore testing students on specifically prescribed objectives becomes easier.

4. Simulated patients, by definition, correspond closely to situations a student-physician will meet in the future and thus they are likely to be perceived by the student as relevant.

Many critics point out that however involved the participants get in a model situation, it is still a game. Simulations cannot make real the consequences of decisions, and this, together with the inevitable but necessary degree of oversimplification, alters their very nature. But most instructional situations are to some extent false: conventional learning in the classroom is also removed – perhaps even more so – from the 'real world'. So, on balance, this is a very useful teaching method which provides experiences which would otherwise be lacking, and which has considerable potential as a means of evaluating students' aptitudes and performance. Simulations almost invariably heighten interest, increase motivation, and may indeed promote further reading and study of related subjects.

Case Studies

Case-studies provide illustrations of methods, activities and problems which cannot be appreciated in their full complexity if introduced in lectures. A situation might be presented to students accompanied by facsimile documents so that the students can discuss the situation and suggest possible ways of handling it. Likewise, a collection of case-studies may be used to allow the students to consider how a particular problem has been tackled in a variety of ways. Another use of case-studies allows students to empathize with a problem and understand better their own development: thus Suczek's (1972) study which focuses on the personality growth of students in their first two years of college, may be of interest to fellow students as well as being instructive for teachers.

There appear to be few reports on how successful case-studies are as a teaching method, although one or two accounts are now beginning to appear. Perkins (1968) has described a course on problems and failures of engineering materials which is based on case-histories that are discussed in seminars. The course increased the ability of students to solve problems independently even in relatively unfamiliar areas. Taylor (1971) has collected materials, including letters, to enable students to study legal and other problems in obtaining planning permission from local authorities. The roles of applicants and officials may be played in a 'game' prior to discussion, and these techniques are widely used in business and management studies.

Sources of information and materials for use in games can be obtained from SAGSET (Society for Academic Gaming and Simulation in Education and Training) and from its publication, for example McAleese (1978) and Megarry (1979). Chemistry-based card games are described by Megarry (1975); card and board games, including mathematics and logic, are published by Longmans. Interactive case-studies have been developed by the Science Education Group at Glasgow University (Reid, 1976). Useful books are by Ellington et al. (1980) on games in science, and by Taylor and Walford (1978) who explain several established games in detail.

11.7 Summary

- This chapter reviews new teaching methods in which teachers play a less dominant but more helpful role.
- The topics of programmed learning, and Keller plan types of instruction were considered under the heading of 'behavioural instruction'. Research in this area suggests that these are effective methods of instruction, particularly at the introductory level.
- Similarly, in language learning highly structured courses seem more appropriate for low-order objectives than for more advanced teaching/learning.
- Computer-based instruction offers the possibility of more effective self-instruction at these higher levels, but at present this is perhaps more true in theory than in practice.
- Still looking to the future, audiovisual aids may be incorporated into computer-based instruction to provide home-based interactive video packages.
- With the increase of cheap and versatile microcomputers, games and simulations may become more commonplace. Such methods of instruction almost invariably heighten interest and increase motivation.

CHAPTER 12

MOTIVATING AND COUNSELLING STUDENTS

Despite teachers' efforts to help students, some still find themselves in difficulties. In this chapter we consider how to prevent such problems which can lead to personal and economic waste. We focus on four concerns: underachieving students, the effects of debilitating anxiety, students with acute difficulties, and how teachers and counsellors might work together better than they presently do.

For various reasons there is a considerable student wastage in higher education. Every year some students decide that they have chosen the wrong course. Others gain poor marks for coursework and fail in their examinations despite good performance at school. Some very able students withdraw because of boredom. Others underachieve because of a debilitating anxiety; and a few suffer from serious emotional problems which require psychiatric treatment.

The resulting loss of funds to institutions of higher education is considerable – if we ignore for the moment the disappointment to students and teachers. In 1976, Dr Janek Wankowski, Senior Lecturer and Counsellor at the University of Birmingham, estimated that his success in rescuing 60 students from failure had saved the University at least £20,000 after allowing for the cost of a counsellor (Raaheim and Wankowski, 1981). At the current rate for undergraduate fees the withdrawal of 60 first-year students entails the loss of more than £100,000 in revenue during the next two years. And since most universities, for various reasons, have a withdrawal rate of about 10 percent per annum, greater success in helping students might save far more. A 10 percent withdrawal rate is an extravagance which institutions of higher education can no longer afford. In the USA the economic advantages of student support services are already appreciated (Garfield and McHugh, 1979).

The growing volume of studies of new methods developed by teachers and counsellors shows that more can be done for underachieving students, and others likely to withdraw. These studies focus on three concerns: (1) aids to underachieving students; (2) modification of emotional states adversely affecting performance; and (3) counselling in acute crises.

12.1   The underachieving student

Chandler (1977) notes several causes of underachievement. We list them here noting, of course, that our descriptions are abbreviated and that students may experience one, or several, of the following difficulties:

1. Some students come from family backgrounds which have no experience of higher education, and problems with parents, families and friends are often at the root of depression and anxiety. Some experience difficulties with the independence of college life following the security of the school. Some are overwhelmed by the competition between individuals concerning excellence in academic life.

2. Some students may have been directed to a subject which is not their first choice because the places were not available (e.g. many students are directed to dentistry instead of medicine). Others may get bored spending three more years on a subject on which they have already spent a considerable time at school. Most students successfully reconcile themselves to problems such as these, but others – a few – withdraw.

3. Some students might have been given inadequate initial guidance about subject choice and start in the wrong department. Such students do better given the chance to transfer. The evidence suggests, however, that students who remain on a course and who remain unhappy are more likely to fail.

4. Some students may have done extra well at school by hard work and rote-learning methods. Such methods are inappropriate in higher education, and these students get into academic, and then emotional, difficulties.

5. Some students may have inappropriate study habits. Some are not used to working on their own, to using libraries, to reading selectively, to evaluating opinions, to doing things without being told how to do them, and so on.

Counsellors can usually help with these kinds of difficulties – personal, emotional and academic. In dealing with underachievement (whatever the causes) a number of counsellors have explored helping with academic problems and teaching methods. Nelson-Jones and Toner (1978), for instance, have identified eight factors involved in students' competence:

1. Planning, organizing and effective use of study time.
2. Effective reading and memorizing.
3. Interpersonal relationships and ability to obtain study help.
4. Writing and note-taking.
5. Meeting academic requirements (this seems closely related to 1).
6. Examination skills.
7. Critical thinking, creativity and contributing.
8. Handling worries and personal concerns.

They note, in addition, two other areas of skill where competence is often important:

9. Coping with numerical and statistical data.
10. Educational decision-making.

Nelson-Jones and Toner review ways in which counsellors may help students with these various areas of concern. In most of them, difficulties may be caused or exacerbated by severe anxiety. Procrastination, for instance, can be due to fear of failure which, in turn, may follow from students setting impossibly high standards for themselves.

Several counsellors have reported on courses which they have conducted that touch on the elements listed by Nelson-Jones and Toner. Many of these courses are concerned with note-taking and study habits (e.g. Demetriou and Parsonage, 1977; Robin et al., 1977; Garfield and McHugh, 1979). The method described by Garfield and McHugh was developed in 1966 for college students mainly in the Pittsburgh area. Sub-objectives are specified in achieving skills in reading and note-taking, so enabling weaker students to learn them step by step. The teacher/counsellor focuses on a particular course which the students are pursuing. His or her role is that of group chairperson, who moulds the small group of students into a supportive learning team. Students are encouraged to learn from each other by asking for clarification; better skilled students may model the learning steps for others, so multiplying the opportunities for peer instruction.

In reading, say, a chapter of a book, the students are advised to engage in seven activities:

1. To read selectively, studying successive short sections of the material. (Chapter surveys are considered too ambitious initially.)
2. To take notes after each section is read, looking for relationships and reflecting these in their notes.

3. To 'knead' these notes, where 'knead' includes activities such as: simple retranslation of a difficult term or sentence; relating main ideas; perceiving relationships threaded through the text; developing new insights. Students are also encouraged to take a fresh look at their text notes – modifying them with underlinings, arrows, brackets and new comments in the margins – until they have clarified or improved their original understanding. If some material is still confusing students are encouraged to return to that portion of text. If this fails, specific questions for clarification are identified for other group members or the teacher to clarify.

4. To make an overview, or brief review, of the notes when the above activities have been completed. This allows a return to the general framework, and a class summary may be useful at the end of each overview.

5. To question notes, i.e. to assume the role of a teacher, questioning textbook and classroom notes section by section. Students dictate questions to the learning counsellor who becomes the student. When at home the student may use another person in this role. Whereas early questions are simple, students progress gradually to asking questions suitable for an examination paper.

6. To rehearse answers, i.e. answering each set of questions orally or in writing, or both, without referring to their notes.

7. To evaluate their answers, estimating the grade they should receive, making comments and corrections, and, perhaps, repeatedly rehearsing and modifying this activity.

In the first session, when students have been sent, or arrive voluntarily at the college learning centre because of poor results, the counsellor encourages them to talk freely about the course and their difficulties. They are assured that the counsellor knows how to go about learning the subject, and the role of the group in learning is explained to them. In the next two sessions new learning behaviours are tried out: the counsellor delivers a lecture adapting the first four steps of the process to the students' subject, and they are encouraged to try the processes at home. In the second of these sessions, students discuss any attempts they have made, and groups begin to work together. In remaining sessions, the counsellor always relates the students' learning activities to the study process and, as the group grows in confidence, the counsellor's role fades. In these ways students' behaviour is shaped until goals are met.

While it might be argued that teaching a single method of reading and note-taking is limiting, because of differences between students and subjects, it seems probable that once students have gained confidence they will modify the method to suit themselves and different situations. It is clear that these training sessions with the counsellor fully involve the students, provide feedback on performance, lead to achievement through understanding, provide interaction with peers and encourage the capacity for independent work. It is also of interest to note that the course is dependent upon students working with materials that they actually need in their learning situations; in other words, the work is seen as directly relevant.

The course described above is typical of many that focus on study habits, note-taking and reading. These courses can be grouped into different kinds on the basis of their underlying philosophies. The courses described below are clearly more behaviouristic in orientation than the one described above.

Bower and Hilgard (1981) describe how study skills for low achievers have been improved by reinforcement procedures. They cite one example where students with study problems were asked to observe and record their study habits for a week. Then an individual reinforcement training procedure was implemented in which each student made an attempt to study in a distraction-free environment, and to reinforce his or her activities with some desired privilege (e.g. going to the cinema) only when a certain minimal level of performance had been achieved (e.g. a certain number of pages read, an essay completed, etc.). As the programme continued the amount of work specified was increased and the reinforcers became less frequent and more abstract. One particular technique favoured by some investigators is to require the students to plot a daily graph of the amount of work done (e.g. the number of pages written for an essay) since, it is argued, monitoring one's achievements in this way can be highly reinforcing.

Another behavioural technique which has achieved some popularity in this area is that of self-control: the research suggests that training in self-control and self-monitoring techniques can enhance the success of study-skill programmes. Greiner and Karoly (1976), for example, compared various techniques in this respect. Students were trained in a particular study strategy – Robinson's (1961) SQ3R method – and received different degrees of training in components of self-control. One group of students, for example, were taught to monitor and to record their study activities as well as to use the SQ3R method. Another group were taught in addition how to reward themselves for completing certain study goals. A third group were instructed in planning activities: how to break down large tasks into smaller, manageable ones; how to timetable their resources so as to avoid cramming, and so on. Greiner and Karoly concluded that the most effective technique was to combine certain treatments: a group that received training in self-monitoring, self-rewarding and planning strategies significantly outperformed other groups on a number of different measures of academic performance.

Alex Main (1980, 1984) has described a rather different approach to study counselling at Strathclyde University. Main tells of how he has found it much more effective to make available a drop-in study centre than to run courses on study skills. At Strathclyde there is such a study centre – a room placed in a teaching building and not within any of the 'caring' agencies elsewhere on the campus. The centre can be visited without appointment and without 'booking in', in other words no records are kept. The centre is supplied with a small collection of books, pamphlets, sound tapes, tape/slide programmes and video-tapes devoted to such topics as time management, essay writing, report writing, mathematical skills, note-taking, reading and exam preparation. These materials vary in standards and format. The important point for Main is that different kinds of materials help different people in different ways.

Students who use the study centre do not need to record their attendance. However, a more personal appointment service is available for those who request it. A rough estimate of the amount of usage so far suggests that an average of 50 students use the centre in a normal week in term time, and that this number is much greater at the beginning of the academic year and just after term exam results are published. Some students visit briefly, some spend several hours, some visit once only, some come back frequently.

Main believes that the existence of a self-help facility helps students in several ways. First, if it is genuinely a 'drop-in' centre, with free access, no prior booking and no supervision, then students do not fear being labelled as 'problems'. The emphasis is on improvement rather than difficulty. Secondly, even the best students want to check out their study methods from time to time and are more likely to do so if there is no bureaucratic hassle about doing so. Thirdly, the set-up can emphasize that students are responsible for their own learning and for deciding about altering or improving their learning styles. Self-help may therefore lead to more lasting effects. Lastly students can time their use of the facility to meet their own individual needs.

Finally, in this section we may note that there is currently much interest on the part of psychologists in teaching learners how to develop skills of learning. Brown et al. (1981), for example, distinguish between three kinds of instruction: (1) blind instruction, i.e. do this, this and this . . . there are no explanations; (2) informed instruction, i.e. do this because . . . the reasons for actions are given; (3) self-controlled instruction, i.e. informed instruction together with instructions on how to monitor, check and evaluate one's progress.

These investigators cite evaluations of self-controlled instruction with college students learning to summarize texts. In this example Brown et al. devised six rules for the students to follow when writing summaries, and taught groups of students to apply these rules and to check that they were using them appropriately. In one study subgroups in four conditions were compared, viz:

1. Self-management: students were given general encouragement to write a good summary, to capture the main ideas, to dispense with trivia and unnecessary words but they were not told any rules for achieving this end.

2. Rules: students were given explicit instructions and modelling in the use of rules.

3. Rules and self-management: students were given the same information as that in groups 1 and 2, but were left to integrate it for themselves.

4. Self-controlled use of rules: students were given additional training in the use of rules: they were shown how to check they had a topic sentence for each paragraph, to check that all redundancies were deleted, all trivia erased, that any lists of items were replaced by superordinates, etc.

The results favoured the fourth group, with the largest gains being made by the most able students.

Another study, by Meichenbaum (1977), describes the use of self-control techniques for developing learning skills in hyperactive children. Essentially Meichenbaum's technique involves talking to oneself about what it is one has to do when carrying out a complex task. The training of impulsive children is basically done in five stages as follows:

1. The therapist demonstrates the task, talking aloud to himself the instruction. The child watches and listens.

2. The child does the task, following the instructions given aloud by the therapist.

3. The child does the task, instructing him or herself out loud.

4. The child does the task, instructing him or herself in a whisper.

5. The child does the task, saying the instructions to him or herself silently.

The instructions for the tasks consist of a set of questions, the answers to which are given in the form of anticipation and rehearsal. Each stage is punctuated by guiding statements (e.g. be careful here, watch it, remember to do this before that) and by self-rewarding statements (e.g. good, doing fine so far, it's coming on, done it!).

The evidence from Meichenbaum's studies suggests that impulsive children can use self-controlled learning techniques: they can learn to regulate and control their impulsivity by using such techniques, and they are able to transfer their skills to different tasks.

This approach can be applied to other areas of instruction. Thus, for example, suppose we took the four kinds of teacher comment found at the end of students' essays as described by Clanchy and Ballard (1983) (see p.137). It is a small step to ask students to turn these notions into questions which they might ask themselves as they are writing. They could ask, for example:

● Is my essay relevant?
● Have I made good use of several different sources?
● Have I presented a reasoned argument?
● Have I presented my essay adequately?

The more difficult thing for the teacher to do next is to devise a list of activities to accompany these questions in order that students can check that they have carried them out. Self-controlled learning thus requires teachers to make the task more structured, and to guide learners in how to monitor, check and evaluate their comprehension as they learn.

12.2 Modifying emotional states which adversely affect performance

The current interest in self-monitoring, self-evaluation and self-control in the area of study skills for underachievers can also be seen when people are concerned with reducing anxiety. Debilitating anxiety inhibits action. This may manifest itself in disorderly study habits, poor organization, fear of tests and examinations, failures of memory, fear of speaking in public even to small groups, vacillation in coming to decisions, and in an inability to cope with academic frustrations. Another less common but injurious emotional state is a feeling of pointlessness, giving rise to apathy which undermines effort.

Some specific anxieties, such as that of speaking in public, may be dealt with by desensitization. This technique involves the person in learning to cope successively with problem situations which are graded in terms of their increasing anxiety level. In terms of public speaking this may, for example, initially involve thinking about performance while in a state of relaxation and stopping at a point before anxiety is aroused, then explaining something to a friend, then reading a brief paper to a counsellor and so on until the person can give a half-hour lecture to a fairly large audience.

Paul (1966) reported on an extensive experiment comparing systematic desensitization with 'insight' methods in reducing fear of public speaking. The experiment initially involved more than 700 speech students, and, from them, the 96 most debilitated by anxiety were selected. Four groups, equated on observable anxiety, received either: (1) modified systematic desensitization; (2) insight-oriented psychotherapy; (3) attention-placebo treatment; or (4) no treatment. Analysis of results showed that desensitization was consistently superior (100 percent success); no differences were found between the effects of insight-oriented psychotherapy and the non-specific effects of attention-placebo treatment (47 percent success) but both groups showed greater reduction in anxiety than the no-treatment controls (17 percent). These improvements were maintained at a follow-up session.

Altmaier and Woodward (1981) compared desensitization with study skills training, and found that the former reduced anxiety more than the latter but that neither led to an increase in academic performance which was measured three months later. However, Deffenbacher et al. (1980) found that anxiety management training and self-controlled desensitization both led to a reduction in anxiety compared with no-treatment controls, and that both treatments led to an improvement in academic performance measured six weeks later. Follow-up studies (Deffenbacher and Michaels, 1981a, b) suggested that while the treatments continued to be effective in reducing anxiety (at 12 and 15 months), there were no significant differences in academic performance between the treatment and the control groups.

As noted in Section 12.1, Chandler (1977) pointed out that a fear of independence adversely affects learning. Counsellors find this a common problem which may lead to a disorientation if students are suddenly expected to act independently. Abercrombie and Terry (1978) commented on students' reactions to change in the authority–dependency relationship during a course designed specifically to encourage autonomous learning. Discussions were held to help both students and tutors come to terms with problems of education for change. They report that, 'among the themes which emerged were: the wish to remain dependent conflicting with the wish and need to become self reliant; feelings of impotence; discomfort due to lack of perceived structure; realistic fears of failure as a result of being independent, and fantasy fears of reprisals from rejected authorities; the exhilaration of feeling emancipated; and recognition that it was possible to have and use internalised as distinct from imposed values'.

When discussing their wish to remain dependent, or to become independent, students made comments such as:

> This educational system has been conditioning you for twenty years to resist thinking for yourself.

> You've got to come to the stage where you say that they don't exist any more. It's irrelevant . . . they're not an authority any more.

> A good deal of the difficulty is still that you, whether you like it or not, whether you reject it or not, still are very dominated by authority . . . Every person has to fight this devil on his own.

Wankowski (1979) has developed a method which enables students to learn through teaching. This obliges them to take responsibility for studying and understanding a subject and to decide how best to present it clearly to a layman. The students who choose this activity tend to be depressed and disenchanted owing to the difficulties they find in studying at university. The method appeals especially to those who, at school, were dependent on feedback from the teachers and so miss the 'knowledge of results' supplied through frequent assessment and interaction in class. In teaching they obtain the response of an audience – in this instance the counsellor who has little knowledge of their subjects – and so obtain feedback on their presentation. Preparing a talk for an interested but inexpert listener allows the students to relax. Thus they are enabled to sort out their material, to formulate it clearly, to decide how best to explain technical points, and so on.

The role of the counsellor is a supportive one. On no account should he or she be 'a model of success, confidence and mastery' in the student's field, since this would be intimidating to a student who feels 'unsuccessful, frustrated and intellectually impotent'. The counsellor needs to be both genuinely ignorant or poorly informed in the student's field and sufficiently interested to read around the chosen topic in order to ask intelligent, but not too demanding questions. Opportunity to reflect on what has happened can be offered in discussion.

Methods of reducing anxieties are usually best left to trained counsellors. However, Wankowski (1979) notes the value of tape-recording in helping students who have difficulty in beginning to write essays or reports, even though they have made careful preparation. This seems to be a common and crippling disability among undergraduates. The students are encouraged to discuss freely the subjects for their essays without too much reflection, while recording what they say. They are then able to use the taped discussion around the subject as the basis for the essay. In the case of a report a descriptive account may be all that is necessary, the student making a resumé.

A different kind of anxiety is identified by Hazell (1976) who studied students who felt 'there is no point in anything'. If they went to the counsellor they were apt to have nothing to say, feeling that this too was a pointless activity. In a few instances this state of mind had developed because students had chosen courses unsuitable to their interests, and so they could be advised to change their area of study. Others, however, seemed to be in a seriously devitalized state, affecting whatever they attempted; activities were, therefore, carried on in a routine, mechanical fashion. Hazell felt that these students lacked a sense of being wanted and valued as persons and might, in some cases, seek someone to hate and fight in order not to feel 'empty'. Students such as these are likely to require prolonged help through individual therapy with a psychiatrist or counsellor. Group therapy as described by Bramley (1979) might also prove helpful.

Rosenfeld (1978) reviews the literature on anxiety in learning and discusses ways by which it may be reduced.

12.3   Counselling in acute cases

Every year psychological and medical counsellors treat a number of students who develop signs of severe strain prior to examinations. This may manifest itself in a number of ways. Some students become continuously anxious, unable to work or sleep as they worry increasingly about possible failure. If they try to study, they cannot take in what they read and they fail even to recall a lecture they have just heard. In cases when anxiety is less intense it may nevertheless reduce a student's efficiency. He or she then puts in more hours of study in the hope of catching up, and so becomes exhausted, and increasingly worried.

In the University of London Malleson (1967) found that about 50 percent of the students who presented had overt symptoms of anxiety. In other cases the manifestation of anxiety took a disguised form. About 30 percent of students complained of increasing torpor, often associated with nocturnal insomnia. These students most commonly visited the university doctors to ask for a stimulant, explaining that their symptoms had appeared at an inconvenient time. The remaining 20 percent presented with physical symptoms, usually of a psychosomatic kind, such as vertical headache or nervous dyspepsia.

The latter groups of students include some who have no insight into the cause of their 'illness'. Not only do they not realize it for themselves, but they fail to accept the explanation when it is given by a doctor. Malleson believed these to be cases of conversion hysteria, where the symptoms can serve as an excuse for failure; for, in the case of genuine illness, a doctor's certificate can save a student's place in college or university.

Some students in the latter group present with the classic *belle indifférence* of hysteria. They are certain that their symptoms have no relation to examination anxiety because they were not worried at all about examinations – quite the reverse. They may even add that they wish they could feel more concerned, for then they would work harder!

In Malleson's view students who show no symptoms prior to an examination but panic during the examination, or suddenly develop crippling symptoms which oblige them to leave the examination hall, have also suffered from pre-examination strain possibly in the form of *belle indifférence* during the preceding weeks. The examination in such cases has acted as 'a last straw to a back already bent'.

When students come for treatment there is usually little time left before the examination; management must therefore consist in giving support until the examination is over. After an initial exploratory interview, Malleson concentrated on giving the students confidence by asserting that such symptoms were common, even in very able students, explaining their cause, and assuring students that they could be remedied. In later interviews he gave guidance about working hours (which were often excessive), stressed the importance of relaxation (when not working the student probably sat in a chair and worried) and gave advice about revision. In some cases drugs were prescribed in sufficient doses to reduce anxiety to manageable proportions, but insufficient to cause intellectual blunting.

Nelson-Jones and Toner (1978) similarly note that practical approaches to examination crises include tranquillizers (assuming no adverse side-effects), emotional support, the opportunity for catharsis so that students may get matters more in perspective, relaxation, and the opportunity to take the examination in a different location.

12.4   Relationships between teachers and counsellors

In this final section of this chapter we examine differences between teachers and counsellors, and look to see how both might work together more profitably. We shall be talking in broad generalities, as, like most things in higher education, there is great variation in how different people and different institutions conduct their daily business.

Indeed, it would appear that no two institutions have the same structure for counselling services. Very few, for instance, seem to combine careers guidance and personal counselling. Some counselling services are offered in a medical setting, whereas others are independent; some deal with only extreme personal problems, whereas most deal with academic problems in addition.

Furthermore, each institution generates its own problems. At the University of Keele, for instance, it is claimed that the residential campus life can lead to feelings of isolation and/or claustrophobia, whereas others claim that city universities have no sense of community life. Keele students report that it is difficult to get away from people you know and that love affairs can have prolonged and agonizing endings.

A questionnaire study carried out by the Appointments and Counselling Service at Keele examined the concerns of students and the sources of help that they turned to (Wyld and Mintz, unpublished). The questionnaire focused on a large range of concerns to see if there were problems that counselling services did not normally come into contact with. Unfortunately only 20 percent of the 400 or so students given the questionnaire responded, so it is not clear how much weight one can put on the findings. Nonetheless, of those who responded, the highest concerns were with examinations, academic performance and essay writing, and the lowest concerns were with drinking, suicidal feelings and drugs.

Of particular relevance to this book, however, was the finding that the main sources of help that these students reported were their friends (26 percent), the counselling service (24 percent) and their tutors (17 percent). This in part depended upon the kind of problem posed. Thus, whereas 70 percent of the students reported going to the Appointments and Counselling Centre with vocational problems, 52 percent turned to their tutors for academic advice and 60 percent turned to their friends and families on more personal matters.

The range of problems presented to the Appointments and Counselling Service at Keele was classified as vocational (about 40 percent), personal (about 25 percent), academic (about 20 percent) and a miscellaneous mixture (about 15 percent), but, of course, these categories overlapped. Currently a staff of four (with back-up secretarial resources) is expected to cope with the problems of a student body of 2500, as well as with problems posed by past students (and staff) who are always welcome. This particular staff–student ratio is higher than that in many other institutions. The question thus arises: what assistance can teaching colleagues give beleaguered counsellors?

Two kinds of assistance seem self-evidently obvious. First, teachers can pay more attention to, and give more help to, underachieving students than they currently appear to do. This is particularly true when it comes to study skills. Secondly, counsellors, on the other hand, can help teachers to develop some of their skills when it comes to assisting with students' personal problems.

Teachers and study skills

Main (1980) argues that academic tutorship should be the responsibility of those who teach, and that it should not be passed on to any central service. He considers that the role he plays as a counsellor does not markedly differ from that which he plays as a teacher. The argument of Main is close to that of Gibbs (1981) which we discussed earlier (p.123). This is that teachers are on the spot, they understand the students' needs and, most importantly, they are seen by the students as the relevant persons to go to with academic problems.

Clearly this argument (put as baldly as this) overstates the case: it is not always true that teachers appreciate students' needs, nor that all students want to discuss academic difficulties with teachers who are closely involved with their assessment. Nonetheless, the point can be made that students study specific disciplines which have specific requirements. Thus advice from a teacher in that discipline can be seen as relevant. In addition, this advice is likely to be more concrete and less abstract, and to include appropriate examples taken from actual and relevant learning situations.

Main (personal communication) argues as follows:

> Who better than the subject-teacher to introduce study skills to new students? To introduce note-taking techniques during the actual lectures when students have to take notes? To discuss the reading skills required for essay-writing at a tutorial when the first assignment of the year is given out? To discuss methods of exam-revision when the first term exam dates are given out? And so on. The teacher of biology or economics or thermodynamics can get across the message that methods as well as content are important in any discipline or profession.

Counsellors and teachers

It may be that many teachers will agree with the arguments put foward by

Main, but that they will want to point out that it is all very well explaining all of these things at appropriate points in time, but how do you deal with students who present themselves later with difficulties, and with the emotional problems consequent upon them? Is there any advice that counsellors can give to teachers in this respect?

At the University of East Anglia Thorne and da Costa (1976) and Thorne (1979) have initiated the Counselling Associates Programme which is offered by the counselling service to all teaching members of the university. Courses are designed to allow the participants to explore their helping abilities. Sixteen persons are selected from among the applicants for each course following interviews by a counsellor. The programme includes such activities as lectures and discussion about how people interact; encounter exercises and games; encounter groups; exercises to increase empathy; role-play of an interview between a counsellor and a client needing help; discussion of peer counselling; and a plenary session in which participants' experiences during the course are discussed.

In consequence there are now about 100 associates who contribute to the work of, and act as ambassadors for, the counselling service. In addition, it is claimed that the experience of communication, self-disclosure and trust among members of the university from all levels enables the collectivity of the university to realize true community values.

Ratagan (1977) has described a single course at a technological university designed to restore a counselling role to tutors in higher education in addition to the established specialized student personnel services. The aim was to develop teachers' interpersonal skills and to help them to see their work in a wider perspective. The programme included discussion of typical student problems and of learning and study skills; and, as in the East Anglia programme, exercises were used to develop empathy. Role-play of inter-actions between tutors and students was video-taped and replayed prior to discussion. Some participants felt that a short course was inadequate to develop the necessary skills and recommended spending more time, for example, in a residential course.

Main (1980) takes a slightly different approach. Main is not enthused about the usefulness of courses but he does agree that teachers can take on more counselling than they do. In order to assist them he describes his own approach. Main indicates that whenever a student presents a problem, whatever its form, his approach follows three 'stages' or phases: (1) listening and exploring; (2) understanding and relating; (3) focusing and assisting.

Listening and exploring are particularly important. Students find it difficult to express their difficulties, to know where to begin, and worry about seeming foolish in the eyes of the teacher. It is necessary at this stage, therefore, to let the students talk around their problem without interruptions. Main uses very neutral openings to get the student talking.

Sorry I wasn't around when you came in yesterday – but I'm glad you were free to come back today.

We haven't met before have we? But I'm sure I've seen you around the Union.

If the student seems withdrawn or ill at ease, Main is sometimes more direct:

Ann (my secretary) didn't mention if you said why you wanted a word with me.

Did I see you the other day looking at some of the tapes in the Study Centre?

These beginnings are followed by more open-ended questions, particularly those that get the student to recapitulate.

Now, have I got it right? You feel . . .

Am I right in thinking you worry about . . .

You said that . . .

This leads on to questions which probe the student concerning how his or her feelings appear to others.

Have you talked about this to any of your teachers?
Has anyone else discussed this with you?
How do you feel X would think about this?

These latter questions establish how far the students have explored their difficulties already, what advice they have received and followed or rejected, and what personal thoughts they have.

Throughout this initial stage Main is careful not to jump to conclusions, or to categorize the student's problems. Quick conclusions or categories can be insulting to a student: problems are individual to them; they need care, and time to be properly explored.

The second phase – understanding and relating – involves the counsellor in supporting the student with his or her problem, and indicating that the counsellor cares about how things will turn out. (Here again, Main advises that it is wise to avoid trite things like 'but of course, that's a common problem', or 'you needn't think you are the first student to come up with that'.) Main finds that he needs to express his desire to understand in order to establish a working relationship with a student.

By means of the first and second stage, it is possible in the third stage – focusing and assisting – to start to focus on possible alternative paths of action. Solutions must arise out of the interaction and from the student if they are to be acceptable. This third stage involves the counsellor and the student in working through and evaluating alternatives together. In every case, however, Main argues, it is important for the counsellor not to give advice, but to focus on the alternatives and to leave the student to make the final decision. The role of the counsellor (in Main's view) at this point is to reinforce and support the decision the student makes, and to help him or her to carry it out.

12.5 Concluding remarks

The argument of this chapter has been that teachers can aid counsellors, and that counsellors can aid teachers. Nelson-Jones and Toner (1978) and Biggs (1976) see the role of the counsellors as one of active cooperation with the teaching staff in facilitating learning. Clearly cooperation is likely to be enhanced if academic staff know more about the counsellors' work and have more experience of working with them. With such knowledge teachers are more likely to be able to help their own students effectively, or, in the event of failure, to be willing to send their students to their counselling colleagues for assistance.

Nonetheless, despite the approach taken in this chapter, there is, in many people's view, a great divide between counsellors and teachers. Their objectives are not the same, and it is difficult, sometimes, for one group to empathize with the other. The counsellor's concern is with helping the student; teachers, on the other hand, have many competing concerns and dealing with problem students is seen (perhaps mistakenly) as an additional burden rather than as part of the job. Counsellors are concerned with the whole person; academics with their subject discipline first, their own individual excellence next and their students third.

Many teachers have great difficulty in empathizing with their students. Academics, by their very nature, have been successful at academic work and they have achieved their position with relative ease. Most enjoy studying and teaching and have forgotten (if they ever knew about) many of the difficulties of being a student. But, as Chandler (1977) puts it, 'The vast majority of students do not find study easy and for them intellectual work is demanding, difficult and sometimes not truly rewarding'. It is only when academics realize this and begin to act upon it that progress will be made in reducing underachievement.

12.6 Summary

● The causes of student underachievement are many and varied. Emotional difficulties can arise from personal and academic problems and interfere with learning.
● Many courses have been run which help underachieving students to cope better with study skills. Some of these courses are more behavioural than others.
● Some successful innovations appear to be drop-in study centres which are divorced from central services, and courses which use academically relevant materials.
● The skills of counsellors and teachers need to be shared if underachievement is to be reduced.

CHAPTER 13

ACADEMIC WRITING AND POSTGRADUATE SUPERVISION

This chapter considers two aspects of professional life: academic writing and postgraduate supervision. In the first part we consider writing as a skill, and we examine the implications of this viewpoint for improving the skills of writing. In the second part difficulties that surround postgraduate supervision are described. Checklists are provided to measure the quality of supervisory practice, and suggestions are made for improving postgraduate study.

One of the requirements of professional people is that they contribute to their profession. This chapter discusses two ways in which academics can do this – ways that have not, until recently, received much attention in general texts on teaching and learning in higher education. These two are (1) contributing to the literature of the discipline, and (2) helping postgraduate students to do the same.

13.1 Academic writing

Contributions to the academic world are often made by way of publications, and a list of publications is seen by many as a tangible indication of effort in this regard. Some academics enjoy the process of publication but many find it extremely difficult. Lowenthal and Wason (1977), in a survey of academics and their writing, gathered responses which fully illustrated this. Some writers enthused about the process of writing: they emphasized that arriving at the end product was by no means the sole reward. Somehow, writing itself, and making sense of what they had written, was part of the pleasure. Others, however, found the experience far less pleasant:

The initial gurgitation of material builds up high pressure of nervous excitement, leading to such physical symptoms as redness in the face, headache, inability to sit down, lapses of concentration and extreme short temper, especially on interruption. Ordering the material presents agonising problems of rethinking and usually destroying whole bodies of the original material: problems of sequencing often lead to inability to write down a coherent sentence . . . The final process (is) well nigh unendurable!

It is possible in a chapter of this kind to say something of value for both kinds of writer? What knowledge and skills has the former got that the latter could easily acquire? What recommendations can experienced colleagues make that might help the novice enjoy the challenge of writing?

The nature of writing

Writing is a skill. Skills are made up of subroutines, all of which are learned, appropriately connected and integrated through practice. Writing, like most skills, involves carrying out many different subroutines – or trying to achieve many different goals – all at the same time.

What are these goals that affect writing? We can order them in terms of a hierarchy, ranging from long-term major goals to short-term immediate subgoals. In doing this we are imposing an order on the goals which, in the act of writing, interweave with no clear order. Nonetheless, when asked to list such goals hierarchically, we might produce something like that shown in *Figure* 13.1. This figure clearly demonstrates the hierarchy, but it does not fully convey the interaction between the levels, and how, at each level, the writer can spend an inordinate amount of time deciding on the actual information to present, and how best to express and sequence it.

Skilled performance is smooth and uninterrupted. Lengthy practice allows the sub-elements of a skill to be integrated so that they require little, if any, conscious attention. Thus skilled performers are able to separate out and pay greater attention to larger units (or goals), while the lesser ones look after themselves. This is not the case for the novice. The novice is hampered by having to pay attention to too many things all at once.

There are two implications in such a view of writing. First, is it possible to separate out groups of skills and to pay attention to them at different points in time? For example, can one separate the composition skills (the setting down of ideas) from the transcription skills (the mechanics of writing) and focus on one set of skills at a time? Secondly, is it possible to work repeatedly in a particular genre so that the various requirements of a particular work (e.g. format and style) become almost second nature?

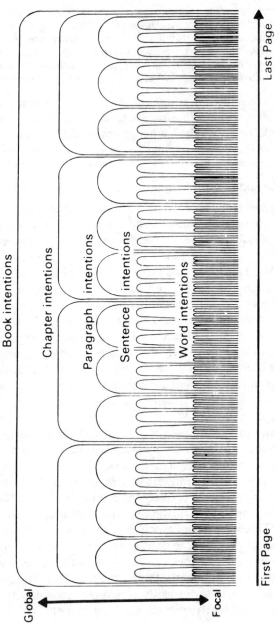

Figure 13.1 Layers of intention in writing a book (from Smith, 1982; reproduced with permission of the author and Heinemann Press)

Composition versus mechanics

One of the first things that many experts tell novices about writing is that it is best to get something down on paper straight away. What they mean is that one should ignore the mechanics and get on with the composition. Elbow (1973) and Wason (1983) have argued cogently for separating composition from transcription skills in writing. In 1970, Wason wrote:

> My own practice, which may have some generality, is to write a complete first draft (of an article) at a single sitting, as quickly as possible, even if it is disjointed and lacking in cohesion.

Thus the first thing to do is to get what you want to say down on paper as quickly as possible. Editing, polishing, changing, resequencing and the like can be left until later. At this stage it does not matter if sentences are incomplete.

Wason argues that this approach is particularly satisfying. Once you have some text before you you are able to question your assumptions, to rethink your conclusions and to develop new lines of inquiry. As one of Wason's colleagues said:

> Writing for me is an experience of knowing what I say. I can make endless schemes of how the piece should run but it never comes out according to plan. Until I have written a paragraph I do not know whether what I am saying is true. Once it is down in black and white I frequently see it is not and then I have to ask myself why it is not. (Lowenthal and Wason, 1977)

Writing genres: the textbook

There is no one kind of textbook, but we can all recognize different genres – the original authored contribution, the edited set of conference papers, the edited selection of previously published papers, and so on. The advice that one can give to budding textbook authors is straightforward. Publishers need to see a synopsis of the text, a full table of contents and at least one sample chapter. It is helpful to provide an estimate of the length of the book, some indication of the number and degree of complication of illustrative matter (tables, diagrams, mathematical equations, etc.), the size of the potential market and an estimated date of delivery. It is sensible to send such materials to publishers who already have a 'list' or series in the field, and it is useful to outline the competition and how the proposed text will differ from it. Publishers prefer original contributions to edited conference papers or edited readings because, one suspects, their costs are greater for the latter.

Writing genres: the scientific article

Few academics get sufficient practice to become skilled textbook writers, although undoubtedly such people do exist. Many more, however, contribute by publishing short papers and scientific articles. Although the requirements are different for different disciplines there may be some value in discussing in general terms the scientific article.

Choice of journal   The choice of a target journal for a publication depends upon the purpose of the article and the requirements of the readers. Some journals are more prestigious than others, and thus might have higher rejection rates, longer editorial processing time and longer delays between acceptance and publication (Gordon, 1978; Watson, 1982). Some people argue, therefore, that it might be advantageous to aim at a new journal which will be initially short of papers than to risk delays and rejection by a more prestigious one. Citation journals will ensure that articles in obscure journals are brought to the attention of the interested reader. Some inside knowledge (gained by asking colleagues) might also be a good thing. What are the rejection rates for particular journals? What are typical dates between submission, acceptance and publication? Do you always see the proofs before publication? Does the journal charge you for publication? Does the editor answer correspondence? Has the editorship changed? Has the editor published on your topic?

Preparing an article   The scientific paper divides neatly into several parts. Typically these are as follows: title; abstract; introduction; materials and method; results; discussion; conclusions; literature cited; acknowledgements.

We noted earlier that Wason tries to write the first draft of a scientific paper in a single sitting. However, many people – experts and novices alike – do not have the time to do this. They can, nonetheless, complete one or more of the parts at one go. We asked five colleagues about how they went about writing scientific articles, and from their responses it is clear that they used a variety of approaches to sequencing the parts. Most of them preferred to do the sections in the order listed, but one preferred to do the introduction first (to clarify his thinking) while others preferred to do it near the end (when most of the work was completed and they now knew where they were going). It was common, however, for the abstract to be written last (Hartley, 1980).

Not only did our colleagues sequence the task differently but they went about the task of writing in different ways. Some points of contrast are as follows:

- Colleague A composed directly with a typewriter (with triple spacing and wide margins at the top, bottom and sides). He revised his manuscript, using a mixture of longhand and typewritten corrections, and continued with this procedure until he had a version (scissored and pasted, if necessary) from which a secretary could produce a clean, final version.

- Colleague B composed and revised his first draft in longhand. He then typed out his second draft, and revised it in longhand. This process continued until a meticulously prepared version, with only one or two corrections per page, was ready for a secretary to produce the final copy.

- Colleague C composed and revised his first and second drafts in longhand. The resulting version was then given to a secretary for typing. Once the text was 'in print' consultation with others took place, leading to major revision, retyping and further minor revisions before a final version was produced.

These accounts are simplifications. As noted earlier, writers do not proceed directly in stages or in sequence. There is much going to and fro. Most of our colleagues wanted to add the word 'usually' to our descriptions of their strategies. Colleague D, in particular, found it difficult to think in terms of a numbered sequence of drafts. Furthermore these procedures might strike many younger colleagues as odd. Colleague E, for example, used a word processor throughout.

There are many textbooks and articles on how to write a scientific paper, and some of these may be helpful to the reader (e.g. see Abshire, 1982). The kinds of tips given are:

1. The *title* should contain the fewest words possible that adequately describe the paper. Careful attention should be paid to the syntax, for ambiguities can result from telegrammatic prose. A useful device seems to be to use a colon to break the title into two parts – a keyword and an explanation.

2. The *abstract* should state clearly the exact problem studied, describe the techniques and the conditions used, and summarize briefly the results and principal conclusions.

3. The *introduction* should discuss the nature and scope of the problem being investigated. This usually entails a brief review of the pertinent literature. Introductions often start by being general but end up focusing on

the specific question that the author is attempting to answer.

4. Both the *materials* and *method* need to be described precisely so that a sufficiently competent worker can repeat the investigation without having to read anything else.

5. The *results* need to provide both 'the big picture' and the 'small details'. The amount of attention paid to the latter is a function of the nature of the article and the amount of journal space permitted. However, if the results are clear then this section might be the shortest one in the paper.

6. The *discussion* section is the hardest to characterize briefly. Day (1977) lists the following points of a good discussion:

a.   Try to present the principles, relationships and generalizations shown by the results. And, bear in mind, in a good discussion you *discuss*: do *not* recapitulate the results.

b.   Point out any exceptions or lack of correlation; define unsettled points.

c.   Show how your results and interpretations agree (or contrast) with previously published work.

d.   Don't be shy. Discuss the theoretical implications of your work, as well as any possible practical applications.

7. The *conclusions* summarize the main findings and state (in the light of the discussion) what conclusions can be drawn. The evidence for making each conclusion needs to be provided.

8. The *literature* cited in the article should be primary source materials. Reference to secondary source materials (such as unpublished data, conference papers, abstracts and theses) can be given in a separate section. The format of this section of the paper can cause the author headaches: close attention needs to be paid to the journal's house-style at this point (and, indeed, throughout, when preparing the final version for publication).

9. The *acknowledgements* acknowledge the assistance of colleagues and any outside financial help, such as grants, contracts or fellowships.

Several journal editors have provided useful guides for authors (e.g. Maher, 1978; Scarr, 1982). Scarr, for example, suggests that the perfect manuscript should present research that is worth doing, and that will make a contribution if well reported. Tips such as these, and guidelines about good writing practice (e.g. Hartley, 1981) are useful, but they cannot fully capture the essence of a physical skill. To give an analogy with driving: a driver's manual is useful, but experience, good instruction and considerable practice are essential to learn the skills of driving. The same is true for writing. In our view, the best way to proceed is to write quickly (following the method of Wason) one section at a time, completing first drafts, revising and editing them (perhaps several times), and finally to consult one's colleagues about what one has written.

Editing written text

Editing, like writing, involves separating out subskills and doing some of them singly and some of them in combination. Thus, for example, one might work systematically through the text and check that each reference in the text and in the bibliography has the same spelling and date, *or* one might check all the different headings to see if their level of use has been consistent, *or* one might consider the clarity of individual sentences, paragraphs and sections.

There are two facets to sentences which make them difficult to understand. One is their length. The other is their vocabulary. The longer a sentence is, usually, the harder it will be. The more technical, verbose and jargon-ridden the vocabulary, the more difficult a sentence is to follow. The same points apply to paragraphs. The longer and the more complex paragraphs are, the harder they will be to understand. One simple way of improving clarity is to pay attention to these two points (Hartley, 1981).

Some techniques which the present authors find useful in editing text are:

1. If the text does not make sense – or if it is difficult to follow – think of how you would explain to someone else what it is you are trying to say. Explain it – out loud, if necessary – and then write down what you said as quickly as you can. Then polish this.

2. Read through the whole text subvocally as a reader might, and note anything that causes you to pause, or query the sense. Adjust the text to match what it is you had to say to yourself to make sense of the pause.

3. Leave the latest version of the text that one has written for a period (say for 12 hours or more) and then come back to it afresh, and apply (2) again.

4. Make copies of the text and ask colleagues or students to read it and to point out any difficulties that they experience. Even better, ask them to circle or underline where they might expect other colleagues (or students) less able or less knowledgeable than themselves to experience difficulties.

For many writers the process of editing text is tedious, especially if the manuscript has to be retyped 3, 4 or 15 times before it is deemed satisfactory. Word-processing systems make this editing process easier.

Two other points about editing can be made here. First, editing can be enjoyable if it is regarded as part of the challenge of producing a clear manuscript and thus one of the skills of writing. Secondly, manuscripts are never finished. One can always modify, polish and change. And, quite probably, editors and referees will make other suggestions and ask for additions, deletions and changes. So it is best to stop somewhere. Deadlines are remarkably helpful in this regard – and if there is no deadline, set your own and keep to it.

Writers' blocks

Nearly all academic writers seem to experience writers' blocks at some time or another (Hartley and Knapper, 1984). Smith (1982) distinguishes between three kinds of blocks to writing. Physical blocks occur when the writer is tired and it just becomes too much of an effort to continue. Procedural blocks occur when the writer cannot decide what to write next. Psychological blocks occur when the words should come, and could come, but the writer cannot bring himself or herself to let the words appear on the paper.

Smith argues that writers may be defeated by the magnitude of the task and/or by the fear that the product will fail to measure up to some standard. Writers may be afraid of a lack of approval from their readers or academic colleagues. They may be afraid because they failed last time, or – more rarely – because they were so successful that now they cannot hope to live up to other people's expectations. They may also be afraid because what they really fear is that what they have to say is really not worth saying. Smith writes, 'This fear has an historical basis. Sitting on the shoulders of many writers is the wraith of a schoolteacher, waiting to jump on every fault of punctuation or spelling, on every infelicity of expression. Writing is so personal and so tangible that we are reluctant to risk displaying ourselves so openly on paper, where we can be questioned on every comma.'

Wason's technique of putting down something, even if it is only alternative beginnings to see what each one looks like, can overcome procedural blocks. It is much harder to dislodge psychological blocks. The most common form of advice given by professional writers is to resolve the block by writing – at least something – every day. Some suggest that one should get into the habit of writing something every time that one sits down at a certain place. Others suggest trying to achieve small but daily subgoals. Psychologists suggest that one can achieve a great deal by rewarding oneself for the achievement of particular goals, however small at first. Blocks, it is argued, can be resolved by lowering one's expectations about what it is that one is likely to produce – initially at least. Finally, some suggest that it is always useful to finish a period of work at a point where it is useful or necessary to rewrite it before carrying on, or to stop in the middle of a section rather than at its end, or even to start by rewriting the last paragraph that was written the time before. The point of these suggestions being that once writing has started, it is easier to carry on. In fact, the most common way of tackling blocks seems to be to leave the material for a while, to do something entirely different, and then to return and try again.

Collaboration

So far we have discussed authors as though they all work alone. However, collaboration between authors is becoming more common in scholarly research and writing (Over, 1982). The advantages and disadvantages of collaboration are many and varied.

Fox and Faver (1982) discuss the findings that emerged from a series of interviews held with 20 collaborative writers. In their paper they describe the intellectual and emotional factors involved in the choice of collaborator(s), and the ways in which the task and the relationships are handled. They suggest that the first step in successful collaboration is to choose one's partner(s) wisely. This involves assessing whether or not the partner shares one's theoretical dispositions, technical competencies and working habits. A good 'fit' between partners can arise if these are matched or complementary. Thus, for example, it might be wise to share a theoretical view, but useful to work with someone whose skills are complementary to your own.

Fox and Faver distinguish between three, overlapping ways of working together:

1. Partners can divide the parts of their project. Here each collaborator works separately on different parts, and reviews and comments on the other's output.

2. Partners can separate the parts of the project. Here each collaborator works separately on the same parts, and then the different versions are melded together.

3. Partners can share the parts of the project. Here the collaborators work together on parts of the project: they might, for example, plan the contents and structure of a book together.

Different factors affect which particular method of operation seems best at a particular time. If the task is fairly routine, then dividing the parts seems sensible enough. More complex tasks, however, would probably benefit from some combination of sharing and separating the parts. If the skills of the collaborators are complementary, then obviously dividing the parts appropriately is a wise procedure. The constraints of time and resources can also dictate who is going to do what and when.

Fox and Faver suggest that scholars working together can avoid a great deal of stress and resentment if they arrive at a written agreement about the workload before the manuscript is actually prepared. Our own experience has not suggested the necessity for such written agreements – trust in one's partner seems sufficient. We have both, individually, enjoyed many different kinds of collaboration as well as the present one for this particular text. The most effective partnerships, from our point of view, have been those where each partner has trusted the other and where each partner has fulfilled his or her obligations on time.

13.2 Postgraduate supervision

In addition to carrying out and writing up research, the teacher in higher education can be expected to supervise postgraduate students – fledglings in the research process. In recent years the difficulties that face postgraduate students have become more prominent. In particular, attention has focused on low completion rates (where completion is defined as the successful submission of a thesis to the appropriate authority). Welsh (1979), for example, reported that postgraduates who began their studies before 1964 showed completion rates of approximately 80 percent in science subjects but only 50 percent in arts subjects by 1970. Similar but even more alarming figures have now been reported by the various research councils.

Clearly, not completing a thesis does not mean that nothing has been achieved. Nonetheless, these completion rates seem far from satisfactory. Data such as these have caused both teachers and learners to reflect on the nature, aims and difficulties of postgraduate study and to make recommendations for action and discussion.

Supervising postgraduates

One of the main areas of postgraduate study discussed in the UK is that of postgraduate supervision. The problems of inadequate supervision have been outlined by many people (e.g. see Rudd, 1975; Hirsh, 1982; Working Party on Postgraduate Education, 1982). Supervision has been deemed to be inadequate from all quarters, although it is not so clear what the remedies should be.

Welsh (1979) interviewed 64 students and their supervisors after their first year of research in various disciplines. She found unanimity in the perceptions of the students and their supervisors about their different roles.

The students expected professional expertise and guidance from their supervisors, they wanted their supervisors to be interested in and enthusiastic about their work, and they wanted them to be well organized and readily available to them for discussion and help. The supervisors also distinguished between their professional and their counselling roles and indicated their willingness to have regular contacts with their students if this was required. Despite this unanimity, Welsh found that half of the students expressed reservations about the supervision that they had received.

The main complaints of the students appeared to be threefold:

1. They indicated that there was a discrepancy between the amount of contact made with the supervisor and the amount desired by the student. In most cases the complaint was that too little contact had taken place (although some did complain of being overdirected).

2. They were unhappy about the nature of the personal relationships between supervisors and students. In Welsh's study approximately 40 percent indicated that they had no social contact with their supervisors outside the department, and, again, approximately 40 percent did not regard their supervisors as the kinds of people to whom they could take non-academic problems. Approximately 25 percent reported that they were seldom given any encouragement by their supervisors, and 15 percent claimed that their supervisor showed little interest in their work.

3. They suggested that there was often a mismatch between students' and supervisors' expectations about the roles to be played by each. Welsh discovered, for example, that some students who thought that the supervisor had a crucial role to play were supervised by ones who saw their role as much less crucial, and vice versa.

Welsh was able to relate many of these criticisms to factors in the situation – such as the amount of research activity carried out by the supervisor, and the area of interest in which the supervisor worked. It was clear that supervisors who accepted research students to work on topics in which they themselves were interested were more likely to produce satisfied postgraduates than those who took on research students with interests in unrelated areas. Welsh found that 47 of her 64 students had supervisors with similar research interests and that 28 of these were satisfied with their supervisors. However, the remaining 17 students had supervisors who worked in unrelated areas: here only three were happy with the supervision that they had received. Also, it appeared the students were more likely to be satisfied with their supervision if their supervisors were relatively young, that is, if they had less than five years' teaching experience.

Methods and styles of postgraduate supervision

Welsh (1979) distinguished (on the basis of her interviews with supervisors) between three styles or methods of supervision:

1. Highly direct in the early stages of research for all students, even the most able ones, then gradually diminishing as the students find their own feet:

> If a postgraduate needs a supervisor all the way through his research period, he shouldn't be doing research.

2. Direct in the initial and final stages of the research period, with a lengthy period of quiescence in the middle:

> I help to formulate a viable research project, I then retreat providing encouragement and advice only if required, and then move back into a prominent role nearer the writing up stage.

3. Direct throughout the entire period:

> The supervisor must at all times be closely aware of what the student is doing.

Her interviews with the students, however, led Welsh to introduce a fourth method:

4. Non-direct – here the supervisor is a remote figure to the student, providing the minimum guidance and having little contact at any stage of the student's research period.

> My supervisor has been inadequate. He never gives specific criticism of my research. He did not object to my chosen topic yet cannot advise me on how to go about it. He allowed me to finish the thesis, read all the chapters, but then gave me a vague warning that all was not right when the thesis was put together. I hesitate to go to other staff members for fear of insulting him.
>
> (Rudd, 1975)

Cutting across these methods of supervision are certain styles of approach which we may caricature as the 'science' and 'arts' approaches respectively. At one end the PhD is a 'training'; at the other it is an 'opportunity for independent thinking'. Different approaches stem from different degrees of emphasis on points along this continuum.

The 'science' approach provides a clear model for the student to follow. Often, for example, in the first term students might be given a problem in their area of interest (or, more likely, in the area of their supervisor's interest) and asked to solve it, or to complete a literature review on the topic. Or the student may be given an experiment to do – one which may be a replication of one already published. Simply stated, the aim of the science approach seems to be to get the apprentice started: the problem is pre-defined or imposed.

In the 'arts' and 'social sciences', however, the students are often left to develop by themselves. Typically it is suggested to them that they read around in an area and try to work up a topic that might be researched. Generally students seem to cast about for three to nine months or even a year before finding something suitable. The task is to formulate a problem. The supervisor's role is much less directive: the aim initially is to make vague suggestions and then to push more firmly later. The attitude of some supervisors seems to be that if students cannot teach themselves they are not worth taking on.

Arts students seem to be the most isolated. One student of our acquaintance, during her studies for a PhD in English, obtained a list of other students in London working on similar topics and formed a discussion group which met regularly. This gave them the support they needed; otherwise students were withdrawing owing to depression and uncertainties which developed during hours of solitary study.

Thus both approaches, in their extreme form, have their advantages and limitations. Nonetheless, across all of these different methods and styles are some common concerns shared, with varying degrees, by all supervisors. These are: how to get the students started; how to maintain their enthusiasm; how to keep them to a reasonable time schedule; how to assist them in 'writing up'.

Experienced colleagues have made a number of suggestions about how supervisors can help in each of these areas, but little has been written about the last two. As far as 'writing up' is concerned, Welsh (1979) and Galbraith (1980) have outlined the difficulties in more detail than most. In her study of 64 postgraduates Welsh found that one-third had not submitted any form of written work in their first year, 40 percent admitted to having no idea of the standard required in a thesis, and a further 35 percent said that they only had a vague idea of what was involved.

Welsh suggested that written work, taking the form of planning proposals, literature reviews and first drafts, should be encouraged. The supervisor needs to give particular attention to the regular achievement of subgoals if the student is to avoid those tempting lures to procrastination. The guides we gave earlier on in this chapter about writing and publishing are, of course, also relevant to postgraduate students, and additional, specialist guides are available (e.g. Howard and Sharp, 1983).

A supervisor's checklist

In 1983 the Science and Engineering Research Council produced a pamphlet entitled *Research Student and Supervisor: an Approach to Good Supervisory Practice*. This pamphlet concluded with the following checklist:

1. Is there a departmental document available to students and supervisors, laying out the department's view on good supervisory practice?
2. What steps are taken to try and make a good match between a supervisor and the prospective student?
3. Is the student given a reading guide for the summer vacation after graduation?
4. Does the student present a report in the first year which is assessed by people other than the supervisor?
5. Does the student see the supervisor often enough?
6. Are there regular occasions when the student's progress and background knowledge of the subject are both assessed?
7. Is the first-year assessment procedure seen as satisfactory by both supervisor and student?
8. Are there occasions when the student has to make a public presentation and are these presentations satisfactory?
9. How is the topic of research refined in the first year?
10. When is a long-term programme of research laid out and has a critical path been defined?
11. Is there a point where the supervisor checks the student's record-keeping to see whether it is systematic?
12. Is it clear by half-way into the second year that it is possible to finish the project in the three years?
13. Does the student get a mock viva between six and twelve months before he is due to submit?

To these items we would add at least five more:

14. Has the student been shown in the first year a typical thesis which might indicate the kind of thing he or she is expected to produce?
15. Has the student been shown the supervisor's termly report (or does he or she obtain any indication of its contents)?
16. Has the supervisor read, commented on and speedily returned any preliminary written materials prepared by the student?
17. Has the student been shown the instructions given to the external examiners about what they are required to look for and comment on?
18. Do supervisors discuss with other members of staff various strategies and tactics for dealing with problems that arise?

The Council's checklist also included seven items for students which it seems appropriate to list here too:

1. Have you tried to plan your work satisfactorily?

2. Have you identified the major difficulties?
3. Do you understand the relevant references?
4. Are your records in good order and could you answer a question on something you did six months ago?
5. Have you drafted the first version of any portion of the work that has been completed?
6. Do other people find your written English difficult to understand?
7. Are there any tables, figures or other matter which could usefully be prepared at an early stage?

Finally in this section, we might observe that the Economic and Social Research Council (ESRC) has taken several steps to improve supervision and completion rates. Both students and supervisors are now required to write an annual report on their progress, and at the end of the grant period a lengthy report is required from both, which sets out in detail their progress to date. If the thesis has not been submitted supervisors are asked to say when they think it will be completed and what steps they propose to take to ensure it. If there have been no publications from the thesis the supervisor is asked to outline his or her plans for encouraging the student to disseminate the results of the research.

In addition, the ESRC has in hand the process of changing the nature of the PhD degree in the social sciences. Departments are being asked to organize a one-year training programme in research methods (on which the students' performance will be assessed). These training programmes are to be taken before beginning the thesis proper. Such a procedure reflects a change in thinking about the nature of the PhD: the emphasis is now being put more clearly on the notion that it involves training in research rather than discovering and reporting original research.

Some different approaches to postgraduate research

In discussing ways of improving the quality of postgraduate supervision a number of writers have made suggestions about how the existing system might be changed. In this section we consider some of these suggestions.

Separating supervising from examining. Many people find the notion that the supervisor should also be the internal examiner somewhat distasteful. They recommend that some other member in the department concerned should take on the internal examiner's role at the appropriate time. To provide another examiner may be possible in large departments but it may not be practical in small ones. Difficulties might also arise, for example, if the supervisor was the head of the department and the internal examiner was a more junior member (especially if the latter wished to fail the thesis). Nonetheless, it would seem reasonable that the supervisor should not be an examiner if this can be arranged.

Group supervision   Several commentators have suggested that the single supervisor should be replaced by either a committee system or by two (or more) joint supervisors. Students would appear regularly before such committees to give an account of their progress and to discuss their future plans. As Rudd (1975) points out, this procedure would not only give students practice at exposition but it would also lead to a more thorough and open review of progress. This openness would make it clear whether or not the student was being adequately supervised.

Relatedly, of course, some movement might be made in the direction of making the final viva and defence of the thesis more open (along US and Canadian lines, for example).

Interim assessment   One way of improving students' completion rates might be to increase or to implement already existing provisions for making some interim assessment on the way. It is fairly common, for example, for some universities to require candidates to submit a Master's thesis after the first year of their research before being allowed to progress to the PhD. However, it is also fairly common for universities to waive this requirement and to allow the student to progress directly to the PhD. The advantages and disadvantages of this approach are many and varied (e.g. see Woodman, 1982).

Clearly different departments might have different views. A comment by the Royal Economic Society quoted in the report of the Working Party on Postgraduate Education (1982) seems appropriate here:

> Many University teachers would regard the taking of a Master's degree in Economics as a good deal more important than the taking of a Ph.D. A Master's degree followed by a Ph.D. is probably the best training of all for someone who wishes to be an academic, but it is doubtful whether the extensive thesis work associated with a Ph.D. is of much value for an Economist wishing to go into business or public service . . . We therefore welcome the trend towards a Master's degree and towards Ph.D.s which involve the equivalent of a Master's degree as a prerequisite.

More flexible requirements for the PhD   Other writers have suggested more dramatic changes in the nature of the PhD and how students might go about achieving one. Baddeley (1979), for instance, called for a rejection of the typical (and in his view, turgid) thesis in favour of a literature review and two published papers. This view was not supported by many colleagues in Baddeley's profession (psychology): most of them wished to see the thesis retained as the main contender among several options (Baddeley, 1983).

Other writers have suggested that there should be more flexibility in the research training given in the first year (e.g. Baum, 1979). The argument is that if students can accomplish a variety of tasks successfully in their first year then they and their supervisors will be better able to judge whether or not they should go on to complete a PhD.

An example of this in practice is provided in the LSE social geography department where in 1972–1973, Professor Michael Wise had 16 or more postgraduate students who shared one small room (as space is at a premium in LSE). These students were taken through systematic exercises – a literature survey, exercises in analysing data, etc. – and had the benefit of discussing their work with peers as well as supervisors/tutors. When they proceeded to a PhD (some were quite content with MSc) they had a supervisor and could choose up to three additional tutors. If students wished to specialize in physical geography, they could be supervised by someone from King's College (LSE and King's have a reciprocal arrangement). In the event that students did not get on well with the supervisor, they could transfer to another tutor. This did not cause ill-feeling.

Joint research Finally, we may note the isolation of postgraduate students. They are few and far between in most departments and, being neither student nor staff, they work in a no-man's land. They have few colleagues who are familiar or interested in the minutiae of their academic research. This isolation (which is particularly acute among foreign students) has been well documented by Rudd (1975) and Welsh (1979). One suggestion worth exploring further in this context is whether or not some forms of joint research might be considered. Certainly the research councils have responded favourably to this notion by providing 'linked studentships', that is, awards for individual students to do their research 'linked' to an ongoing research team. While welcoming these developments, however, the Working Party on Postgraduate Education (1982) felt it necessary to comment that it was not easy to achieve satisfactory training of students within group research, and that there could be conflict between training in group research and traditional PhD requirements.

Conclusions

All of the considerations discussed in this final section of this chapter were clearly in the minds of members of the Working Party on Postgraduate Education (1982). They concluded their report on postgraduate training with the following recommendations:

A. On research training we recommend

(i) all research students be given a thorough grounding in research techniques as an integral part of their training

(ii) the choice of research topics should be heavily influenced by the staff and, where appropriate, also from outside the academic institution; this is to ensure that the topic is a suitable subject for research training, that it is likely to prove a rewarding investigation, that it is of practical benefit where this is possible, that competent supervision is available and that the work can be completed within the time available

(iii) since a great deal of substantive scientific research is carried out in groups, students should, wherever possible, work either in related groups or as part of an ongoing substantive research project; if this leads to PhD theses different in form from the present and at variance with current university regulations then the regulations should be amended

(iv) there should be frequent contact between supervisors and students, with part supervision from outside the institution whenever this is feasible, and regular checks on the quality of supervision preferably by a supervising committee

(v) towards the end of the student's first year there should be detailed and careful consideration of his suitability to continue with research training

(vi) much more attention should be paid to completion of the research investigation within three years and the thesis presented at the latest one year afterwards (we recognise that in the social sciences this might mean some reassessment of the nature of the PhD degree).

B. To the Research Councils that

(i) they should take into account the benefits of larger departments in allocating research quotas

(ii) they should routinely maintain and publish statistics of submission rates for PhD students whom they support by individual universities, and they should take such steps, up to and including the withdrawal of quotas, as are necessary to ensure that completion usually takes place within four years

(iii) they should also discriminate in favour of those institutions and departments which effect the policies at A(i) – (vi) above

(iv) they should harmonise their regulations in respect of their awards.

These salutary remarks remind one that postgraduate supervision is not a trivial matter. Good supervision requires time and effort – and a moral obligation from both supervisor and student.

13.3   Summary

- This chapter reviewed two aspects of professional life – academic writing and postgraduate supervision.
- If writing can be viewed as a skill then certain implications ensue: subroutines can be practised separately, and practice in different genres can make performance almost second nature.
- Most writers experience writers' blocks of one kind or another at certain times. Many resolve such blocks either by doing something else for a while, or by leaving off writing at a point from where it is easy to pick it up again.
- One fruitful way of proceeding is to write in collaboration with someone else. This can be rewarding if partners trust each other and complete their obligations on time.
- Many postgraduate students find 'writing up' difficult, and low completion rates for postgraduate students have drawn attention to the difficulties of postgraduate supervision.
- Supervision seems more satisfactory when students research topics in which their supervisors share an interest, and when their supervisors are relatively young.
- There are many different methods and styles of supervisory practice, ranging from the 'science' to the 'arts' model. New approaches involve separating supervising from examining, moving towards group supervision, using interim assessments, making the PhD requirements more flexible and exploring group or joint research.

PART FIVE

EVALUATION

CHAPTER 14

EVALUATING STUDENTS, COURSES AND TEACHERS

This chapter is divided into four parts. Part One sets the scene and indicates how, today, techniques of assessment are much more varied than in the past. Part Two examines the assessment of students: attention is drawn to the unreliability of the essay examination, attempts to make it more reliable and alternative methods of examining. Part Three examines the more general and ongoing effects of courses on students and teachers. Finally, in Part Four the evaluation of teaching is considered: particular attention is paid to the advantages and limitations of student ratings for improving courses and for providing evidence of teaching effectiveness.

14.1 Changing practices in evaluation

The changing practices in teaching and learning in higher education that we have discussed in earlier chapters are inevitably reflected in changing methods of evaluation. *Table* 2.3 (p.36) showed, for instance, how the different kinds of objectives that we discussed in Chapter 2 were related to different methods of teaching, and to different techniques of evaluation. Today there is more emphasis on evaluating the process of learning, and less on evaluating what is recalled or retained at the end of a course, and a greater interest in the contributions that can be made with continuous or course-work assessment. Above all there is much more variety in assessment than used to be the case.

Continuous assessment

When the NUS (1969b) argued in favour of continuous assessment, they meant 'a system of assessment by which all aspects of a student's work during his time at college are taken into account – tutorial essays, practicals, seminar contributions, dissertations, etc. as well as written examinations'. In this way, they claimed, teachers and students alike would get continued feedback on performance. In discussing such methods they found different responses: 'On the one hand staff and students speak of the continued strain involved in this system, but others speak of a reduction in nervous tension and a feeling that the individual had a fair chance to demonstrate his capabilities . . . If judgement is based on a candidate's performance over three years it is more difficult for society to brush it aside.' They appreciated the possibility that students might be more concerned about any bias they suspected in tutors' judgements when marking coursework, and the problems of external examiners called on to compare essays or projects which were essentially different in kind, but they felt that such a varied form of continuous assessment was fairer to students and more meaningful to employers.

In the USA continuous assessment often takes the form of weekly or fortnightly tests in which grades are assigned to contribute towards the students' overall assessment at the end of the year. Those who favour this system claim that it encourges hard work. In one inquiry, however, Burke (1968) found that students assessed in this way reported adverse effects both on their own work and on teaching. In another study, which compared students frequently graded with those who were not, the results suggested that the former tended to cram for exams, and to cut courses not directly relevant to them (Johnson and Abrahamson, 1968).

Coursework assessment

An alternative to continuous assessment, designed to avoid the continued strain on the staff of marking, and on the students of constant preparation, is to introduce intermittent assessment of coursework. With a procedure of this kind, the two best essays out of three for a term may be included in the assessment, or three experiments chosen for discussion in a viva, and so on. Staff agree that under such a system students may not always work hard, but they prefer this to continuous assessment if the latter leaves no time for thought or for intensive pursuit of special interests.

Methods such as these are still relatively rare. Legge (1981) weighs advantages and disadvantages of coursework assessment – in this instance in psychology. He sees it as being less concentrated than the end-of-term examination; it prevents failure due to a 'bad day'; the threat of an unseen paper is removed; there is closer simulation of occupational activities where there is access to various resources so that one need not work 'out of one's head'; achievement is likely to be high. On the other hand, students can, in theory, concentrate only on the topics which they present for assessment; they may not be motivated to study on a broad front; and there are many deadlines to meet which may encourage plagiarism or cheating under stress. This, in turn, involves stress on staff in policing, and, since coursework submissions are substantially longer than examination scripts, different criteria are needed in marking.

When discussing the pros and cons of continuous or coursework assessment, differences between students are seldom mentioned. Commonly it is said that mature students and those more intellectually advanced are likely to appreciate a form of assessment which allows them to study in depth, whereas younger and less well-equipped students vary in their attitudes towards continuous testing. At Bradford University different first-year students said of the *same* system of assessment:

> It's a lot easier to work gently all through the year than to make a mad rush just before exams.

> I don't mind continuous assessment for practicals but I'd prefer a major exam on theory. I think continuous assessment is more strain.

> It's a bit difficult really, because you want to do extra work like background reading but you must use the time to revise for tests.

It is for the last of these reasons that some advanced students prefer examinations, whereas those who have built up inhibitions about examinations prefer to be assessed more continuously.

Studies of coursework assessment are few and far between. It is generally acknowledged that including coursework with other examination marks raises the final mark obtained, but this effect is often exaggerated by both staff and students (Hartley and Branthwaite, 1977). Two inquiries (Carpenter, 1975; Chansaker and Rautray, 1980) both reported that students put their main efforts into those parts of the course that were assessed. A study by Hartley and Branthwaite (1976) suggested that students tended to tailor their strategies to whatever system of evaluation was being used. Thomas (1976), however, reported that coursework assessment had a broadening rather than a limiting effect in the German department at Warwick.

Self- and peer assessment

Boud and Lublin (1983) argue that it is important that students should develop a capacity for self-assessment for several reasons: (1) self-assessment is a necessary component of independent or autonomous thinking; (2) students should move from dependence on external assessment to independent self-assessment; (3) realistic self-assessment is an essential component of professional practice.

Today, self- and peer assessments are being increasingly encouraged. As we saw in Chapter 11, much self-assessment is built into computer-assisted learning and PSI or Keller plan courses where proctors learn to assess other students' work and to discuss it with them. Bruffee (1978) finds that a much deeper understanding is achieved by peer tutors. Learning to criticize their own work or that of their peers gives students insights into what is required and, presumably, it increases their ability to assess their own performances.

A particularly interesting investigation of self- and peer assessment is reported by Boud and Lublin (1983). In the first class following a mid-term examination engineering students were randomly allocated an (unnamed) paper from one of the other students in the class (of over 100 students). They marked the paper in their own time, following model answers and a marking schedule prepared in advance by the staff. Each student exchanged the marked paper the following week in return for his or her own paper. The students then marked their own paper, using the same criteria, and unaware of the marks they had been given. Finally, the two marks were compared. If they were within 10 percent of each other the student was awarded his or her own self-mark. If the discrepancy was greater than 10 percent then the paper was re-marked by a member of staff. In addition the staff sampled other papers at random to discourage mark fixing. Boud and Lublin do not report on the amount of agreement between the students; they do comment, however, that the students liked the procedure, and that there were considerable savings in staff time as far as marking was concerned.

It seems questionable whether self- and peer assessment should be included in a final assessment. Orpen (1982) reports assessment both by lecturers and by peers of essays written by students in organizational behaviour and political philosophy courses. There was no significance between them in (1) the average mark assigned, (2) the variation of the marks, (3) the extent to which their marks agreed with each other, (4) the relationship between the marks they gave and the writer's performance in end-of-course examinations. Orpen argues that since they proved equally valid and reliable it might be reasonable to allow peer marking in place of marking by lecturers from time to time. Gilbert (1976) suggests that peer assessment may be more consistent than that of instructors, while Sims (1976) finds that students are generally fair and objective markers.

A useful survey of findings concerning peer and self-assessment, with a substantial bibliographic reference, has been written by Boud (1980).

14.2 Evaluating students: assessment by examinations

The content of examinations

A number of psychologists and teachers collected evidence about the limited content of some examinations during the 1960s and 1970s. In the USA McGuire (1963) used taxonomies of educational objectives to analyse the content of objective tests used in medical examinations. She found that 78 percent of test items fell into the lowest category of 'isolated recall', 5 percent required recognition of learning of a fact or concept, 11 percent involved ability to generalize, leaving only 7 percent in five higher categories; of these, 'unfamiliar application' and 'ability to synthesize' remained unrepresented. McGuire felt that this reflected a relatively unconscious choice of factual material by the examiners. Similar results have been obtained in Britain by Spurgin (1967), Black (1968), and Beard and Pole (1971) in physics and biochemistry examinations.

Objective tests

The problem of low-level objectives and factual recall is felt by some to be an acute one with objective tests. Objective tests require candidates simply to select the correct answer from a number of alternatives. Because reading and answering the questions take so little time a large number of items can be set and all of the syllabus can be covered; this usually gives rise to a wide range of marks which differentiates effectively between candidates. Such tests are not only quick to administer but they are also easy to mark. The results compare well with other criteria of success and have the advantage that they are available for students and teachers to see almost immediately after the examination is completed.

Critics of objective tests have claimed, and some still claim, that objective tests can only test factual information, that guessing distorts results and that intelligent students may obtain answers by a process of deduction relating to the test constructor's strategy rather than by reference to the subject matter. The last of these criticisms applies of course only to tests which are poorly constructed, so that they give unintentional clues, and there is a variety of ways of allowing for guessing (e.g. see Rowley and Traub, 1977). Moreover, objective tests can be devised which require students to apply principles, to match related items, to interpret data or to make a judgement (Bloom, 1956; Iliffe, 1966). Several medical teachers have employed multiple-choice tests over a period of time and found them useful (e.g. Illingworth, 1963; Young and Gillespie, 1972; Sanderson, 1973).

The criticism that objective tests are difficult and time consuming to construct seems to be amply justified. But once a bank of suitable questions has been collected and classified it may be drawn on by different bodies to set their own examinations. In America, and more recently in Britain, it is possible to program a computer to select items from a bank with proportions of questions relating to different subject matter (at stated levels of difficulty) as well as different kinds of cognitive skill. These more complex types of objective tests now offer new possibilities for both teaching and testing. It is possible, for example, to use computer-assisted instruction in which progress depends upon the particular choices of answers in a series of multiple-choice questions.

It is interesting to observe that, in so far as objective tests are applicable in higher education, it may prove feasible to set up 'absolute' standards which will allow for comparisons between students of successive years or different colleges. Since the questions used in examining are not normally made available to students it is possible to repeat some of them in successive years, thus providing a limited basis for comparison.

Essay examinations

The rationale for essay writing, and its continued inclusion in coursework assessment or examination papers, has been examined by Coffman (1971). Coffman claims that the major purpose of education is to prepare individuals to interact with each other in the realm of ideas. The basic tool of this interaction is language; and educated people are those who can react appropriately to questions or problems in their field as they recognize them. Such people are able to marshal evidence to support a position and they are able to extend their range of understanding to contribute to the advancement of ideas and constructs within their field. Thus they perform by speaking or writing and the essay is an appropriate sample of performance.

Despite this, and other similar claims, the use of essays in examinations is questionable. Henderson (1980) criticizes such claims in detail and comes to the conclusion that they are all open to attack at one level or another. Rowntree (1977), in an interesting book on assessment and its purposes, comments that Britain is too essay ridden and especially too examination essay ridden.

The main difficulty with the essay examination is that the process is unreliable (and hence invalid) on three main counts: (1) student variability on the day is not taken into account; (2) independent examiners allocate different marks to the same scripts; (3) the same markers will give different marks to the same scripts if they mark them again after an interval of time. These three characteristics of essay marking have been well known for a long time. Marshall and Powers (1969) cite studies which demonstrated the last two in the 1880s and 1910s, long before the 'classic revelations' of Hartog and Rhodes (1936). Similar studies, with similar findings, have been reported ever since. It would seem, for one reason or another, that the unreliability of essay marking has to be rediscovered every year.

In addition to these major sources of unreliability in marking there has been disturbing work which shows that the quality of handwriting, the length of the essay, the effects of marker fatigue, and the position of the script in a series (e.g. after a run of good answers or after a run of poor ones) can all affect the mark given.

The problem, therefore, for many investigators who value the essay examination is to see what can be done to make it more reliable. A number of techniques and methods of examining have been considered, and we shall report on some of them in turn. At the outset, however, we need to point out that none of these solutions entirely solves the problems raised by the three types of unreliability described above. This is not to say that new forms of examination are worse (or better) than the essay type: they are different, and they each produce their own problems. Examiners always need to think, therefore, of what method or what *combination of methods* is appropriate for measuring the achievement of particular objectives.

Improved marking schemes When the tutor marking of essay assignments proved unreliable at the Open University, Byrne (1979) analysed the questions and the guidance notes supplied to tutors and sought their views by questionnaire and interview. He concluded that both the questions and the notes contributed to variation because of their ambiguity and lack of explicitness; guidance was lacking on the weighting of multi-point questions and on the scope of questions; there was misleading guidance on length and insufficient detail. Attention was therefore paid to these factors, raising, of course, the inevitable problem that an agreed marking scheme implies that there is an agreed answer to the question.

Limiting essay topics A more promising method of increasing the reliability of marking essays is to limit the essay topic in some way. Some exam papers in science and social science subjects require answers which are partly in essay form and partly in the form of worked examples. Insofar as these answers are often mathematical, greater reliability can be expected. Gronlund (1976) gives several examples of areas which are more suited to restricted responses: explaining cause–effect relationships, describing the applications of principles, presenting relevant arguments, formulating tenable hypotheses and formulating valid conclusions. Another way of restricting the essay topic, suggested by Henderson (1980), is to incorporate within the question itself the dimensions along which the answer will be assessed. Ambiguity can be reduced by making it clear that the answer should be addressed to a particular audience, or written from a particular point of view.

Increasing the number of markers   Perhaps the most common way of attempting to increase the reliability of marking is to double or even treble mark the answers. Studies of this procedure (e.g. Hill, 1977) indicate, however, that this is likely to reduce marks to a common level of mediocrity and to mask extreme differences, apart from being time consuming. McVey (1975) found that agreement between markers tended to be high under normal circumstances. However, in an experiment when the names of candidates were deleted in addition to the marks being given independently, the greatest difference for any candidate on any one paper was 28 percent, whereas it was no more than 10 percent before these precautions were taken.

Leaving names on scripts, of course, allows for all sorts of bias (conscious and unconscious) to manifest itself. In an ingenious study of project marking Bradley (1984) showed, for example, how, on borderline cases, competent men were given higher marks than competent women, less competent men were given lower marks than less competent women, and how, overall, women students were marked down relative to men.

Other forms of written examination

Increased reliability in essay marking seems to be unattainable unless abilities and skills are analysed in some detail, more specific questions are devised to test them, multiple markers are employed, and names are removed from scripts. To counteract these difficulties a number of variations on the essay examination can be found.

The open-book examination The open-book examination matches more closely the situation in the professions in that students can look up facts and figures they forget, or find the relevant information, provided that their prior knowledge is sufficient to enable them to do so quickly. On the whole students welcome the opportunity to look up data which they need only for the duration of an examination, and anxiety is reduced. An investigation by Kalish (1958) of the open-book method showed no difference either in anxiety or success between students using this method and the traditional one, whereas studies by Feldhusen (1961) and Jehu et al. (1970) found no effects on examination scores although anxiety was reduced.

Those who argue against the open-book system and in favour of the traditional one claim that the stress of a timed examination is a better test of performance in a situation which requires quick effective action leading to prompt decisions and to the production of rapidly prepared reports. But this implies that there must be a choice between the methods, whereas a consideration of objectives in relation to professional requirements may decide between these methods or show that both are desirable.

Prepared time tests, or 'seen' papers Other modifications of traditional examinations include seen papers which allow the students several weeks to work on the subject prior to a timed examination. When this was first tried it was claimed that results showed little difference in the expected rank order of candidates but that performance was generally improved. However, some students claim that the method puts too much of a premium on memory or that, having plenty of time for thorough preparation, they try to scribble down everything they know once they get into the examination room (Flood-Page, 1967). The latter criticism suggests that this kind of test is most effective in showing whether students are able to select information, employing it to the best advantage; but their emphasis on 'getting it all down' indicates that they believe that their teachers give more credit for the quantity of information than for its intelligent use.

Open books and 'seen' papers are as open to criticism on grounds of low reliability as are traditional written papers. The fact is that where teachers have different objectives and different philosophies they give credit for different kinds of achievement; consequently, agreement between their marks may be low.

Projects We have already discussed the value of projects in learning in Chapter 10. Since many departments use them, there are numerous systems of assessment in existence. Harris and Dowdeswell (1979) review five such methods:

1. *Contracts*, developed in the USA, which involve a written agreement between a student and supervisor regarding the nature of the project, its mode of conduct and the end product required. The authors list steps in a possible routine.

2. Assessment relating to *objectives*, where objectives and marks to be assigned to them are agreed in advance.

3. *Ranking*, where supervisors have a large number of projects to assess. They read through them quickly, assigning them to one of three categories, e.g. top 10 percent, bottom 10 percent and middle. Subsequently supervisors group them in smaller categories before assigning marks.

4. *Performance*, where marks are assigned to previously agreed categories, e.g. skill in exposition, use of literature, originality, scope of the work, etc., to personal qualities such as resourcefulness, perseverance, initiative, ability to work in a team; or to a combination of these.

5. *Romantic* is entirely subjective. There is no agreed procedure.

Harris and Dowdeswell provide illustrations of materials related to these different methods in appendices. The authors also comment on the use of multiple markers, continuous or end-point moderation and problems arising in marking projects produced by a group of students.

The relationships between project marks and the marks obtained in traditional examinations are a matter of discussion. In a geography department at Newcastle University, less than half the undergraduates with a mark of A in research projects obtained examination marks as high as B+ (Whiteland, 1966). This bears out the claim made by students (as well as psychologists) that creative individuals are not necessarily good examinees. Hudson (1966) found evidence that some distinguished men obtained poor degrees at Oxford and Cambridge, with a third of Fellows of the Royal Society having gained a second-class degree or worse at some time during their university career. No doubt these findings are one reason for the introduction of open-ended experiments and research projects for undergraduate students; prowess in these is a better indication of ability in research than is ability to pass traditional examinations.

Assessing practical work and oral skills

The assessment of practical work now takes into account wider objectives in the training of scientists, such as the ability to ask appropriate questions or to develop hypotheses and set up well-constructed experiments to test them.

Investigations of oral and practical tests show similar sources of unreliability in marking but to these must be added (1) the effects of personality (Holloway et al., 1967) and (2) volubility on the part of the candidate – as more fluent candidates tend to gain higher marks (Evans et al., 1966). In an American study of oral examinations grading became less stringent during the course of each day's examinations and also on each succeeding examination day (Cotton and Peterson, 1967).

A study which offers some explanation of variability between examiners is that of Natkin and Guild (1967) who asked six teachers to grade the practical work of 65 dental students. They discovered that the teachers did not observe the same errors. Although there was greater agreement when a carefully planned marking system was issued, the main causes of differences continued to be in what the examiners observed.

A promising new development is described by Harden and Cairncross (1980) who are using an Objective Structured Practical Examination (OSPE). They find this a reliable and valid alternative to the usual kind of practical examination which can be adapted to a teacher's needs. The main features of OSPE are:

1. Separate assessment of process and product through observation of performance (using a checklist) and assessment of end result.
2. Adequate sampling of skills and content to be tested.
3. An analytical approach to the assessment.
4. Objectivity.
5. Feedback to teacher and students.

The OSPE method goes a considerable way towards the analysis of specific abilities and the use of short tests which have been recommended to increase the reliability of examining. It is also more efficient in terms of time and numbers.

Other new approaches to examining practical work, oral skills or the medical examination of patients include the use of tapes and video-tapes to provide a permanent record thus enabling more examiners to see and hear the performance and to assess it at their leisure. But, although it is certainly possible to see or hear better, so far there is little evidence that the assessments of examiners are appreciably more reliable. Nevertheless, a collection of permanent records can provide material which should make it practical to train some examiners to a higher level of consistency.

Combining and comparing marks

Anyone who marks papers and sees examination results in different institutions of higher education will know that the same group of students may perform very differently in different topics within the same subject, or in different subject matters in a combined subjects examination.

Several research workers have drawn attention to the different proportions of degree classes between subjects. The Robbins Report (Committee on Higher Education, 1963), for instance, cited percentages of first-class degrees, ranging from 4 percent in history to 14 percent in mathematics. Doubtless these findings are partly due to the ease with which high, or low, scores can be obtained in subject matter which is either right or wrong compared with that in which a range of judgements is legitimate. Yet it would be possible to adjust these proportions – as is done already for O- and A-level examiners with different standards – if there was not evidence that university examiners tend to have preconceived ideas as to the appropriate proportions of failures and first-class degrees in their subjects. Hohne (1965), for example, showed that improved student quality was not reflected in better examination results.

The chief problem in convincing teachers in higher education that valid comparisons can be made across different subjects is that different populations of students are being compared and their numbers may be small. In O- and A-level examinations where thousands, or tens of thousands of candidates take a range of subjects, it seems reasonable to expect almost equal means and standard deviations in all the main subjects. No one is likely to object if a computer program is used to standardize scores in order to assign approximately equal numbers of students to each grade, A – F. But in higher education, unless objective tests are used, it is usually impossible to separate out the effects on marks of students' different abilities, the influence of courses and of teaching, and bias or severity in marking by examiners. Elton's (1968) finding that in three departments of physics which had identical entry standards, 38, 42 and 72 percent of the students gained honours degrees, suggests that the quality of teaching differed. In order to be fully valid, of course, such a conclusion requires that the final examination should be the same for all students. When different examination papers are set in different colleges, as is usually the case, then the effects due to the teaching and the effects due to the difficulty of the papers are confounded. No standard of comparison exists except through external examiners who may draw on experience of marking in a number of colleges and departments to reduce major discrepancies.

Not only are there differences between institutions but also there are differences *within* institutions in the ways in which marks are arrived at for combining purposes. At the University of Keele, for instance, it has been noted that in arriving at a final mark in one subject (which is then to be combined with the final mark in another subject) different departments set different numbers of papers and different kinds of papers, utilize coursework differently and vary in their utilization of viva procedures and external examiners.

Attempts to combine or compare marks statistically are thus of some interest. Leblond et al. (1975) reported that when standardized scores were computed from raw marks in chemistry, the students' mark order differed very little. Two students (five percent) dropped into a lower class division, but not students rose into a higher division. Of six borderline cases, standardization raised the marks of three of them and lowered the marks of the other three, one of whom might have been awarded a lower class. Small changes of this kind seem to be so common an experience that some departments standardize scores only in the event of difficulty with borderline cases.

Hartley and Branthwaite (1977) used computer simulations of results to decide on the relative weightings of various assessments. They found that including a modest amount of coursework, in addition to the examination results, made little difference to the overall results, but that the procedure seemed fairer and was liked by students.

King (1976) compared marks obtained by eight assessment methods in geography finals over a period of three years. On average, the correlations were about 0.50 between the methods in 1973 and 1974, but dropped to 0.27 in 1975, suggesting that the methods were tapping skills and abilities which differed more in the third year. Correlations between the marks for the dissertation and other assessment methods were 0.38, 0.56 and 0.12 in the three successive years. King comments that in a multi-faceted assessment pattern, 'the more types of ability and skill it attempts to take into account, the less easy and less meaningful it becomes to summarise and combine the results . . . The translation of a combined numerical score into a degree class is essentially an arbitrary procedure'.

King (1976) suggests that departments might experiment with profile assessment in parallel with degree classifications. A profile gives a set of grades (or marks) for different aspects of the total performance; *Figure* 14.1 provides an example. Kempa and Ongley (1979), as a result of an inquiry

Figure 14.1 An example of an experimental profile report form. (Reproduced with permission from Kempa and Ongley, 1979)

EXPERIMENTAL PROFILE REPORT FORM

Name of Institution: _____

Type of course taken by student: _____

Qualification (including overall
grade) gained or predicted: _____   If predicted,
                                                        tick here   ☐

QUALITY ASSESSED	ASSESSMENT				
	A	B	C	D	E
Knowledge of basic chemical facts, laws, principles					
Ability to apply knowledge in problem-solving situations					
Ability to interpret chemical information and data					
Calculative and mathematical competence					
Deductive and reasoning ability					
Basic *practical* skills, in relation to manipulation and observation					
Design and execution of practical investigations (e.g. projects)					
Persistence and application in the study of chemistry					
Ability to work independently, i.e. with minimum supervision and guidance					
Communicative skills, in both oral and written work					

Subject bias: (Please place a tick against subject areas in which the student has been particularly successful)

Inorganic Chemistry	_____	Organic Chemistry	_____
Physical Chemistry	_____	Theoretical Chemistry	_____
Experimental work	_____	Applied Chemistry	_____

into university marks for chemistry, concluded that it was feasible to report the results of such an assessment in a profile.

14.3   Evaluating courses and curricula

In earlier chapters we have given a number of examples of course evaluation which have shown that many people think that examinations and tests can only be considered as *one aspect* of evaluation. Such people are likely to be keen on exploring how students and teachers react to courses as they are going on. Evaluations have been made of teachers', students' and post-graduates' attitudes to courses, of personality characteristics in relation to performance, of procedures and interactions in the classroom, and of administration and how decisions are made.

Anderson and Ball (1978), in their book on the profession and practice of evaluation, consider several different purposes of course evaluation. As in any field where experts come from a range of specialities there are many points of view, and these are reflected in the diverse conceptions and methodologies of evaluation. Some evaluators still follow traditional lines, designing carefully designed experiments or, if these are impossible, quasi-experiments, from which 'hard' data are obtained from pre- and post-tests and from questionnaires; these data are presented in tables or subjected to analysis prior to interpretation. Other evaluators find it more meaningful to use 'illuminative' research, advocated in Britain by Parlett and his colleagues (Parlett and Miller, 1974; Parlett and Hamilton, 1978). These evaluations depend in interviews, participant observations, case-studies, and inquiries into attitudes and opinions, etc., which are normally regarded as 'soft' data by the traditionalists. The studies of physics teaching described in books edited by Bliss and Ogborn (1977) and Ogborn (1977b) were conducted with such methods. It is argued that no experimental approach on its own can supply information to show what features within a situation contribute to success or how this comes about.

Some evaluators, using a range of methods, have combined traditional and illuminative approaches. For example, the validity of responses to a questionnaire may be checked by the close observation of a few representative students for several days by participant observers. Brew (1978) and Brew and McCormick (1979) describe how they used a range of methods in evaluating the effects of an Open University Course on the digital computer following its introduction at the University of Essex. The methods included case-studies, questionnaires, study diaries, conversations and interviews, together with computer-marked assignments and a final examination. Their aim was 'to describe and analyse the total context of the experiment, including the attitudes of its participants and other people affected by its implementation, its effects on the institution in which it took place, the effects of the institution on it, but also the relationship between these factors in so far as they impinged upon the innovation'.

Illuminative methods involve researchers collaborating with people in the departments or institutions they evaluate. This can give valuable impetus to curriculum development as teachers gain insights into the effects of their courses and their contexts. Both Hall (1979) at Adelaide, and Hewton (1982) at Sussex, stress the importance of working with representatives of a department in bringing about educational changes within it.

One effective method of promoting changes is described by Mathias and Rutherford (1982). At Birmingham University, between 1974 and 1978, a group of university teachers collaborated in discussing evaluation, academic staff in pairs from similar subjects evaluated each other's courses, and the results were presented to the full group of staff involved. In each pair, the evaluator discussed the lecturer's course with him or her before using a variety of evaluative techniques. These varied with the nature of the course, the kinds of problems and issues arising and the time available. Lectures might be video-taped and analysed. Discussions with students were spread over a period of time, a number of questionnaires might be administered for students to complete, focusing on general or specific features of the course, and the evaluation might be extended to the post-examination period. Informal training was given to group members on interviewing and on questionnaire design and analysis. After the first year, an experienced evaluator worked with a new member. This flexible and adaptable approach served to reveal differing views of the course by teachers and students. Discussion in the group contributed further to staff development by broadening perspectives and developing evaluation skills.

Some students, of course, have independently decided to evaluate courses. At the University of New South Wales, the Students' Union has published an annual *Alternative Handbook* since 1975. Their aim is to provide a different sort of information on courses and staff from that found in official university publications. In 1979, it contained surveys by students taught in the university (Roe and Vasta, 1980). The information is gathered by questionnaire, containing sections on lectures, tutorials/seminars, practical experience, assessment and grading. A general section ends with invitations to comment on books found useful, on staff members, etc. Such alternative handbooks are now a feature of many institutions in higher education (e.g. see Payne and Lipschitz, 1982).

Validating courses

During the 1970s 'validation' began to become a widely used term in educational circles, particularly in connection with the CNAA. Church and Murray (1983) define validation (in this context) as 'the consideration of a course of study which leads up to and includes the decision on its approval or re-approval'. More explicitly they define it as 'the process of scrutinising a proposed degree scheme, and of deciding whether or not it should be approved as being of an appropriate standard for the award to which it is intended to lead, and, if this proves to be the case, of then specifying the conditions which must be fulfilled if the course is actually to run'.

Validation, of course, is not the entire province of the CNAA. Universities, for instance, validate, and so do other bodies such as the Technician Education Council (TEC), the Business Education Council (BEC) and various professional bodies (e.g. The Central Council for the Education and Training of Social Workers). However, as noted in Chapter 1, about one-third of all students who are studying for a degree attend CNAA-validated courses. The CNAA approves courses in pure and applied sciences, social sciences, business and management studies, arts and humanities, education, and art and design. It validates approximately half of the teacher education courses in England and Wales, and the bulk of the training of teachers in further education. The Council also awards Masters and PhD degrees.

The early work of the CNAA was mainly concerned with validating proposals from institutions making their first applications. More recently the Council has been concerned with validating additional courses or developments in existing institutions – thus there has been a change of emphasis. This change is reflected in the revised procedures which were introduced in 1979–1980. Up until that date most CNAA degree courses were approved for a five-year period, which meant that colleges had to start preparing for revalidation often before the first intake of students had completed the course. The principal innovation in 1979–1980 was the introduction of approval for an indefinite period of time for well-established courses but with on-site reviews (say every five years). The next main change was to allow the colleges a greater freedom to modify their approved courses (within previously agreed limits). Finally, more flexibility was introduced into the whole process of validation, allowing for more discussions at an earlier stage and less 'confrontation' between the CNAA and a department applying for validation.

There are several accounts of the work of the CNAA in practice, and of how the experience affects practitioners (e.g. Alexander and Wormald, 1983; Billing, 1983). McNay and McCormick (1982) provide a lengthy and informative account in *Case Study 3* of the Open University's Third Level Educational Studies Course, 'Curriculum Evaluation and Assessment in Educational Institutions'. This case-history includes a discussion of the following stages of a CNAA validation (each with illustrative documents):

- the preliminaries;
- the documentation;
- the internal scrutiny;
- the CNAA's initial consideration;
- the announcement of the visit;
- the day of the visit;
- the judgement and its basis;
- the aftermath.

Billing (1983) reports that the CNAA has been criticized periodically for making its decision on the basis of a one-day site visit. However, as Billing points out, there is far more than just the site visit under consideration, and the preparation of the course submission for the CNAA involves a considerable amount of time and effort. There is a great deal of documentation. McNay and McCormick (1982) report that some colleges have been known to submit proposals in boxed sets of 10 volumes like Christmas presents. In theory, however, the submission is supposed to be a summary of a fuller course description which could be made available to students as a course handbook.

When considering a proposal the Council concentrates on three factors: (1) the Council's knowledge about the college as a whole; (2) the quality and experience of the staff who will be associated with the course if it is approved; (3) the papers submitted by the college which define the aims and intentions of the proposed course and specify how it is intended that these should be achieved.

Harrison (1983) reports that some staff complain about the long and sometimes tortuous chain of communications between the college and validating panel; about the lack of personal communication between the development team and the panel (with consequent uncertainty about what the panel would require), and of panels which appear to change their minds during negotiations. Many more staff complain about the costs of preparing such submissions, particularly in terms of the time they have to spend preparing and revising their proposals which, they say, detracts from their primary task of teaching. Others, of course, feel that the necessary discussions and interactions between members of a department, and the discussions of aims and objectives can only be beneficial.

Validation and students

Harrison (1983) presents an interesting account of the effects of validation upon students. One student, for example, complained that his lectures had been totally disrupted for four weeks prior to a CNAA visit, and he asked, pertinently, why such work could not have been done in the vacation.

Harrison points out that a validating body can affect directly the impact of a course on students in various ways: validation affects the content of the course; the course structure and the teaching methods; and the assessment standards and procedures. Validation affects students indirectly, too, via its judgements concerning the staff and their resources. It seems that with accumulated experience the CNAA has learned how to check course proposals to make sure that they can be taught satisfactorily in terms of students' workload, timetable, the timing of assignments and numerous other practical details which vitally affect students' progress.

When validating first submissions, no attempt is made by the CNAA to assess whether or not the objectives of the course have been met. Approval is given on trust, as it were, that the course will achieve its aims and objectives, provided that the procedures and resources set out in the proposal are maintained. When validating resubmissions, however, evidence can be collected to assess how effective the course has been, and to justify any modifications. Here the opinions of students may be helpful, and most departments use a variety of procedures for consulting students about their courses, ranging from having students as members of key committees to informal contacts in the corridor. Many CNAA visiting panels now arrange for a formal meeting with at least some current students (and possibly recent graduates) during their visitation, and most CNAA panels expect to see at least a written report on the impact of the course on students in any revalidation proposal. Procedures such as these encourage departments to consult with their students about course administration, methods and content, and to pay serious attention to their desires and difficulties.

The impact of the CNAA on higher education has been considerable. It has forced people to consider what they are doing, what they want to do and how they can best accomplish it. It has led to considerable debate about the importance of standards, methods and assessment. It has encouraged greater planning, control and feedback. Other institutions who do not validate or who have to validate courses have been forced to take note of what is happening and to ponder on the implications for themselves.

14.4   Evaluating teaching

Changing attitudes to evaluation

The main purposes of evaluating teaching are (1) to improve teachers' skills and knowledge about teaching and (2) to use the information obtained about a person's teaching skills for certification or in decisions concerning promotion. Evaluations may be made by colleagues and by students.

In Britain, as we noted in Chapter 1, almost all universities have now appointed an individual or a committee, or have set up a unit to promote staff development activities, but Britain still lags behind in making arrangements for evaluating teaching. New teachers are on probation for three years, during which time the head of department is required to ensure that their performance is adequate. Unless adverse comments are made before certification, it is assumed that subsequent teaching performance will be satisfactory.

There is some evidence, however, that compared with opinions in the 1960s, teachers are now more favourable to the idea that some measure of teaching performance can be used as a criterion for promotion. Blank (1978) found that faculty with high research and scholarly productivity were more favourable to the use of student evaluations than they were to more general criteria of 'teaching effectiveness'.

Evaluations by colleagues can, however, raise problems. Such evaluations are unlikely to be reliable unless colleagues have numerous opportunities to see each other in action in the classroom. Moreover, teachers with different value systems may find it difficult to evaluate fairly each other's work. Nevertheless, Cohen and McKeachie (1980) consider that colleagues may be the best persons to interpret data on student outcomes and teaching, and to make judgements in areas of scholarship and motivation.

Student evaluation of teaching

In the USA, faculty involvement in the evaluation of colleagues' teaching has now given way to a greater use of student ratings. The most common way in which students evaluate teaching is to use some sort of rating scale, checklist or questionnaire. One example of a lecture evaluation form was given in Chapter 8 (pp.170–171); *Figure* 14.2 provides another. In a book surveying experience of students' evaluation of teaching in America, Flood-Page (1974) gives a number of illustrative questionnaires and lists arguments for and against their use in the light of American experience.

Figure 14.2   Example of a lecture evaluation form. The numbers in each column indicate the number of students (out of 43) who ticked this particular column.

The Lecturer:	BAD 1	2	3	4	GOOD 5
1 Presented his material clearly and logically	0	4	10	22	7
2 Enabled you to understand the basic principals of the subject	0	2	10	17	14
3 Could be clearly heard	7	15	11	8	2
4 Made his material intelligibly meaningful	1	5	12	19	6
5 Adequately covered the ground	1	5	18	15	4
6 Maintained continuity in the course	0	6	13	15	9
7 Showed an expert knowledge of his subject matter	2	2	13	17	9
8 Adopted an appropriate pace in the lecture	0	4	9	14	16

Figure 14.2 shows a typical finding: student ratings are likely to go across the scale provided, and there is no way in which one particular teacher will be able to satisfy all the different needs of each member of the class. Thus after one series of lectures Falk (1966) reports that students wrote a variety of opinions:

These lectures were the best I've had this year.

Congratulations on an exceedingly workmanlike job of teaching as opposed to purely lecturing.

Gives students the impression that they are back in the schoolroom. By this I mean over-simplification, over-classification.

Made a fascinating period of history very flat.

Ongley (1975) found that some students praised highly a conscientious teacher who covered the syllabus thoroughly in well-planned lectures whereas others looked for originality and provision of information which was not readily accessible, preferring that basic information should be obtained in private study.

Even when behaviours are specified in detail, variations in performance and differences in judgement still pertain. Like examiners, students

observe different things. Nonetheless, the chief value of this kind of assessment is to inform teachers of their strengths and weaknesses and to help
them to improve their teaching. In terms of *Figure* 14.2, for example, it
seems that this lecturer needs to speak more clearly, or to use a microphone,
and that more effort should be made to shift the majority of judgements
towards the good end of the scale.

The main debate about student ratings, of course, concerns itself with the
validity and reliability of such ratings. The questions at issue are questions
like:

● Are ratings of effectiveness related to academic performance?
● What factors affect students' appreciation of teaching?
● Are the ratings consistent between groups?
● Can student ratings detect changes in teacher performance?

There have been a number of studies on these issues (e.g. see Costin et al.,
1971; Centra and Rose, 1976; Reavis, 1979), and the review by Nadeau
(1977) is helpful in teasing out the findings from this research.

We shall report as an example the results from one typical study. Marsh
(1982a, b) developed the SEEQ scale (Students' Evaluation of Educational
Quality). During six years, over 50,000 forms were completed by students
at the University of California, Los Angeles, from more than 50 academic
departments. Every item on the final scale was judged relevant by 80–95
percent of students, and the three most frequently mentioned items were:
(1) the instructor's style of presentation held your interest during class; (2)
the instructor's explanations were clear; (3) the instructor was enthusiastic
about teaching the course. Ratings were reliable if they were based on the
responses of 10–15, or more, students.

Evidence for the validity of the ratings was inferred from three findings:

1. Students learned more with the teachers who were rated more favourably.
2. Items rated by graduate and undergraduate students over a period of
several years correlated 0.83.
3. Staff ratings of their own performance proved closely similar to
ratings by students in one study; in a second study, ratings by students and
teachers correlated 0.45 on the same component of teaching effectiveness
but only 0.02 on different components.

The teachers involved indicated that the student ratings were useful for
improving their courses and/or the quality of their teaching: 80 percent said
that they were potentially useful while 59 percent said that they actually had
been useful. Marsh suggests that feedback from students' ratings would be

even more effective if it was coupled with a candid discussion with an external consultant.

However, not all studies find high correlations between student ratings and teachers' self-evaluations. Centra (1980) reported a correlation of only 0.21. He found, in this instance, that teachers rated themselves more highly than students rated them (although he considered that students' ratings were generous). In the absence of high validity, Centra felt that self-ratings would be of little value in aiding personnel decisions but could be of value in improving teaching. He suggests, however, that a self-report of a teacher's activities over the year would have value for both purposes.

Some British universities already require such reports. At the University of Bradford, for instance, self-reports are collected from the staff by heads of departments for the deans of faculty, who put them together to form departmental reports. Views differ as to whether these are, or should be, used when promotion is considered. In *Response to Adversity*, Williams and Blackstone (1983) comment: 'Teaching performance should be given as much weight as research in any evaluation of lecturers and to help achieve this . . . there should be regular reviews of individual performance based on self-appraisal'. Such procedures take us directly to the issues of staff development – and back to Chapter 1.

14.5 Concluding remarks

The assessment of students, of courses and of teachers is clearly a complex matter. There is no single agreed way of doing these things: different philosophical perspectives interact with different practical constraints to produce a variety of more or less satisfactory procedures. If we were asked, however, to give advice to teachers on the basis of the information presented in this chapter, the kinds of things we would have to say would be as follows:

- Discuss with colleagues who teach your subject matter in other institutions how they go about assessing their students.
- Discuss with colleagues who teach *different* subject matters in your own institution how they go about assessing their students.
- Explore with your students the effects of different assessment procedures. Discover how they react to and prepare for different methods, whether there are wide individual differences here, and what information they find it helpful for departments to provide.
- If coursework is not included in your end-of-year assessments try to introduce it in a modest form. Explore the effects of different weighting schemes, and consider the effects of scaling the results from different

examination papers in order to be fairer to students when combining marks.

● Try to assess whether or not other objectives (apart from the recall of basic knowledge) are being assessed by your departmental procedures. Consider how improvements might be made here.

● Always, when marking for examination purposes, try to ensure that more than one marker assesses the materials.

● On occasions, try to persuade students to assess their own and their fellow students' work, and to compare their assessments with yours. Such a procedure will make the students more aware of the subjective nature of assessment.

● If you have not been evaluated by students before (and even if you have), try developing personal lecture evaluation forms for your own lectures and courses. Feedback from such forms can be useful when revising and planning courses for subsequent years.

14.6 Summary

● Aims, teaching methods and techniques of assessment are all inter-related.

● Changing aims in higher education and changing socioeconomic factors have been accompanied by changing techniques of assessment.

● Most techniques of assessment, both old and new, are unreliable in one way or another: student variability on the day is not taken into account and (with the exception of objective tests) different markers will allocate different marks to the same piece of work.

● Difficulties such as these can be overcome by using multiple markers and pooling data from different kinds of assessments made over a period of time. Such procedures match more closely the skills and abilities that students are expected to acquire.

● Just as there have been changes in ways of assessing students, so there have been changes in ways of assessing teachers and courses. The procedures used to validate courses can both directly and indirectly affect student learning.

● Teaching effectiveness can be evaluated by fellow colleagues and by students. The main aim of procedures used here should be to help teachers improve their skills and knowledge about teaching. Not surprisingly, however, administrators also express an interest in these procedures because of their concern with teaching quality and promotions.

BIBLIOGRAPHY

Abboud, C.V. and Bunderson, C.V. (1971) *A Computer-assisted Instruction Program in the Arabic Writing System*. Technical Report No. 4, CAL Laboratory, University of Texas at Austin.

Abercrombie, M.L.J. (1960) (1969) *The Anatomy of Judgment*. London: Hutchinson. Education Edition – Harmondsworth: Penguin.

Abercrombie, M.L.J. (1979) *Aims and Techniques of Group Teaching*, 4th ed. Guildford: Society for Research into Higher Education.

Abercrombie, M.L.J. and Terry, P. (1978) *Talking to Learn: Improving Teaching and Learning in Small Groups*. Guildford: Society for Research into Higher Education.

Abshire, G.M. (1982) A bibliography of writings on writing. *IEEE Transactions on Professional Communication PC–25*, 3, 211–219.

Adamson, H., Hughes, P. and Edgecombe, A. (1979) Home experiments for first year university students. *Journal of Biological Education* 13(4), 297–302.

Agutter, P.S. (1979) Precision testing: a method for improving students' written work in biochemistry. *Journal of Biological Education* 13(1), 25–31.

Aiken, E.G., Thomas, G.S. and Shennum, W.A. (1975) Memory for a lecture: effects of notes, lecture rate and informational density. *Journal of Educational Psychology* 67(3), 439–444.

Alexander, R. and Wormald, E. (1983) Validation in teacher education. In Church, C.H. (ed.) *Practice and Perspective in Validation*. Guildford: Society for Research into Higher Education.

Allen, P.H.G. (1968) Engineering projects for engineering undergraduates. In *Innovations and Experiments in University Teaching Methods*. Report of the third conference organized by the University Teaching Methods Unit, University of London Institute of Education.

Altmaier, E.M. and Woodward, M. (1981) Group vicarious desensitization of test anxiety. *Journal of Counseling Psychology* 28(5), 467–469.

Aluri, R. (1982) Application of learning theories to library use instruction. *Libri* 31(2), 140–152.

Anderson, R.C., Reynolds, R.E., Schallert, D.L. and Goetz, E.T. (1977) Frameworks for comprehending discourse. *American Educational Research Journal* 14(4), 367–381.

Anderson, S.B. and Ball, S. (1978) *The Profession and Practice of Program Evaluation*. San Francisco: Jossey Bass.

Andriesson, J.J. and Kroon, D.J. (1980) Individualised learning by video disc. *Educational Technology* 20(3), 21–25.

Argyle, M. (1983) *The Psychology of Interpersonal Behaviour*, 4th ed. Harmondsworth: Penguin.

Armstrong, M. and Boud, D. (1983) Assessing participation in discussion: an exploration of the issues. *Studies in Higher Education* 8(1), 33–44.

Association of University Teachers (1969) *Report to Council*. Working Party of University Teachers, No. 276, February 1969. London: AUT.

Ayscough, P.B. (1976) CAL – boon or burden? *Chemistry in Britain* 12(11), 348–352.

Baddeley, A. (1979) Is the British Ph.D. system obselete? *Bulletin of the British Psychological Society* 32, April, 129–131.

Baddeley, A. (1983) The working party on postgraduate education. *Bulletin of the British Psychological Society* 36, January, 9–12.

Barnett, S.A. (1958) An experience with free discussion groups. *Universities Quarterly* 12(2), 175–190.

Baum, T. (1979) A good two-one – and then what? *The Guardian*, 26 October 1979.

Beard, R.M. (1967) *Small Group Discussion in University Teaching*. London: University Teaching Methods Unit, University of London Institute of Education.

Beard, R.M. (1968) *Research into Teaching Methods in Higher Education*. London: Society for Research into Higher Education.

Beard, R.M. (1971) Programmed learning – co-operative ventures. *Chemistry in Britain* 7, 324–326.

Beard, R.M., Bligh, D.A. and Harding, A.G. (1978) *Research into Teaching Methods in Higher Education*, 4th ed. Guildford: Society for Research into Higher Education.

Beard, R.M., Healey, F.G. and Holloway, P.J. (1974) *Objectives in Higher Education*, 2nd ed. Guildford: Society for Research into Higher Education.

Beard, R.M., Levy, P.M. and Maddox, H. (1964) Academic performance at university. *Educational Review* 16(3), 163–174.

Beard, R.M. and Pole, K.E. (1971) Content and purposes of biochemistry examinations. *British Journal of Medical Education* 5(1), 13–21.

Beard, R.M. and Senior, I.J. (1980) *Motivating Students*. London: Routledge & Kegan Paul.

Beattie, G.W. (1982) The dynamics of university tutorial groups. *Bulletin of the British Psychological Society* 35, April, 147–150.

Becher, R.A. (1971) The effectiveness of higher education. In *Innovations in Higher Education*. Proceedings of the Annual Conference of the Society for Research into Higher Education, 1971.

Becker, A.D. (1978) A survey and evaluation of teleconferencing. In Brook, D. and Race, P. (eds) *Aspects of Educational Technology 12*. London: Kogan Page, pp. 212–218.

Betts, D.S. and Walton, A.J. (1970) A lecture match or 'Anything you can do I can do better'. *Physics Education* 5(6), 321–325.

Biggs, D.A. (1976) The student counsellor as a team member. *British Journal of Guidance and Counselling* 4(1), 28–37.

Billing, D. (1983) Practice and criteria of validation under the CNAA. In Church, C.H. (ed.) *Practice and Perspective in Validation*. Guildford: Society for Research into Higher Education.

Bishop, Lloyd K. (1971) *Individualising Educational Systems*. New York: Harper & Row.

Black, P.J. (1968) University examinations. *Physics Education* 3(2), 93–99.

Black, P.J. (1971) Group discussion in the planning and reporting of group projects. In *Varieties of Group Discussion in University Teaching*. London: University Teaching Methods Unit, University of London Institute of Education.

Black, P.J., Dyson, J.G. and O'Connor, D.A. (1968) Group studies. *Physics Education* 9(1), 18–22.

Blackman, D. (1980) Images of man in contemporary behaviourism. In Chapman, A.J. and Jones, D.M. (eds) *Models of Man*. Leicester: British Psychological Society.

Blank, R. (1978) Faculty support for evaluation of teaching: a test of two hypotheses. *Journal of Higher Education* 49(2), 163–176.

Bligh, D.A. (1971) *What's the Use of Lectures?* Harmondsworth: Penguin.

Bligh, D.A. (1977) The Cynthia syndrome. *Bulletin of Educational Research* 13(1), 21–24.

Bligh, D.A., Ebrahim, G.J., Jaques, D. and Warren-Piper, D. (1975) *Teaching Students*. Exeter University Teaching Services.

Bliss, J. and Ogborn, J. (eds) (1977) *Students Reactions to Undergraduate Science*. Nuffield Foundation Higher Education Learning Project, Physics. London: Heinemann.

Blizard, P.J., Trastotenoyo, M.S., Haryono, R. and Adinoto, S. (1979) The educational bureau – a key organization for facilitating educational development and change. *Higher Education* 8(1), 9–40.

Bloom, B.S. (1956) *Taxonomy of Educational Objectives. 1. Cognitive Domain*. New York: David McKay.

Boud, D.J. (1980) *Self and Peer Assessment in Higher and Continuing Professional Education: An Annotated Bibliography*. Occasional Publication No. 16. Sydney: Tertiary Education Research Centre, University of New South Wales.

Boud, D.J., Dunn, J.G., Kennedy, T. and Thorley, R. (1980) The aims of science laboratory courses: a survey of students, graduates and practising scientists. *European Journal of Science Education* 2(4), 415–428.

Boud, D.J. and Lublin, J. (1983) Student self-assessment. In Squires, G. (ed.) *Innovation Through Recession*. Guildford: Society for Research into Higher Education.

Bowden, J.A. (1980) Independent learning of laboratory techniques. In Winterburn, R. and Evans, L. (eds) *Aspects of Educational Technology 14*. London: Kogan Page, pp. 74–77.

Bower, G.H. and Hilgard, E.R. (1981) *Theories of Learning*, 5th ed. New York: Appleton, Century Crofts.

Bradley, C. (1984) Sex bias in the evaluation of students. *British Journal of Social Psychology* 23, 2, 147–153.

Bramley, W. (1979) *Group Tutoring: Concepts and Case Studies*. London: Kogan Page.

Brancher, D.M. (1975) Projects and the development of general education. *European Journal of Engineering Education* 1(1), 35–40.

Branthwaite, J.A., Trueman, M. and Hartley, J. (1980) Writing essays: the actions and strategies of students. In Hartley, J. (ed.) *The Psychology of Written Communication: Selected Readings*. London: Kogan Page.

Brennan, J.L. and Percy, K.A. (1976) *What Do Students Want? An Analysis of Staff and Student Perceptions in British Higher Education*. Paper presented at The Second Congress of the European Association for Research and Development in Higher Education, Louvain-la-Neuve (cited by Raaheim and Wankowski, 1981).

Brew, A. (1978) Developing a methodology for an evaluation. *Assessment in Higher Education* 3(3), 168–185.

Brew, A. and McCormick, B. (1979) Student learning and an independent study course. *Higher Education* 8(4), 429–441.

Brewer, I.M. (1977) A case study of an innovative method of teaching and learning. *Studies in Higher Education* 2(1), 33–54.

Brewer, I.M. (1979) Group teaching strategies for promoting individual skills in problem solving. *Programmed Learning and Educational Technology* 16(2), 111–128.

Brewer, I.M. and Tomlinson, J.D. (1981) SIMIG: the effect of time on performance and modular instruction. *Programmed Learning and Educational Technology* 18(2), 72–85.

British Medical Students Association (1965) *Report on Medical Education – Suggestions for the Future*. London: British Medical Association.

Bromley, D.B. (1974) *The Psychology of Human Ageing*, 2nd ed. Harmondsworth: Penguin.

Brophy, J.E. and Good, T.L. (1970) Teachers communication of differential expectations for children's classroom performance: some behavioural data. *Journal of Educational Psychology* 61(5), 365–374.

Brown, A.L., Campione, J.C. and Day, J.D. (1981) Learning to learn: on training students to learn from texts. *Educational Researcher* 10(2), 14–21.

Brown, G.A. (1976) Using microteaching to train new lecturers. *University Vision* 15, 24–31.

Brown, G.A. (1978) *Lecturing and Explaining*. London: Methuen.

Brown, G.A. (1979) *Learning from Lectures*. Department of Education, University of Nottingham.

Brown, G.A. and Bakhtar, M. (eds) (1983) *Styles of Lecturing*. University of Loughborough, UK ASTD Publications.

Brown, G.A. and Tomlinson, D. (1979) How to . . . improve lecturing. *Medical Teacher* 1(3), 128–135.

Brown, R. (1965) *Social Psychology*. New York: The Free Press.

Brown, S., Nathenson, M. and Kirkup, G. (1982) Learning from evaluation at the Open University II. Helping students to learn from audio-visual media. *British Journal of Educational Technology* 13(3), 217–236.

Brown, W.F. and Holtzman, W.H. (1955) A study attitudes questionnaire for predicting academic success. *Journal of Educational Psychology* 46(2), 75–84.

Bruffee, K.A. (1978) The Brooklyn Plan: attaining intellectual growth through peer-group tutoring. *Liberal Education* **64**, 447–468.

Bruhns, I. and Thomsen, O.B. (1979) Concerns of new university teachers. *Higher Education* **8**(1), 99–110.

Brumby, M.N. (1979) Problems in learning the concept of natural selection. *Journal of Biological Education* **13**(2), 119–122.

Brumby, M.N. (1982) Consistent differences in cognitive styles shown for qualitative biological problem solving. *British Journal of Educational Psychology* **52**(2), 244–257.

Burke, R.J. (1968) Student reaction to course grades. *Journal of Experimental Education* **36**, 11–13.

Butcher, H.J. (1968) *Human Intelligence: Its Nature and Assessment.* London: Methuen.

Buzan, T. (1974) *Use Your Head.* London: BBC Publications.

Byrne, C. (1979) Tutor marked assignments at the Open University: a question of reliability. *Teaching at a Distance* **15**, 34–43.

Carpenter, N. (1975) Continuous assessment and student motivation in management studies. *International Journal of Electrical Engineering Education* **71**(2), 205–210.

Case, C.L. (1980) The influence of modified laboratory instruction on college student biology achievement. *Journal of Research in Science Teaching* **17**(1), 1–6.

Cassie, W.F. and Constantine, T. (1977) *Student's Guide to Success.* London: Macmillan.

Centra, J.A. (1978) Types of faculty development programs. *Journal of Higher Education* **49**(2), 151–162.

Centra, J.A. (1980) The how and why of evaluating teaching. *Engineering Education* **12**(1), 5–12.

Centra, J.A. and Rose, B. (1976) Student ratings of instruction and their relationship to student learning. Educational Testing Service Research Bulletin. Princeton, NJ: Educational Testing Service, p. 17.

Chandler, E. (1977) *Student Counselling: When and Why.* Exeter University Teaching Services, University of Exeter.

Chansaker, B.A. and Rautray, V. (1980) How relevant is continuous assessment? A business studies experience. *Assessment and Evaluation in Higher Education* **6**(1), 49–56.

Child, D. and Smithers, A. (1973) An attempted validation of the Joyce-Hudson scale of convergence–divergence. *British Journal of Educational Psychology* **43**(1), 57–61.

Choppin, B.H.L. et al. (1973) *The Prediction of Academic Success.* Slough: NFER.

Church, C.H. and Murray, R. (1983) Of definitions, debates, dimensions. In Church, C.H. (ed.) *Practice and Perspective in Validation.* Guildford: Society for Research into Higher Education.

Clanchy, J. and Ballard, B. (1983) *How to Write Essays.* London: Longman.

Clavering, E. (1980) The use of computers as aids to learning. In Winterburn, R. and Evans, L. (eds) *Aspects of Educational Technology 14.* London: Kogan Page, pp. 211–216.

CNAA (1979) *The Council: Its Place in British Higher Education.* London: CNAA.

Coffman, W.E. (1971) Essay examinations. In Thorndike, R.L. (ed.) *Educational Measurement*, 2nd ed. Washington: ACE.

Cohen, P.A. and McKeachie, W.J. (1980) The role of colleagues in the evaluation of college teaching. *Improving College and University Teaching* **28**(4), 147–154.

Collier, K.G. (1983) *The Management of Peer-Group Learning: Syndicate Methods in Higher Education*. Guildford: Society for Research into Higher Education.

Collingwood, V. and Hughes, D. (1978) Effects of three types of university lecture notes on student achievement. *Journal of Educational Psychology* **70**(2), 175–179.

Colson, G. (1963) *Voice Production and Speech*. London: Museum Press.

Committee on Higher Education (1963) *Higher Education* (Robbins Report). London: HMSO.

Cooper, B. (1964) *Writing Technical Reports*. Harmondsworth: Penguin.

Costin, F., Greenough, W.T. and Menges, R.J. (1971) Student ratings of college teaching: reliability, validity and usefulness. *Review of Educational Research* **41**(5), 511–535.

Cotton, T. and Peterson, O.L. (1967) An assay of medical students' abilities by oral examination. *Journal of Medical Education* **42**(5), 1005–1014.

Cowan, J., McConnell, S.G. and Bolton, A. (1969–70) *Learner Directed Group Work for Large Classes*. Edinburgh: Department of Civil Engineering, Heriot-Watt University.

Cox, K. (1982) Planning workshop content and process. *Newsletter*, February. Sydney: The University of New South Wales Centre for Medical Education and Research Development.

Crombag, H.F.M., De Wijkerslooth, J.L. and van Tuyll van Serooskerken, E.H. (1972) *On Solving Legal Problems*. (Full version in: *Over het Oplosson van Casusposities*.) Groningnen: H.D. Tjeenk Willink.

Crombag, H.F.M. and van Tuyll van Serooskerken, E.H. (1970) *Het CI – Kurriculum in de Fakulteit de Rechtsgeleerdheid: een tussentijds verslag* (The first-year curriculum in law school: a preliminary report). Leiden: Bureau Onderszoek van Onderwijs, R.U. Leiden, rapport nr. 2.

Cronbach, L.J. and Snow, R.E. (1977) *Aptitudes and Instructional Methods: A Handbook for Research on Interactions*. New York: Irvington.

Crossley, C.A. (1968) Tuition in the use of the library and of subject literature in the University of Bradford. *Journal of Documentation* **24**, 91–97.

Cryer, P. and Rider, J.G. (1977) A 'do-it-yourself' demonstration laboratory. *Physics Education* **12**(6), 384–393.

Dahlgren, L.O. (1981) Teaching and learning of basic concepts in economics. *Research and Development in Higher Education 5*. The National Swedish Board of Universities and Colleges.

Dahlgren, L.O. and Marton, F. (1978) Students' conceptions of subject matter: an aspect of learning and teaching in higher education. *Studies in Higher Education* **3**(1), 25–35.

Dallos, R. (1975) Programmed learning and personality: a review and preliminary study. *Programmed Learning and Educational Technology* **12**(1), 12–20.

Daly, D.W. and Dunn, W.R. (1980) An alternative approach to learning in under-graduate mathematics. In Winterburn, R. and Evans, L. (eds) *Aspects of Educational Technology 14*. London: Kogan Page, pp. 104–110.

Darke, M. (1968) Teaching design methods. *Royal Institute of British Architects Journal*, January, pp. 29–30.

Davies, D.M. (1968) Teaching sheets as an aid to learning. In *Innovations and Experiments in University Teaching Methods*. London: University Teaching Methods Research Unit, Department of Higher Education, University of London Institute of Education, pp. 88–89.

Davies, E.R. (1978) Helping postgraduate demonstrators in the laboratory. *Studies in Higher Education* 3(1), 81–85.

Davies, G. and Higgins, J. (1982) *Computers, Language and Language Learning*. London: CILT.

Davies, I.K. (1976) *Objectives in Curriculum Design*. London: McGraw Hill.

Davies, I.K. (1981) *Instructional Technique*. New York: McGraw Hill.

Day, R.A. (1977) How to write a scientific paper. *IEEE Transactions on Professional Communication PC–20*, 1, 32–37.

DeCecco, J.P. (1971) *Conviction, Choice and Action: An Honorable and Practical Educational Psychology*. Paper available from the author, Department of Psychology, San Francisco State College.

Deffenbacher, J.L. and Michaels, A.C. (1981a) Anxiety management training and self-control desensitisation – 15 months later. *Journal of Counseling Psychology* 28(5), 459–462.

Deffenbacher, J.L. and Michaels, A.C. (1981b) A 12-month follow-up of homogeneous and heterogeneous anxiety management training. *Journal of Counseling Psychology* 28(5), 463–466.

Deffenbacher, J.L., Michaels, A.C., Michaels, T. and Daley, P.C. (1980) Comparison of anxiety management training and self-control desensitisation. *Journal of Counseling Psychology* 27, 232–239.

Demetriou, B. and Parsonage, J.R. (1977) Chemistry for electrical engineers. *Journal of Chemical Education* 54(4), 221.

Dick, W. and Carey, L. (1978) *The Systematic Design of Instruction*. Glenview, Ill.: Scott Foresman.

Domino, G. (1971) Interactive effects of achievement orientation and teaching style on academic achievement. *Journal of Educational Psychology* 62(5), 427–431.

Driskell, J. (1976) A study of the effectiveness of a guided note-taking and study-skills system upon the level of academic success among entering University of Idaho freshmen. *Dissertation Abstracts* 37, 1305–A.

Duchastel, P. (1979) Retention of prose materials: the effect of testing. *Journal of Educational Research* 72, 299–300.

Duchastel, P. (1980) Extension of testing effects on the retention of prose. *Psychological Reports* 47, 1062.

Duchastel, P. and Nungester, R. (1981) Long-term retention of prose following testing. *Psychological Reports* 49, 470.

Du Feu, V.M. (1968) The language laboratory and minimal skills courses. In *Innovations and Experiments in University Teaching*. London: University Teaching Methods Unit, University of London Institute of Education.

Eble, K.E. (1972) *Professors as Teachers*. London: Jossey Bass.

Elbow, P. (1973) *Writing Without Teachers*. London: Oxford University Press.

Ellington, H.I., Percival, F. and Addinall, E. (1980) The potential role of games and simulations in science education. In Winterburn, R. and Evans, L. (eds) *Aspects of Educational Technology 14*. London: Kogan Page, pp. 90–94.

Elsey, B. (1982) Mature students experience of university. *Studies in Adult Education* **14**, Sept., 69–77.

Elstein, A.S., Spaafka, S.A. and Bordage, G. (1979) Problem solving applications of research to undergraduate instruction and evaluation. *Programmed Learning and Educational Technology* **16**(4), 296–302.

Elton, L.R.B. (1968) Success and failure in university physics courses. *Physics Education* **3**(6), 323–329.

English, H.B., Welborn, E.L. and Killian, C.D. (1934) Studies in substance memorisation. *Journal of General Psychology* **11**(2), 233–260.

Entwistle, D. (1960) Evaluations of study skills courses: a review. *Journal of Educational Research* **53**(7), 243–252.

Entwistle, N.J. (1972) Personality and academic attainment. *British Journal of Educational Psychology* **42**(2), 137–151.

Entwistle, N.J. (1974) *Sylbs, Sylfs and Ambiverts: Labelling and Libelling Students*. University of Lancaster, Department of Educational Research.

Entwistle, N.J. and Brennan, T. (1971) The academic performance of students: 2. Types of successful students. *British Journal of Educational Psychology* **41**(3), 268–276.

Entwistle, N.J., Nisbet, J.B., Entwistle, D.M. and Cowell, M.D. (1971a) The academic performance of students: 1. Predictions from scales of motivation and study methods. *British Journal of Educational Psychology* **41**(3), 258–267.

Entwistle, N.J., Percy, K.A. and Nisbet, J.B. (1971b) Preliminary report to the Rowntree Trust. University of Lancaster, Department of Educational Research.

Entwistle, N.J. and Wilson, J.D. (1977) *Degrees of Excellence: The Academic Achievement Game*. London: Hodder & Stoughton.

Epstein, H.J. (1970) *A Strategy for Education*. London: Oxford University Press.

Epstein, H.J. (1972) An experiment in education. *Nature* **235** (5335), 203–205.

Erskine, C.A. and O'Morchoe, C.C.C. (1961) Research on teaching methods: its significance for the curriculum. *Lancet* **1**, 709–711.

Evans, C. (1980) The use of student led groups or syndicates in French literature courses. *British Journal of Educational Technology* **11**(3), 185–200.

Evans, L.R., Ingersol, R.W. and Smith, E.J. (1966) The reliability, validity and taxonomic structure of the oral examination. *Journal of Medical Education* **41**(7), 651–657.

Eysenck, H.J. (1947) Student selection by means of psychological tests – a critical survey. *British Journal of Educational Psychology* **17**(1), 20–39.

Eysenck, H.J. (1965) *Fact and Fiction in Psychology*. Harmondsworth: Penguin.

Eysenck, H.J. (1972a) Personality and attainment: an application of psychological principles to educational objectives. *Higher Education* **1**(1), 39–52.

Eysenck, H.J. (1972b) Personality and learning. In Wall, W.D. and Varma, V.P. (eds) *Advances in Educational Psychology I*. London: University of London Press.

Falk, B. (1966) The preparation and in-service training of university staff. *Australian Journal of Higher Education* **2**, 200–206.

Falus, I. and McAleese, W.R. (1975) A bibliography of microteaching. *Programmed Learning and Educational Technology* **12**(1), 34–53.

Feldhusen, J. (1961) An evaluation of college students' reactions to open book examination. *Educational and Psychological Measurement* 21(3), 637–646.

Ferguson, C., Gray, T.G.F., Harvey, T.M. and King, W. (1976) Audio visual guidance for laboratory teaching. *European Journal of Engineering Education* 1(3), 190–196.

Flood-Page, C. (1967) Worrying about examinations. *Cambridge Institute of Education Bulletin* 3(6), 2–7.

Flood-Page, C. (1971) *Technical Aids to Teaching in Higher Education*. Guildford: Society for Research into Higher Education.

Flood-Page, C. (1974) *Student Evaluation of Teaching: The American Experience*. Guildford: Society for Research into Higher Education.

Fontana, D. (1981) *Psychology for Teachers*. London: Macmillan.

Forman, D. (1972) *Revision Strategies of Second-year Students and Exam Performance*. Unpublished dissertation, University of Keele.

Fox, D. (1981) How polytechnic lecturers perceive their roles and training needs – some implications for staff development. *Bulletin of Educational Research* 22, 15–22.

Fox, M.F. and Faver, C.A. (1982) The process of collaboration in scholarly research. *Scholarly Publishing* 13(4), 327–339.

Freeman, J., Carter, G. and Jordan, T. (1978) Cognitive styles, personality factors, problem solving skills and teaching approaches in electrical engineering. *Assessment in Higher Education* 3(2), 86–121.

Freemantle, M.H. (1976) Keller Plans in chemistry teaching. *Education in Chemistry* 13(2), 50–51.

Freemantle, M.H. and Blackler, T.C. (1975) A personalised system of instruction in physical chemistry. In *Progress in Chemical Education*. Sheffield Polytechnic, pp. 56–60.

Fry, E. (1963a) *Teaching Faster Reading – A Manual*. Cambridge: Cambridge University Press.

Fry, E. (1963b) *Reading Faster*. Cambridge: Cambridge University Press.

Furniss, B.S. and Parsonage, J.R. (1975) Student assessment on entry to chemistry courses. *Research in Assessment*. Chemical Society Assessment Group, pp. 52–56.

Gabb, R.G. (1978) Student rating of the components of a successful self-instructional course. *Programmed Learning and Educational Technology* 15(4), 284–290.

Gadzella, B.M. (1982) Computer-assisted instruction in study-skills. *Journal of Experimental Education* 50(3), 122–126.

Gage, N.L. (ed.) (1963) *Handbook of Research on Teaching*. Chicago: Rand McNally.

Gagné, R.M. (1977) *The Conditions of Learning*, 3rd ed. New York: Holt, Rinehart and Winston.

Gagné, R.M. (1980) Is educational technology in phase? *Educational Technology* 20(2), 7–14.

Galbraith, D. (1980) The effect of conflicting goals on writing: a case study. *Visible Language* 14(4), 364–375.

Gale, J., Jolly, B. and Devine, M. (1976) Choice and design of an individual learning package – audiotape and booklet. In Clarke, J. and Leedham, J. (eds) *Aspects of Educational Technology 10*. London: Kogan Page, pp. 135–138.

Galton, M.J., Holloway, J.H., Raynor, J.B. and Tomlinson, M.J. (1976) Introducing chemistry at university. *Education in Chemistry* 13(2), 38–40.

Gardner, P.H. and Winslow, J.D. (1982) *Language Needs in Higher Education: Identifying the Needs of Students of Courses in the Public Sector H.E. Containing a Significant Foreign Language Element.* London: Department of Education and Science/The London Chamber of Commerce and Industry.

Garfield, L. and McHugh, E.A. (1979) Learning counselling: a higher education student support service. *Journal of Higher Education* 49(4), 382–392.

Garland, J. and Munn, C. (1983) Micro-computers and teaching biology. *CAL News* 21, February.

Garland, P.B., Dutton, G.F. and Macqueen, D. (1977) Audio-tutorial aids for teaching biochemistry. *Studies in Higher Education* 2(2), 167–171.

Gaunt, H.M. (1978) Tape/pictures in the laboratory. *British Journal of Educational Technology* 9(3), 176–180.

Geiger, R.L. (1980) The changing demand for higher education in the seventies. Adaptations within three national systems. *Higher Education* 9(3), 255–276.

Gibbs, G. (1981) *Teaching Students to Learn.* Milton Keynes: Open University Press.

Gibson, J.N. (1970) Paper in a symposium on attitudes measurement in exploratory studies. *Bulletin of the British Psychological Society* 23, 323–324.

Gilbert, J.K. (1980) The use of models in science and science teaching. *European Journal of Science Education* 2(1), 3–11.

Gilbert, N.S. (1976) Classmate versus instructor evaluation of learning. *Improving College and University Teaching* 24(2), 119–121, 123.

Glaser, R. (1979) Trends and research questions in psychological research on learning and schooling. *Educational Researcher* 8(10), 6–13.

Glen, J.W., Whitworth, R.W. and Biddiscombe, R. (1983) Introducing students to the scientific literature. *Teaching News* No. 20, University of Birmingham.

Gohdin, W.R., Mammen, E.W. and Dodding, J. (1970) *The Art of Speaking Made Simple*, rev. ed. London: W.H. Allen.

Goodlad, S. (1975) *Project Methods in Higher Education.* Guildford: Society for Research into Higher Education.

Goodlad, S. (1977) *Socio-technical Projects in Engineering Education.* Stirling: University of Stirling, The General Education in Engineering (GEE) Project.

Gorbutt, D. (1974) The new sociology of education. In Reid, I. and Wormold, E. (eds) *Sociology and Teacher Education.* London: Social Section, ATCDE.

Gordon, M.D. (1978) The role of referees in scientific communication. In Hartley, J. (ed.) (1980) *The Psychology of Written Communication: Selected Readings.* London: Kogan Page.

Graves, V. (1976) Tape/slide in individual learning for medical topics. In Clarke, J. and Leedham, J. (eds) *Aspects of Educational Technology 11.* London: Kogan Page, pp. 145–148.

Greenaway, H. (1971) *Training of University Teachers.* Pamphlet 2, July. Guildford: Society for Research into Higher Education.

Greenaway, H. and Harding, A.G. (1978) *The Growth of Policies for Staff Development.* Research into Higher Education Monograph No. 34. Guildford: Society for Research into Higher Education.

Greiner, J.M. and Karoly, P. (1976) Effects of self control training on study activity and academic performance. *Journal of Counseling Psychology* 23(6), 495–502.

Gronlund, N.E. (1976) *Measurement and Evaluation in Teaching*, 3rd ed. New York: Macmillan.

Grubb, R.E. and Selfridge, L. (1964) Computer tutoring in statistics. *Computers and Automation*, March, 20–26.

Hall, W.C. (1979) An approach to evaluating tertiary courses. *Programmed Learning and Educational Technology* 16(2), 136–139.

Hammersley, J.H. (1968) On the enfeeblement of mathematical skills by 'modern mathematics' and by similar soft tack in schools and universities. *Bulletin of the Institute of Mathematics and its Applications* 4, 1–22.

Hammond, K.R. and Kern, F. (1959) *Teaching Comprehensive Medical Care*. Cambridge: Harvard University Press.

Harden, R.M. and Cairncross, R.G. (1980) Assessment of practical skills: the objective structured practical examination. *Studies in Higher Education* 5(2), 187–196.

Hardesty, L., Lovrich, N.P. and Mannon, J. (1982) Library-use instruction: assessment of the long-term effects. *College and Research Libraries* 43(1), 38–46.

Hardy, J.E. (1974) Writing good papers: the art and technique. In Pauk, W. (ed.) *How to Study in College*, 2nd ed. Boston: Houghton Mifflin.

Harri-Augstein, S., Smith, M. and Thomas, L. (1982) *Reading to Learn*. London: Methuen.

Harris, N.D.C. and Dowdeswell, W.H. (1979) Assessment of projects in university science. *Assessment in Higher Education* 4(2), 94–118.

Harrison, R. (1983) Students and validation. In Church, C.H. (ed.) *Practice and Perspective in Validation*. Guildford: Society for Research into Higher Education.

Harrow, A.J. (1972) *A Taxonomy of the Psychomotor Domain*. New York: McKay.

Hartley, J. (1972a) New approaches in the teaching of psychology: an annotated bibliography. *Bulletin of the British Psychological Society* 25(89), 291–304.

Hartley, J. (1972b) Evaluation. In Hartley, J. (ed.) *Strategies for Programmed Instruction*. London: Butterworth.

Hartley, J. (1974) Programmed instruction 1954–1974: a review. *Programmed Learning and Educational Technology* 11(6), 278–291.

Hartley, J. (1976) Lecture handouts and student notetaking. *Programmed Learning and Educational Technology* 13(2), 58–64.

Hartley, J. (ed.) (1980) *The Psychology of Written Communication: Selected Readings*. London: Kogan Page.

Hartley, J. (1981) Eighty ways of improving instructional text. *IEEE Transactions on Professional Communication* PC–24, 1, 17–27.

Hartley, J. (1983) Notetaking research: re-setting the scoreboard. *Bulletin of the British Psychological Society* 36, 13–14.

Hartley, J. (1984) How can tutors help students to write essays? In Shaw, K.E. (ed.) *Aspects of Educational Technology 17*. London: Kogan Page, pp. 74–79.

Hartley, J., Bartlett, S. and Branthwaite, J.A. (1980) Underlining can make a difference – sometimes! *Journal of Educational Research* 73(4), 218–224.

Hartley, J. and Branthwaite, J.A. (1976) All this for two percent: the contribution of course-work assessment to the final grade. *Durham Research Review* 8(37), 14–20.

Hartley, J. and Branthwaite, J.A. (1977) Course-work assessment: computer-aided decision making. In Hills, P. and Gilbert, J. (eds) *Aspects of Educational Technology 11*. London: Kogan Page, pp. 301–306.

Hartley, J. and Cameron, A. (1967) Some observations on the efficiency of lecturing. *Educational Review* **20**(1), 30–37.

Hartley, J. and Davies, I.K. (1977) Programmed learning and educational technology. In Howe, M.J.A. (ed.) *Adult Learning*. London: Wiley.

Hartley, J. and Davies, I.K. (1978) Notetaking: a critical review. *Programmed Learning and Educational Technology* **15**(3), 207–224.

Hartley, J. and Hogarth, F. (1971) Academic motivation and programmed learning. *British Journal of Educational Psychology* **41**(2), 171–183.

Hartley, J. and Knapper, C.K. (1984) Academics and their writing. *Studies in Higher Education* (in press).

Hartley, J. and Marshall, S. (1974) On notes and notetaking. *Universities Quarterly* **28**(2), 225–235.

Hartley, J.R. (1978) An appraisal of computer-assisted learning in the U.K. *Programmed Learning and Educational Technology* **15**(2), 136–151.

Hartog, P. and Rhodes, E.C. (1936) *The Marks of Examiners*. London: Macmillan.

Hawkins, S., Davies, I.K., Majer, K. and Hartley, J. (1981) *Getting Started: Guides for Beginning Teachers*, 2nd ed. Oxford: Blackwell.

Hawkridge, D. (1981) The telesis of educational technology. *British Journal of Educational Technology* **12**(1), 4–18.

Hazell, J. (1976) The problem of pointlessness – a challenge for counselling. *British Journal of Guidance and Counselling* **4**(2), 156–170.

Hegarty, E.H. (1978) Levels of scientific enquiry in university science laboratory classes: implications for curriculum deliberations. *Research in Science Education* **8**, 45–57.

Henderson, E.S. (1980) The essay in continuous assessment. *Studies in Higher Education* **5**(2), 197–204.

Henman, M. (1981) *Orientations of Staff and Students Towards the Study of Pharmacology*. Paper read at the Pharmacology Conference, held at the University of Bradford, April 1981.

Hereford, S. (1979) The Keller Plan (PSI) within a conventional academic environment: an empirical 'meta-analytic study'. *The Journal of Engineering Education* **70**(3), 250–260.

Herzberg, F. (1966) *Work and the Nature of Man*. Cleveland, Ohio: World Publishing.

Hewton, E. (1982) *Rethinking Educational Change: A Case for Diplomacy*. Research into Education Monographs. Guildford: Society for Research into Higher Education.

Highet, G. (1976) *The Immortal Profession*. New York: Weybright and Talley.

Hilgard, E.R. and Bower, G. (1975) *Theories of Learning*, 4th ed. Englewood Cliffs, NJ: Prentice Hall.

Hill, B.J. (1969) The analysis of objectives for lecture courses in the physical sciences and engineering. In *Conference on Objectives in Higher Education*. London: University Teaching Methods Unit, University of London Institute of Education.

Hill, B.J. (1977) The double marking of scripts in university examinations in engineering. *Assessment in Higher Education* 2(2), 87–103.

Hill, J.E. and Nunnery, D.K. (1971) *Personalising Educational Programs Utilising Cognitive Style Mapping.* Pamphlet from the authors, Oakland Community College, 2480 Opdyke Road, Bloomfield Hills, Michigan 48013, USA.

Himmelweit, H.T. (1950) Student selection – an experimental investigation. *British Journal of Sociology* 1, 328–346.

Hirsh, W. (1982) Postgraduate training of researchers. In Oldham, G. (ed.) *The Future of Research.* Guildford: Society for Research into Higher Education.

Hofstein, A. and Lunetta, V.N. (1982) The role of the laboratory in science teaching: neglected aspects of research. *Review of Educational Research* 52(2), 201–217.

Hogg, D.R. (1973) Student attitudes to programmed learning. *Education in Chemistry* 10(1), 7–9.

Hohne, H.H. (1965) Success and failure. *Scientific Faculties of the University of Melbourne.* Melbourne: Australian Council for Educational Research.

Holloway, P.J., Hardwick, J.L., Morris, J. and Start, K.B. (1967) The validity of essay and viva-voce examining techniques. *British Dental Journal* 123, 227–232.

Hooper, R. (1977) *National Development Programme in Computer Assisted Learning: Final Report of the Director.* London: The Council for Educational Technology.

Hounsell, D. (1982) *Learning and Writing.* Paper available from the author, Institute for Research and Development in Post Compulsory Education, University of Lancaster, Lancaster.

Howard, K. and Sharp, J.A. (1983) *Management of a Student Research Project.* London: Gower Press.

Hudson, L. (1966) *Contrary Imaginations.* London: Methuen.

Hudson, L. (1968) *Frames of Mind.* London: Methuen.

Hunter, R.L.C. (1971) Some reflections on the relevance of educational thought for Scottish law teaching. *Juridical Review* 16, 1–19.

Iliffe, A.H. (1966) Objective tests. Reprinted in Davies, I.K. and Hartley, J. (1972) *Contributions to an Educational Technology.* London: Butterworth.

Illingworth, C. (1963) The multiple choice or objective examination: a controlled trial. *Lancet* 2, 1268–1271.

Imrie, B.W., Blithe, T.M. and Johnston, L.C. (1980) A review of Keller principles with reference to mathematics courses in Australia. *British Journal of Educational Technology* 11(2), 105–121.

Jahoda, M. and Thomas, L.F. (1966) The mechanics of learning. *New Scientist* 30, 114–117.

James, D.E. (1967) *A Students Guide to Efficient Study.* London: Pergamon.

James, R.L. (1967) An investigation into the reading efficiency of students at a technical teaching training college. *British Journal of Educational Psychology* 37(3), 391–393.

Jamison, D., Suppes, P. and Wells, S. (1974) The effectiveness of alternative instructional media: a survey. *Review of Educational Research* 44(1), 1–67.

Jehu, D., Picton, C.J. and Futcher, S. (1970) The use of notes in examinations. *British Journal of Educational Psychology* 40(3), 335–337.

Jevons, F.R. (1970) Liberal studies in science – a successful experiment. *Education in Chemistry* 7, 98–99.

Jewell, T.D. (1982) Student reactions to a self-paced library skills workbook program: survey evidence. *College and Research Libraries* 43(5), 371–378.

Johnson, P.C. and Abrahamson, S. (1968) The effects of grades and examinations on self-directed learning. *Journal of Medical Education* 43(3), 200–204.

Johnston, R.F. and Fiel, N.J. (1967) *Structured Learning and Training Environments: A Preparation Laboratory for Advanced Mammalian Physiology*. Project Report No. 203, March. Michigan State University.

Johnstone, A.H. and Percival, F. (1976) Attention breaks in lectures. *Education in Chemistry* 13(2), 49–50.

Johnstone, A.H. and Wham, A.J.B. (1979) A model for undergraduate practical work. *Education in Chemistry* 16(1), 16–17.

Jolly, B. (1972) A review of issues in live patient simulation. *Programmed Learning and Educational Technology* 19(2), 99–107.

Jolly, W.P. and Turner, C.W. (1979) The transition from school to university: some experimental induction programmes for engineering students. *Studies in Higher Education* 4(1), 39–46.

Jones, R.T. (1969) Multiform assessment: a York experiment. *Cambridge Review* 15, 43–47.

Kalish, R. (1958) An experimental evaluation of the open book examination. *Journal of Educational Psychology* 49(4), 200–204.

Keller, F.S. (1968) 'Good-bye teacher . . .'. *Journal of Applied Behaviour Analysis* 1, 78–89. Reprinted in Hartley, J. and Davies, I.K. (eds) (1978) *Contributions to an Educational Technology, Vol. 2*. London: Kogan Page.

Kempa, R.F. and Ongley, P.A. (1979) *Profile Assessment in Chemistry*. Report available from the first author, University of Keele, Keele, Staffordshire, ST5 5BG.

King, R. (1976) Data on student performance under different kinds of assessment. *Assessment in Higher Education* 2(1), 31–45.

Klein, J. (1965) *The Study of Groups*. London: Routledge & Kegan Paul.

Knights, S. and McDonald, R. (1977) Adult learners in university courses. In Billing, D. (ed.) *Course Design and Student Learning*. Guildford: Society for Research into Higher Education.

Knutson, A.L. (1960) Quiet and vocal groups. *Sociometry* 23, 36–40.

Kozma, R.B. (1982) Instructional design in a chemistry laboratory course: the impact of structure and aptitudes on performance and attitudes. *Journal of Research in Science Teaching* 19, 261–270.

Kulik, J.A., Kulik, C.C. and Smith, B. (1976) Research on the personalised system of instruction. *Programmed Learning and Educational Technology* 13(1), 23–30.

Kyle, W.C., Penick, J.E. and Shymansky, J.A. (1979) Assessing and analyzing the performance of students in college science laboratories. *Journal of Research in Science Teaching* 16, 545–551.

Lacey, P.A. (1983) The politics of vitalizing teaching. In Lacey, P.A. (ed.) *Revitalizing Teaching Through Faculty Development. New Directions in Teaching, Vol. 15*. San Francisco: Jossey Bass.

Larkin, J.H. and Reif, F. (1976) Analysis and teaching of a general skill for studying scientific text. *Journal of Educational Psychology* 68(4), 431–440.

Laurillard, D. (1979) The process of student learning. *Higher Education* 8(4), 395–410.

Lavin, D.E. (1967) *The Prediction of Academic Performance*. New York: Wiley.

Leblond, E., Rutherford, R.J.D. and Trickey, D.S. (1975) A case study of the effect of linear standardization of examination marks on final degree classification in applied chemistry. *Progress in Chemical Education*. Sheffield Polytechnic, pp. 94–99.

Legge, D. (1981) Trends in assessment in psychology. *Assessment and Evaluation in Higher Education* 6(2), 165–174.

Leith, G.O.M. (1969) Learning and personality. In Dunn, W.R. and Holroyd, C. (eds) *Aspects of Educational Technology 2*. London: Methuen, pp. 101–110.

Lewin, K. (1947) Group discussion and social change. In Newcomb, T.M. and Hartley, E.L. (eds) *Readings in Social Psychology*. New York: Holt, Rinehart and Winston.

Lewis, R. and Tomlinson, N. (1977) Examples of tutor–student exchange by correspondence. *Teaching at a Distance* 8, 39–46.

Lloyd, D.H. (1968) A concept of improvement of learning responses in the taught lesson. *Visual Education*, October, 23–25.

Long, N.R. and Povey, T.A. (1982) Audio-tapes in distance teaching: a New Zealand experience. *Teaching at a Distance* 21, 60–65.

Lovell, R.D. (1980) *Adult Learning*. London: Croom Helm.

Lowe, B. (1982) Teaching problem solving to undergraduate engineering students. *British Journal of Educational Technology* 13(2), 137–152.

Lowenthal, D. and Wason, P.C. (1977) Academics and their writing. *Times Literary Supplement*, 24 June, p. 782.

Lunt, H.N. (ed.) (1973) *Language and Language Teaching: Current Research in Britain, 1971–72*. London: Centre for Information on Language Teaching and Research, 20 Carlton Terrace, London WC2.

Lunt, H.N. (ed.) (1976) *Language and Language Teaching: Current Research in Britain, 1973–74*, 2nd ed. London: Longman.

Lunt, H.N. (ed.) (1978) *Language and Language Teaching: Current Research in Britain, 1975–77*, 3rd ed. London: Longman.

Lunt, H.N. (ed.) (1983) *Language and Language Teaching: Current Research in Britain, 1977–83*. Duplicated typescript. London: CILTR.

MacDonald, C. (1981) *Textbook Buying and Reading Habits of Undergraduate Students*. Unpublished MPhil thesis: University of Bradford.

Macdonald-Ross, M. (1971) Practical work in science. A talk given at the University of Birmingham, 24 November.

Macdonald-Ross, M. (1973) Behavioural objectives: a critical review. *Instructional Science* 2(1), 1–50.

MacIntosh, N. (1976) *A Degree of Difference*. Guildford: Society for Research into Higher Education.

Mack, D. (1978) *The Workshop Way*. Report on the National Working Conference held at the University of Stirling, 9–12 June 1978. CCTUT Occasional Publication No. 1.

MacKenzie, K. (1974) Some thoughts on tutoring by written correspondence in the Open University. *Teaching at a Distance* 1, 45–51.

312   Teaching and Learning in Higher Education

MacKenzie, K. (1976) Student reactions to tutor comments on the tutor marked assignment. *Teaching at a Distance* 5, 53–58.

Maddox, H. (1963) *How to Study*. London: Pan.

Maddox, H. and Hoole, E. (1975) Performance decrement in the lecture. *Educational Review* 28(1), 17–30.

Maher, B. (1978) A reader's, writer's and reviewer's guide to assessing research reports in clinical psychology. *Journal of Consulting and Clinical Psychology* 46(4), 835–838.

Mahon, H.F. (1977) Student response to differential learning tasks in CML. *Programmed Learning and Educational Technology* 14(2), 168–175.

Main, A. (1980) *Encouraging Effective Learning*. Edinburgh: Scottish Academic Press.

Main, A. (1984) Study counselling at Strathclyde. In Zuber-Skerritt, O. (ed.) *Video in Higher Education*. London: Kogan Page.

Malleson, N. (1967) Treatment of pre-examination strain. In *A Handbook on British Student Health Services*. London: Pitman Medical, ch. 6.

Mann, P.H. (1974) *Students and Books*. London: Routledge & Kegan Paul.

Markle, S.M. (1969) *Good Frames and Bad*, 2nd ed. New York: Wiley.

Marris, P. (1964) *The Experience of Higher Education*. London: Routledge & Kegan Paul.

Marsh, H.W. (1982a) SEEQ: A reliable, valid and useful instrument for collecting students evaluations of university teaching. *British Journal of Educational Psychology* 52(1), 77–95.

Marsh, H.W. (1982b) Students' evaluations of tertiary instruction: testing the applicability of American surveys in an Australian setting. *Australian Journal of Education* 25(2), 77–95.

Marshall, J.G. and Powers, J.M. (1969) Writing neatness, composition errors, and essay grades. *Journal of Educational Measurement* 6(2), 97–101.

Marton, F. and Saljö, R. (1976) On qualitative differences in learning: 1. Outcome and process. *British Journal of Educational Psychology* 46(1), 4–11.

Matheson, C.C. (1981) *Staff Development Matters. Academic Staff Training and Development in Universities of the United Kingdom. A Review: 1961–1981*. London: CCTUT.

Mathias, H. and Rutherford, D. (1982) Lecturers as evaluators: the Birmingham experience. *Studies in Higher Education* 7(1), 47–56.

McAleese, R. (1978) *Perspectives on Academic Gaming and Simulation: Vol. 3. Training and Professional Education*. London: Kogan Page.

McClelland, D.C. (1970) *The Achieving Society*. New York: Free Press.

McClelland, D.C., Atkinson, J.W., Clark, R.A. and Lowell, E.L. (1953) *The Achievement Motive*. New York: Appleton Century Crofts.

McDonald, R. and Knights, S. (1979) Learning from tapes: the experience of home-based students. *Programmed Learning and Educational Technology* 14(2), 168–175.

McElroy, A.R. and McNaughton, F.C. (1979) A project based approach to the use of biological literature. *Journal of Biological Education* 13(1), 52–57.

McGregor, D. (1960) *The Human Side of Enterprise*. New York: McGraw-Hill.

McGuire, C. (1963) A process approach to the construction and analysis of medical examinations. *Journal of Medical Education* **38**(7), 556–563.

McKeachie, W.J. (1963) Research on teaching at the college and university level. In Gage, N.L. (ed.) *Handbook of Research on Teaching*. Chicago: Rand McNally.

McKenzie, J. (1977) Computers in the teaching of undergraduate science. *British Journal of Educational Technology* **8**(3), 214–224.

McNay, I. and McCormick, R. (1982) *Case Study 3 of Curriculum Evaluation and Assessment in Educational Institutions*. Milton Keynes: Open University.

McVey, P.J. (1968) Student evaluation of lectures. In *Innovations and Experiments in University Teaching Methods*. London: University Teaching Methods Unit, University of London Institute of Education.

McVey, P.J. (1975) The errors in marking exam. scripts in electrical engineering. *International Journal of Electrical Engineering Education* **12**(3), 203–216.

Megarry, J. (1975) A review of science games – variations on a theme of rummy. *Simulations and Games* **6**(4), 423.

Megarry, J. (1979) *Perspectives on Academic Gaming and Simulation: Vol. 4. Human Factors in Gaming and Simulation*. London: Kogan Page.

Meichenbaum, D. (1977) *Cognitive Behaviour Modification: An Integrative Approach*. New York: Plenum.

Melton, R. (1978) Resolution of conflicting claims concerning the effect of behavioural objectives on student learning. *Review of Educational Research* **48**(2), 291–302.

Meyer, E. and Veenstra, V. (1980) *Teaching Bread and Butter: A Practical Guide to Effective Teaching and Learning*. Johannesburg: McGraw Hill.

Miller, G. (ed.) (1962) *Teaching and Learning in Medical School*. Boston: Harvard University Press.

Miller, P.M. and Dale, R.R. (1972) The academic progress of male and female first year university students compared. *Research in Education* **8**, 56–60.

Mitzel, H.E. (1974) An examination of the short range potential of computer managed instruction. *CMI Conference Planning Abstract*. November. Chicago: Executive House.

Moreira, M.A. (1980) A non-traditional approach to the evaluation of laboratory instruction in general physics courses. *European Journal of Science Education* **2**(4), 441–448.

Morris, F.C. (1950) *Effective Teaching: A Manual for Engineering Instructors*. New York: McGraw Hill.

Morris, F.C., Surber, C.F. and Bijou, S.W. (1978) Self-pacing versus instructor-pacing: achievement, evaluation and retention. *Journal of Educational Psychology* **70**(2), 224–230.

Morrow-Brown, C. (1978) *Summary of Research into Sources of Grade Variation in Exams. and Other Forms of Assessment*. Paper from the Student Assessment Research Group, Institute of Educational Technology, Open University.

Mosel, J.N. (1964) The learning process. *Journal of Medical Education* **39**(4), 485–496.

Moss, G.D. (1977) Staff development by post or 'the mountain to Mohammed'. *Impetus* **7**, 26–29.

Moss, G.D. and McMillen, D. (1980) A strategy for developing problem-solving skills in undergraduate classes. *Studies in Higher Education* 5(2), 161–171.

Mullinger, L. (1977) A cautionary genetic tale. *Journal of Biological Education* 11(4), 261–265.

Naaera, N. (1972) *Objectives for a Course in Physiology for Medical Students.* Aarhus, Denmark: University of Aarhus.

Nadeau, G.G. (1977) Student evaluation of instruction: the rating questionnaire. In Knapper, C.K., Geis, G.L., Pascal, C.E. and Shore, B.M. (eds) *If Teaching is Important* . . . Canada: Clarke Unwin.

National Union of Students (1969a) *Report of the Commission on Teaching in Higher Education.* Presented to Liverpool Conference, April 1969. London: NUS.

National Union of Students (1969b) *NUS Executive Report on Examinations.* Presented to Liverpool Conference, April 1969. London: NUS.

Natkin, E. and Guild, R.E. (1967) Evaluation of preclinical laboratory performance. *Journal of Dental Education* 31, 152–161.

Neidt, C.O. and Sjogren, D.D. (1968) Changes in students attitudes during a course in relation to industrial media. *Audio Visual Communication Review* 16(3), 268–279.

Nelson-Jones, R. and Toner, H.L. (1978) Approaches to increasing student learning competence. *British Journal of Guidance and Counselling* 6(1), 19–34.

Neufeld, V. and Barrows, H.S. (1974) The 'McMaster Philosophy': an approach to medical education. *Journal of Medical Education* 49(11), 1040–1050.

Newton, J. and Seville, A.H. (1977) Syndicate studies for the systems and management degree. *Physics Education* 12(4), 217–220.

Nicholson, N. (1977) Counselling the adult learner in the Open University. *Teaching at a Distance* 8, 62–69.

Norton, L.S. (1981a) The effects of notetaking and subsequent use on long-term recall. *Programmed Learning and Educational Technology* 18(1), 16–22.

Norton, L.S. (1981b) Patterned note-taking: an evaluation. *Visible Language* XV(1), 67–85.

November, P.J.C. (1978) The tutorial–tape–document learning package. *Studies in Higher Education* 3(1), 91–95.

Nuffield Foundation (1974–1976) *Newsletters* Nos. 5, 6 and 7. London: Nuffield Lodge, Regents Park.

O'Connell, S., Wilson, A.W. and Elton, L.R.B. (1969) A pre-knowledge survey for university science students. *Nature* 222, 52.

Ogborn, J. (ed.) (1977a) *Small Group Teaching in Undergraduate Science.* London: Heinemann.

Ogborn, J. (ed.) (1977b) *Practical Work in Undergraduate Science.* London: Heinemann.

Ongley, P.A. (1975) Student assessment of university teachers and teaching through the closed questionnaire. In *Research in Assessment.* London: Chemical Society Assessment Group, pp. 57–62.

Open University (1980) *Plain English. Living with Technology. A Foundation Course.* Milton Keynes: Open University Press.

Orpen, C. (1976) Personality and academic attainment: a cross-cultural study. *British Journal of Educational Psychology* 46(2), 220–222.

Orpen, C. (1982) Student v lecturer assessment of learning: a research note. *Higher*

Education 11(5), 567–572.

Over, R. (1982) Collaborative research and publication in psychology. *American Psychologist* 37(9), 996–1001.

Parlett, M.R. and Hamilton, J.G. (1978) Evaluation as illumination. Reprinted in Hartley, J. and Davies, I.K. (eds) *Contributions to an Educational Technology Vol. 2.* London: Kogan Page.

Parlett, M.R. and Miller, C.H.L. (1974) *Up to the Mark.* Guildford: Society for Research into Higher Education.

Pask, G. (1975) *Conversation, Cognition and Learning.* Amsterdam: Elsevier.

Pask, G. (1976) Styles and strategies of learning. *British Journal of Educational Psychology* 46(2), 128–148.

Pauk, W. (1974) *How to Study in College.* Boston: Houghton Mifflin.

Paul, G.L. (1966) *Insight Versus Desensitization in Psychotherapy.* Stanford, Calif.: Stanford University Press.

Payne, V. and Lipschitz, V. (1982) *The Alternative Prospectus,* rev. ed. London: Wildwood House.

Pearlmutter, A.F. and Pearlmutter, F.A. (1977) Classroom time utilization in a self-study biochemistry course for medical studies. *Biochemical Education* 5(1), 5–8.

Pentony, P. (1968) A study of students in academic difficulties. *Australian Journal of Higher Education* 3(2), 179–185.

Perkins, J. (1968) A problem-solving approach to teaching a survey course. *Journal of Engineering Education* 66(8), 845–847.

Perry, W. (1976) *Open University.* Milton Keynes: Open University Press.

Perry, W.G. (1970) *Forms of Intellectual and Ethical Development in the College Years: a Scheme.* New York: Holt, Rinehart and Winston.

Peters, R.S. (1958) *The Concept of Motivation.* London: Routledge & Kegan Paul.

Peterson, H.A., Ellis, M. Toohill, N. and Kloess, P. (1935) Some measurement of the effects of reviews. *Journal of Educational Psychology* 26(1), 65–72.

Phillips, R.J. (1981) *An Investigation into the Revision Tactics Used by Finalists.* Unpublished dissertation, University of Keele.

Pilkington, T.L. (1976) Filmstrip/tape programme for continuing in-service training in long-stay hospitals. In Clarke, J. and Leedham, J. (eds) *Aspects of Educational Technology 10.* London: Kogan Page, pp. 276–280.

Piper, D.W. and Glatter, R. (1977) *The Changing University: A Report on Staff Development in Universities.* Windsor: NFER.

Pitcher, J. (ed.) (1978) *HELPIS: 1978* (Higher Education Learning Programmes Information Service Catalogue), 5th ed. London: British Universities Film Council.

Poller, R.C. and Seeley, M.E. (1977) A learning aids laboratory. *Education in Chemistry* 14(2), 51–52.

Popham, W.J. (1968) Probing the validity of arguments against behavioural objectives. In Popham, W.J., Eisner, E.W., Sullivan, H.J. and Tyler, L.L. (1969) *Instructional Objectives.* Chicago: Rand McNally.

Postlethwaite, S.H. (1972) *The Audiotutorial Approach to Learning Through Independent Study: Integrated Experiences.* Minneapolis, Minn.: Burgess Publishing Co.

Poulton, E.C. (1961) British courses for adults on effective reading. *British Journal of Educational Psychology* **31**(2), 128–137.

Pramanik, A. and Dring, D. (1977) An evolving teaching laboratory for first year students of electrical and electronic engineering. *International Journal of Electrical Engineering Education* **14**(1), 17–25.

Prosser, A.P. (1967) Oral reports on laboratory work. In *Teaching for Efficient Learning*. Report of the Second Conference of the University Teaching Methods Unit, University of London Institute of Education.

Raaheim, K. and Wankowski, J. (1981) *Helping Students*. Oslo: Sigma Forlag.

Ramsden, P. (1979) Student learning and perceptions of the academic environment. *Higher Education* **8**(4), 411–428.

Ramsden, P. and Entwistle, N.J. (1981) Effects of academic departments on students' approaches to studying. *British Journal of Educational Psychology* **51**(3), 368–383.

Ratagan, B. (1977) Counselling training for tutors in higher education. *British Journal of Guidance and Counselling* **5**(1), 98–101.

Reavis, C.A. (1979) A study of the effects of prefactory remarks on teacher evaluation. *Journal of Educational Research* **72**(3), 173–177.

Reed, B., Hutton, J. and Bazalgette, J. (1978) *Freedom to Study: Requirements of Overseas Students in the U.K.* London: Overseas Students Trust (78 Vauxhall Bridge Road, London SW1V 1EZ).

Reed, R. (1981) Selecting a micro-computer. *Bulletin of Educational Research* **21**, 12–16.

Reid, N. (1976) Simulations, games and case studies. *Education in Chemistry* **13**(3), 82–83.

Rendel, M. (1975) Men and women in higher education. *Educational Review* **27**(3), 192–201.

Renner, J.W. and Paske, W.C. (1977) Comparing two forms of instruction in college physics. *American Journal of Physics* **45**(9), 851–859.

Resnick, L.B. (1973) Hierarchies in children's learning: a symposium. *Instructional Science* **2**(3), 311–361.

Rickards, J.P. (1980) Notetaking, underlining, inserted questions and organisers in the text: research conclusions and educational implications. *Educational Technology*, June, 5–11.

Riecken, H.W. (1958) The effect of talkativeness on ability to influence group solutions to problems. *Sociometry* **21**(4), 309–321.

Robin, A.L. (1976) Behavioural instruction in the college classroom. *Review of Educational Research* **46**(3), 313–334.

Robin, A.L., Fox, R.M., Martello, J. and Archable, C. (1977) Teaching note-taking skills to underachieving college students. *Journal of Educational Research* **71**(2), 81–85.

Robinson, F.P. (1961) *Effective Study*, 2nd ed. New York: Harper & Row.

Robinson, J.N. (1977) Teaching economics to adults: the use of a game. *Adult Education* **49**(5), 290–293.

Roderick, G., Bell, J. and Hamilton, S. (1982) Unqualified mature students in British universities. *Studies in Adult Education* **14**, September, 59–68.

Roe, E. and Vasta, E. (1980) Assessment in higher education, the current Australian scene. *Assessment and Evaluation in Higher Education* 5(2), 218–253.

Rogers, C. (1969) *Freedom to Learn.* New York: Merrill.

Rogers, C. (1983) *Freedom to Learn for the 80's.* New York: Merrill.

Rogers, J. (1977) *Adult Learning,* 2nd ed. Milton Keynes: Open University Press.

Romiszowski, A.J. (1974) *The Selection and Use of Instructional Media.* London: Kogan Page.

Rosati, P.A. (1973) *A Comparison of the Personalised System of Instruction with the Lecture Method in Teaching Elementary Dynamics.* University of Western Ontario.

Rose, C. (1978) *The Pathways and Pitfalls to Instructional Improvement.* ERIC Document 144 145.

Rosenfeld, R.A. (1978) Anxiety and counselling. *Teaching Sociology* 5(2), 149–166.

Ross, D. (1972–1977) *Courses in Legal Practice.* Melbourne: Leo Cussen Institute for Continuing Education.

Rowell, J.A. and Renner, V.J. (1975) Personality, mode of assessment and student achievement. *British Journal of Educational Psychology* 45(2), 232–236.

Rowley, G.L. and Traub, R.E. (1977) Formula scoring, number right scoring and test taking strategy. *Journal of Educational Measurement* 14(1), 15–22.

Rowntree, D. (1976) *Learn How to Study,* rev. ed. London: Macdonald and Jane's.

Rowntree, D. (1977) *Assessing Students: How Shall We Know Them?* London: Harper & Row.

Rudd, E. (1975) *The Highest Education.* London: Routledge & Kegan Paul.

Ruddock, J. (1978) *Learning Through Small Group Discussion: A Study of Seminar Work in Higher Education.* Guildford: Society for Research into Higher Education.

Rushby, N. (ed.) (1981) *Selected Readings in Computer Based Learning.* London: Kogan Page.

Rutherford, D. and Mathias, H. (1983) Staff development and innovation theory. In Squires, G. (ed.) *Innovation Through Recession.* Guildford: Society for Research into Higher Education.

Saljö, R. (1979) Learning about learning. *Higher Education* 8(4), 443–451.

Sanderson, P.H. (1973) Prediction of student performance by multiple choice testing. *British Journal of Medical Education* 7(4), 251–253.

Scandura, J.M. (1977) A structural approach to instructional problems. *American Psychologist* 32, 33–53.

Scarr, S. (1982) An editor looks for the perfect manuscript. In *Understanding the Manuscript Process – Increasing the Participation of Women.* Committee of Women in Psychology and Woman's Program Office. American Psychological Association.

Schmuck, R.A. and Schmuck, P.A. (1971) *Group Processes in the Classroom.* Dubque, Iowa: W.C. Brown & Co.

Schonell, F.J., Roe, E. and Middleton, I.G. (1962) *Promise and Performance.* Brisbane: University of Queensland Press.

Science and Engineering Research Council (1983) *Research Student and Supervisor: An Approach to Good Supervisory Practice.* Swindon: SERC, Polaris House, North Star Avenue, Swindon.

Seale, C. (1977) The discussion group. *Journal of Further and Higher Education* 1(1), 22–25.

Settle, G. (1981) *A Classification of Tutors' Comments on a Mathematic Assignment.*

Paper from the Student Assessment Research Group, Institute of Educational Technology, Open University.

Sheffield, E.F. (ed.) (1974) *Teaching in the Universities: No One Way.* Montreal: McGill University Press.

Short, A.H. and Tomlinson, D.R. (1979) The design of laboratory class work. *Studies in Higher Education* **4**(2), 223–242.

Shymansky, J.A. and Penick, J.E. (1979) Use of systematic observations improve college science laboratory instruction. *Science Education* **63**(2), 195–203.

Sims, E.J. (1976) Student evaluation of composition. *Improving College and University Teaching* **24**(2), 72.

Skinner, B.F. (1974) *About Behaviourism.* New York: Random House.

Skinner, B.F. (1978) *Reflections on Behaviourism and Society.* New York: Prentice Hall.

Smith, F. (1982) *Writing and the Writer.* London: Heinemann Educational.

Snow, R.E. (1977) Individual differences and instructional design. Reprinted in Hartley, J. and Davies, I.K. (eds) (1978) *Contributions to an Educational Technology, Vol. 2.* London: Kogan Page.

Sommers, J.N. (1982) Responding to student writing. *College Composition and Communication* **33**(2), 148–156.

Spears, J. and Zollman, D. (1977) The influence of structured versus unstructured laboratory on students' understanding of the process of science. *Journal of Research in Science Teaching* **14**(1), 33–38.

Spitzer, H.F. (1939) Studies in retention. *Journal of Educational Psychology* **30**(9), 641–656.

Spurgin, C.G. (1967) What earns the marks? *Physics Education* **2**(6), 306–370.

Squires, G. (1974) Innovation in university teaching. *Programmed Learning and Educational Technology* **11**(1), 5–9.

Squires, G. (1981) Mature entry. In Fulton, O. (ed.) *Access to Higher Education.* Guildford: Society for Research into Higher Education.

Stanton, H.E. (1978) Improving lecturer performance through confidence building. *Journal of Suggestive-Accelerative Learning and Teaching* **3**(2), 123–128.

Steedman, W. (1974) The chemical literature – an undergraduate course. *Education in Chemistry* **11**(3), 93.

Stewart, I.C. (1980) A modified version of the Keller Plan in an advanced financial accounting course. *Accounting and Finance* **20**(2), 111–123.

Stones, E. and Anderson, D. (1972) *Educational Objectives and the Teaching of Educational Psychology.* London: Methuen.

Stuart, J. and Rutherford, R.J.D. (1978) Medical student concentration during lectures. *The Lancet* **2**, 514–516.

Suczek, R.F. (1972) *The Best Laid Plans.* San Francisco: Jossey Bass.

Sugarman, R. (1978) A second chance for computer-aided instruction. *Institute of Electrical and Electronics Engineers Spectrum* **15**(8), 29–35.

Surprenant, T.T. (1982) Learning theory, lecture, and programmed instruction text: an experiment in bibliographic instruction. *College and Research Libraries* **43**(1), 31–37.

Sutton, R.A. (1977) The interface between school and university. *Physics Education* **12**(5), 304–310.

Syrett, J. (1982) Videotex: the implications for technology. In Knapper, C.K. (ed.) *Expanding Learning Through New Communication Technologies*. San Francisco: Jossey Bass.

Szreter, R. (1983) Opportunities for women as university teachers in England since the Robbins Report of 1963. *Studies in Higher Education* 8(2), 139–150.

Tawney, D.A. (1979) *Learning Through Computers*. London: Macmillan.

Taylor, J.A. (1971) *Instructional Planning Systems: a Gaming Approach to Urban Problems*. Cambridge: Cambridge University Press.

Taylor, J. and Walford, R. (1978) *Learning and the Simulation Game*, 2nd ed. Milton Keynes: Open University Press.

Taylor, W. (1980) Effective university teaching. *Education News* 17, 14–18.

Teather, D.C.B. (1968) Programmed learning in biology. *Journal of Biological Education* 2, 119–135.

Teather, D.C.B. (1976) Media in continuing education at a distance. *Continuing Education in New Zealand* 8, 3–10.

Thomas, R.H. (1976) The necessity for examinations – and their reform. *Studies in Higher Education* 1(1), 23–30.

Thoresen, C.E. (ed.) (1973) *Behaviour Modification in Education*. Chicago: NSSE.

Thorne, B. (1979) The study skills workshop. *British Journal of Guidance and Counselling* 7(1), 101–113.

Thorne, B. and da Costa, M. (1976) A counselling service as a growth centre. *British Journal of Guidance and Counselling* 4(2), 212–217.

Tomlinson, R.W.S., Pettingale, K.W., McKerron, C. and Anderson, J. (1973) A report of the final MB examination of London University. *British Journal of Medical Education* 7(1), 1–9.

Travers, R. (ed.) (1973) *Second Handbook of Research on Teaching*. Chicago: Rand McNally.

Trenaman, J.M. (1967) *Communication and Comprehension*. London: Longman.

Trent, J.W. and Cohen, A.M. (1973) Research on teaching in higher education. In Travers, R. (ed.) *Second Handbook of Research on Teaching*. Chicago: Rand McNally.

Trickey, D.S. (1974) Modifications to organic chemistry lectures. In Haynes, L.J., Hills, P.J., Palmer, C.R. and Trickey, D.S. (eds) *Alternatives to the Lecture in Chemistry*. London: Chemical Society.

Trueman, M. and Hartley, J. (1979) How do students use lecture handouts? In Page G.T. and Whitlock, Q. (eds) *Aspects of Educational Technology 13*. London: Kogan Page, pp. 62–66.

Tsai, S.Y.W. and Pohl, N.F. (1978) Student achievement in computer programming: lecture vs. computer-aided instruction. *Journal of Experimental Education* 46(2), 66–70.

Tubbs, M.R. (1968) Seminars in experimental physics. *Physics Education* 3(4), 189–192.

Universities Central Council of Admissions (1969) *Statistical Supplement to the Sixth Report*. London: UCCA.

University Grants Committee (1964) *Report of the Committee on University Teaching Methods* (Hale Report). London: HMSO.

University Grants Committee (1965) *Report of the Committee on Audio-visual Aids in*

Higher Scientific Education (Brynmor Jones Report). Department of Education and Science and Scottish Education Department. London: HMSO.

Uren, O. (1968) The use of texts in language skill development – some problems. In *Innovations and Experiments in University Teaching Methods*. London: University Teaching Methods Unit, University of London Institute of Education.

Van Humbeeck, G., Boving, R. and Van Broekhoven, R. (1982) A computer managed training in problem solving. *Higher Education* 11(4), 475–483.

Veness, T. (1968) Developments in social psychology. *Penguin Social Science Survey*. Harmondsworth: Penguin.

Vernon, M.D. (1962) *The Psychology of Perception*. Harmondsworth: Penguin.

Wakeford, J. (1968a) *The Teaching Methods and Techniques in Sociology*. Paper read at British Sociological Association Teachers' Section Conference, Bedford College, University of London, January 1968.

Wakeford, J. (1968b) *The Strategy of Social Inquiry*. London: Macmillan.

Walkden, F. and Scott, M.R. (1980) Aspects of mathematical education. *International Journal of Mathematical Education in Science and Technology* 11(1), 45–53.

Wallis, D., Duncan, K.D. and Knight, M.A.G. (1966) The Halton Experiment and the Melksham Experiment. In *Programmed Learning in the British Armed Forces*. London: HMSO.

Walton, H.J. (1968) Sex differences in ability and outlook of senior medical students. *British Journal of Medical Education* 2(2), 156–162.

Wankowski, J.A. (1973) *Temperament, Motivation and Academic Achievement* (2 vols.). University of Birmingham Educational Survey.

Wankowski, J.A. (1979) Educational counselling and learning-through-teaching. *British Journal of Guidance and Counselling* 7(1), 72–79.

Wason, P.C. (1970) On writing scientific papers. Reprinted in Hartley, J. (ed.) (1980) *The Psychology of Written Communication: Selected Readings*. London: Kogan Page.

Wason, P.C. (1983) *Trust in Writing*. Paper available from the author, Department of Phonetics and Linguistics, University College, London.

Watson, J.S. (1982) Publication delays in natural and social behavioural science journals. *American Psychologist* 37(4), 448–449.

Weinberg, E. and Rooney, J.F. (1973) The academic performance of women students in medical school. *Journal of Medical Education* 48, March, 240–247.

Welsh, J.N. (1979) *The First Year of Postgraduate Research Study*. London: Society for Research into Higher Education.

White, J.H. (1971) *Teaching Introductory Psychology: An Experience with 80–120*. Paper available from the author, Department of Psychology, The University of Guelph, Ontario, Canada.

Whiteland, J.W.R. (1966) The selection of research students. *Universities Quarterly* 21(1), 44–47.

Williams, G. (1977) Personal contacts between institutions of secondary and higher education. *Higher Education Bulletin* 5(2), 159–179.

Williams, G. and Blackstone, T. (1983) *Response to Adversity*. Guildford: Society for Research into Higher Education.

Williams, P. (ed.) (1981) *The Overseas Student Question*. London: Heinemann.

Winfield, I. (1982) Some developments in the use of videotape replay facilities.

Teaching at a Distance **21**, 83–86.

Woodhall, M. (1981) Overseas students. In Fulton, O. (ed.) *Access to Higher Education*. Guildford: Society for Research into Higher Education.

Woodman, S. (1982) Interim assessment: what price? *Teaching News No. 16*. University of Birmingham.

Woodworth, R.S. and Schlosberg, H. (1954) *Experimental Psychology*, 3rd ed. London: Methuen.

Working Party on Postgraduate Education (1982) *Report*. Cmnd 8537. London: HMSO.

Wright, E. (1968) A research project for clinical medical students. In *Innovations and Experiments in University Teaching Methods*. London: University Teaching Methods Unit, University of London Institute of Education.

Young, S. and Gillespie, G. (1972) Experience with the multiple-choice paper in the primary fellowship examination in Glasgow. *British Journal of Medical Education* **6**(1), 44–52.

Zinn, K.L. (1978) Computer assisted learning in the United States. *Programmed Learning and Educational Technology* **15**(2), 126–135.

INDEX OF NAMES

Page numbers in italics refer to bibliographic details

INDEX OF SUBJECTS